FLARE OUT
AESTHETICS 1966-2016

First published in 2016 by The Visible Press, London
This edition © The Visible Press, 2016

Texts and images by Peter Gidal © Peter Gidal, 2016

Designed by Sam Ashby
Printed in China through World Print Ltd

All rights reserved
No part of this book may be reproduced in any form by any electronic or mechanical means (including photocopying, recording, or information storage and retrieval) without written permission from the publisher

British Library Cataloguing in Publication Data
A catalogue record for this book is available from the British Library

ISBN 978-0-9928377-1-6

www.thevisiblepress.com

PETER GIDAL

FLARE OUT
AESTHETICS 1966-2016

EDITED BY MARK WEBBER AND PETER GIDAL

THE VISIBLE PRESS

This book is dedicated to those who have been so encouraging in many ways from the beginning, just through the force of their generosity; being treated as an equal long before there was cause, being allowed to be, and work, together and gain enormously thereby – teachers, theatre-people, writers and theoreticians, artists – this holds equally for some incredibly supportive publishers and of course for friends (short term and long term) from the beginning to the present.

Thanks are due for such beautiful pictures – and permissions – to Gerhard Richter, Thérèse Oulton, and last but not least Andy Warhol (albeit in the future anterior).

Working with Mark Webber has been particularly unanxious, his and María Palacios Cruz's care – editorial and with all aspects of the book throughout – unwavering.

CONTENTS

Preface by Mark Webber 11
Introduction by Peter Gidal 17

Theory and Definition of Structural/Materialist Film (1975) 37
Further Footnotes (1976) 69
Problems 'relating to' Warhol's Still Life 1976 (1978) 79
The Anti-Narrative (1979) 89
Technology and Ideology in/through/and Avant-Garde Film:
    An Instance (1980) 116
Samuel Beckett's Ghost Trio (1981) 135
Against Sexual Representation in Film (1984) 148
Fugitive Theses re Thérèse Oulton's Paintings (1984) 158
Dialogue and Dialectic in Godot (1986) 169
The Anti-Zoom (A Little Polemic Against Metaphor) (1987) 173
In Representation or Out? Some Condensed Notes on Aesthetics
    and Politics (1988) 176
Endless Finalities (Richter's Abstract Paintings) (1993) 179
The Polemics of Paint (Richter in the Nineties) (1995) 187
NO EYE: Theoretical Reflections on the Eye, Metaphor and
    Film/Video (1995) 206
Once is Never: Warhol's Saturday Disaster & Blow Job (2001) 210
Against Metaphor (1998, revised 2005/2015) 218

Miscellany

Letter to Artforum (1971) 239
Letter to Screen (1976) 240
Letter to Afterimage (1976) 242
Eight Hours or Three Minutes (1971) 248
Notes on my Film Work (1975) 249

Filmography 253
Bibliography 255

PREFACE

Flare Out: Aesthetics 1966-2016 is the first anthology of essays by film-maker and theorist Peter Gidal. Gidal has, since the 1960s, been recognized as one the foremost film-makers in the field of independent/experimental/avant-garde cinema. It is within this context that he is perhaps best known, and through which I became interested in his work. It may therefore be surprising for some readers to discover that about half of this book does not directly address cinema at all, and that rarely in its pages does he directly refer to his own film work. We have chosen to focus on Gidal's most significant essays on aesthetics, many of which are now out-of-print, and to present the broad range of his concerns over a fifty-year period. The uncompromising nature of his film-making is consistent through his prose, which likewise demands active engagement from the reader.

Peter Gidal's film work has been closely identified with others associated with the London Film-Makers' Co-operative (LFMC), an artist-led organisation that combined distribution, exhibition and a film workshop in order to establish a viable, alternative production base for truly independent film-making. Gidal became involved in the Co-op at an early stage in its history – it had been founded in 1966, shortly before he arrived in London – and contributed towards its transition from being solely a distribution agency into one that facilitated production and had a regular screening programme. Throughout the 1970s, much of the discourse around British avant-garde cinema was stimulated by the films and theoretical work of Gidal and his LFMC colleague Malcolm Le Grice. Aware of the lack of critical attention given to the Coop and related film activity, both film-makers began to regularly contribute to art magazines and journals, later expanding their theories in book length form. Writing was part of their creative practice, distinct from but inextricably linked to their film work.

The book *Andy Warhol: Film and Paintings*, published by Studio Vista and Dutton in 1971, was the first widely circulated example of Gidal's prose (notably, he was one of the first to consider all aspects of Warhol's work on equal terms). He began to contribute regularly to *Time Out* (mainly previews to promote the Co-op cinema programme that he was responsible for from 1971-74), and wrote book and exhibition reviews for *Art and Artists* and *Studio International*, concurrent with his more theoretical writing.

Arguably his most important text on film remains "Theory and Definition of Structural/Materialist Film" (1975). Here, Gidal attempts to delineate a form of film-making that was then prevalent at the LFMC. The 'materialist' designation distinguishes that practice from the American tendency of 'structural film' that had become a dominant form of avant-garde cinema in the west. In British and European film-making, it was the physical material of film – the presence of the celluloid strip, of 'film-as-projected' (and for 'expanded cinema' the technology of projection) – that was fundamental to the shaping of innovative work.

Gidal's manifesto had first been sketched out in the article "Film as Film" for *Art and Artists* (1972), then elaborated twice in *Studio International* (1974 and 1975). He considers the 1975 revision as definitive and it is that version that is restored in this volume. The text was further revised (at the request of the publisher) for inclusion in the *Structural Film Anthology*, which was edited by Gidal to accompany an eighteen programme screening series he organised for the National Film Theatre in London, May 1976.

In a brief postscript to his introductory text in the second edition of the *Structural Film Anthology* in 1978, Gidal identified three talks and two published letters that had, up to that point, elaborated upon the original essay. All are included in this new collection.

"Further Footnotes" (1976) was a paper given at the LFMC seminar "Theory of Avant-Garde Film Practice", convened in the wake of a special number of *Studio International* devoted to avant-garde film (November/December 1975 – Gidal's "Theory and Definition" is in this issue, along with the first publication of Peter Wollen's "The Two Avant-Gardes"). Malcolm Le Grice joined Gidal and Wollen at the Co-op seminar, and all three participated in a discussion moderated by Tony Rayns. These dialogues continued later that year during the Edinburgh Film Festival's conference on "Psychoanalysis and the Cinema", at which Gidal delivered a 'condensed' version of "The Anti-Narrative". A third paper, the complexly articulated "Technology and Ideology in/through/and Avant-Garde Film", was delivered at "The Cinematic Apparatus" conference at the University of Wisconsin, Milwaukee, in February 1978.

The writing on film continued, eventually resulting in the *Materialist Film* book (Routledge, 1989), but through the 1980s and beyond his thoughts on cinema were primarily manifest in his film-making rather than being explicated in language (his current filmography lists thirty-two titles). However, Gidal has also written extensively on the dramatist Samuel Beckett, on the artists Thérèse Oulton and Gerhard Richter, and has continued his close analysis of Andy Warhol's work. In these polemical essays on different art forms, Gidal writes with an intense enthusiasm in attempting to understand and explain the works in their specificity.

His long-term associations with Richter and Warhol are outlined in his introduction to this book, and evidenced by the many published articles on their work. Samuel Beckett, a preoccupation since Gidal's teenage years, is the subject of the book *Understanding Beckett: A Study of Monologue and Gesture in the Work of Samuel Beckett* (Macmillan, 1986) and numerous essays, three of which are present in this collection.

Gidal's first piece on Thérèse Oulton's work was commissioned for her celebrated solo show at London's Gimpel Fils gallery in late 1984. The exhibition's large-scale, abstract oil paintings established the artist's reputation; Gidal's catalogue essay received a significant amount of (in his view) undue attention for its distinctive, iconoclastic prose. Fourteen years later, the two collaborated to produce *Against Metaphor*, a small, limited edition book of fifty signed copies. A suite of eight gravure etchings by Oulton interspersed the text. The essay it contained was rewritten in both 2005 and 2015, and is published here for the first time in its substantially revised form.

Three letters, a passage on Warhol and duration, and some brief statements on Gidal's own film works are included in the miscellany. His letter to *Artforum*, referencing Annette Michelson's June 1971 article on Michael Snow, was taken up by Michelson and printed as the first item of "Foreword in Three Letters" in the special film issue of the magazine that she guest edited (September 1971). Michelson's pointed retort to Gidal, which also discussed the broader field of art and film criticism, was followed by a third letter written at her invitation by Jonas Mekas. Gidal has remarked that since the appearance in print of this heated exchange, and despite other moments of personal and political discord, he and Michelson have remained friends. (Michelson was present at the previously mentioned LFMC seminar and reportedly lamented the fact that few public debates in the US were conducted with such seriousness.)

The 1976 letter to *Screen* protests against the lack of attention given by the journal towards the important body of work being produced in and around the London Film-Makers' Co-operative at that time, citing articles by Peter Wollen and editor Ben Brewster as evidence of this exclusion. The journal abandoned plans for a special issue (guest edited by Malcolm Le Grice) in 1973 and few critiques of avant-garde film have graced its pages since. Also in 1976, Gidal responded to Anne Cottringer's unfavourable review of "Theory and Definition of Structural/Materialist Film" in *Afterimage*. This letter did not appear until two years later when the next issue of the irregularly published magazine had been completed.

The dates 1966 to 2016 are identified in the subtitle of this book yet no texts are present from either year. Reflecting on this period in his introduction, Gidal determines 1966 as the starting point for his writing practice: theory, art, aesthetics, politics, film, etc. Previously, in "The Anti-Narrative" he had declared that his project since that same year has been "the distance between knowledge and perception". That project continues today, and can be traced through the polemical texts included herein. The author's original and radical voice remains provocative throughout.

The artist, curator and writer Ian White made a characteristically eloquent statement when he wrote: "The impossibly torrid force and flux of Gidal's writing is remarkable, a system of language parallel to a system of film-making, at once urgent, difficult, subjective, closed, contradictory and jubilant."

Mark Webber

The Visible Press is Mark Webber and María Palacios Cruz. We thank Peter Gidal for his generosity of time and spirit, and for his enthusiasm for the project. We are also grateful to the following individuals that have assisted in the production of this book: Sam Ashby, Gerhard Richter and Konstanze Ell, Thérèse Oulton, Ksenya Blokhina, Matt Wrbican and Greg Burchard, Neil Printz, Samo Gale, Julie Zeftel, Valentina Bandelloni and David Galley, Don McMahon and Isabel Flower, Mike Sperlinger and Josephine Pryde, Stuart Comer, Cerith Wyn Evans, Erika Balsom, Ben Cook, Jing Ye and Yu-Ling Chou.

INTRODUCTION

First Draft

Practice makes perfect. Doubtless not the case. Somewhere, or some time, one has the wish to write and then the writing being such pleasure, it goes on and seems natural even, whilst doing what is anything but natural. In its simplest sense: reforming words, changing, editing, even, whilst as a fifteen year-old 'naturally' carrying out such a desire to write – in my case, a poem *In der Welt unserer Zeit*,[1] or a reader's letter "of jews and jazz and zwerenz' gripes …"[2] or, later, years later: *mis*remembering having loved Hölderlin's poem of a person "vor der kahlen weissen Wand …" i.e. "a blank calcified wall behind, protecting your self from its own self, lost" – when the poem (refound last year) turned out to have been my own, albeit heavily influenced, was one of the (mis)rememorations for me in February 1964 when first seeing Warhol's film *Blow Job*. That then led to a (slight) book by that name, nearly half a century later. The temporal rememberings over a long time becoming (became) themselves duration, duration as a concept, concrete/abstract, the being of one's practice, as imperfect as anything else.

---

[1] In der Welt unserer Zeit / muss man glauben und warten / und in stillem Hunger schweigen. / In der Welt unserer Zeit muss man / sich bewahren vor sich selbst: / vor seinem eigenen Sein / Verstecken spielen. / Und dabei geht man verloren. / Man sieht sich selbst nicht mehr, / nicht einmal sich selbst. / Der Mensch spielt Versteck / mit verlorenen Gegenständen / und findet sich nicht. / Sein Schatten ist eine Wand, / eine kahle weiss-graue Wand. / Sein Herz ist ein Motor, / seine Seele ein Gewirr; / sein Mund ist ein Himmel / mit verlorenen Sternen. / In der Welt unserer Zeit / muss man glauben und warten / und in stillem Hunger schweigen.
  "In der Welt unserer Zeit", *Montanablatt*, No. 44, March 1963.

[2] *twen*, December 1962.

Writing the above as a first draft, by hand (August, 2015) in a notebook late at night. The writings here assembled are seen by me as mainly writing itself, its impetus and pleasures, via the way one tries in words/with words to make something, including some idea, ideas, which are also sometimes concepts, motored by a polemical will to make at least some intervention in thought. That impetus, I think, is – however motivated – political in its outcome when it 'succeeds', when the disagreement with previous ideas in the culture, or present ones – a negativity constantly against, a 'no', always, whether from one's personal, my personal psychoanalytic past and its needs, or just because antagonism to convention is in particular cases a polemical and therefore theoretical necessity – can produce another series of thoughts in conflict. The true meaning of dialectical without the worries, at this stage, as to whether those dialectics are similar or not to previous historical ones, whether or not disputation itself is a metaphysical activity having no concrete relevance to some, whereas to others is as concrete as stone(s).

Even saying *historical* is to some a polemical attack, as when I in the 1970s often argued that experimental films like *Room Film 1973* are historical, in history, namely that history of *that* present and presence. The arguments and polemics and therefrom theory at times *for* something, namely an experimental film practice that was a process against recognition – as recognition means something already-known – continued for some decades, whilst those with to me strange and often reactionary beliefs in the world and its pre-given representations struggled daily to keep their phantasms alive, finding manifold ways of denigrating an anti-representational experimental film practice. Often writing thus became part of a social struggle; yet the struggle in the writing itself was and is for me always primary. Not out of some formalist(ic) love of most writing which I find simply not writing but an image of a pre-existent religiosity, belief, the known, a (narcissistic) collaboration with power.

It should be said that even writing of my using language is really expressing attempts at attempts, and one of these most recently is the previously unpublished version of *Against Metaphor*, written in 1998 and edited for the tenth or fifteenth time.[3] In some cases the impetus to enunciate such ways of writing occurs whilst speaking, and the transcriptions of the spoken word's recorrective thought processes might give an insight into that.

I've begun this introduction it seems by jumping in feet first. As opposed to what? I hope so in any case.

This collection is not meant to be, as many others are, a tome too difficult to lift, too academic to want to read, an overview yet again of already easily definable positions. It is a selection of fifty years of writing (a phrase shocking to me) with always the intent, if not the result, of using language to put the reader into a position of thinker in the present, simultaneously with and against the text in front of them.[4]

And for me whilst writing, in the process itself, it is at its best like that. That's why Nietzsche's note about reading stuff by himself that he doesn't recognize, that seems written by someone else, is something to identify with; something of a paradox for someone writing against identification. I react badly reading others' works when they immediately begin to quote so and so,

---

3   In 1988 "Against Metaphor" had been printed in a small volume – 3 x 5½ inches, handbound – with etchings *on*, not *against*, metaphor by Thérèse Oulton in an edition of fifty copies to give to friends after the British Library, the V&A, and others obtained it for their libraries.

4   "This inscription, not only of Gidal's resistance to (distanciation from) the lure of the sensual, sublimated visual object but also of the spectator's possibility of similar resistance is not just a parallel resistance to the sensual object(s) photographed in the image, it is an attempted inscription of the spectator's possibility of resistance to the identification with the pleasure of the film-maker in that object or even (resistance to) an identification with the film-maker's act of resistance. The film work presented as a film work an attempt to permit the spectator to utilise, appropriate, transform the film unencumbered by the ego of the film-maker – its terms are public rather than private – a public discourse." Malcolm Le Grice in *Independent Cinema Documentation File No. 1: Peter Gidal*, British Film Institute, 1979.

some philosopher, artist, political power figure, as if the unconscious need is overpowering (and overdetermined) to give one's own work spurious validity by identifying with power.

The dominance (hegemony) of certain names, and worse, the vehement refusal to investigate their identification with certain known acceptably kosher figures from the past and those power figures' objective oppressions, gives me certainly the wish – despite the ideological impossibility – to remain 'outside', *other*, an other amongst others. Secondly as to the Nietzsche quote: about not recognizing one's own work or better, not being at one in some imaginary identification with anything let alone one's self, means the process and the presence of a writing as such is not annihilated.[5]

The reader-viewer's position, as in my concept of the viewer/viewing *film-as-projected*, not deconstructed and analysed later, is a fundamental difference from the dominant ideology's literary and cinematic experience, and these essays all engage – in the political sense of *engagé* – with that.

Seeing everything as a problem reminds me of some of the wonderful students at the RCA. I taught at the Royal College of Art from 1971 till they fired me in 1983 (and then fired those whom they'd used to facilitate it, the latter surprised when they in turn were unceremoniously let go having done what they (didn't know they) were hired to do), and experimental filmmaking and theory was vanquished from the RCA. Straightforward historical falsifications still rebound in some recent books, taking as tragedy what began as farce: experimental filmmakers-to-be forced at the Film Co-op into straightjackets of practice, unconsciously mimicking the cartoon of victims being dragged into Structural/Materialist seminars I tacked to my office door in 1976. The extremely heterogeneous making of radical experimental film in Britain in the 1970s and 1980s, and the writing of film theory,

---

5   Rememoration is another matter causing recoil if there's something imagined to be *there*.

from those days, from that ghetto, can be found if the will is there. But this isn't a book of film theory. The film writings became, sometimes, aesthetic theory; thus it seemed right to say *which* practice it is that it is the consequence of – not linked but not inextricably *un*-linked: film.

These essays are essays in aesthetics, having several impetuses (impeti?): my love of Samuel Beckett's work since first reading *Endgame* in 1963 on a mountain in Switzerland, not as romantic as it sounds, being only a reference in tribute to my boarding school. My love of Samuel Beckett's work has persisted over half a century and I have included here some essays which in their use of language are halting, difficult, impossible, as they should be when (ostensibly) dealing with his use of words, a materiality of the word whether to be read or heard, in *Not I*, or in *Waiting for Godot*, or in *Worstward Ho*, or the *Texts for Nothing*. Those still are pieces inseparable from my ostensible self and in relation to which the struggle to deal with their language-use forced in the best sense a similar struggle. (I don't mean similar, as it sounds normative, I mean ... what is the word?) My book on Beckett's use of monologue and gesture (*Understanding Beckett*, 1986) – another such struggle, perhaps the most extreme – is a separate matter: nothing in this collection is from that or any other book: *Materialist Film* (1989), *Andy Warhol: Films and Paintings* (1971). The decision was made with The Visible Press to keep only to the extreme theoretical, polemical, materialist essays, in all their durational brevity or length.

One of the Beckett pieces, "NO EYE" was given as a paper, to near total incomprehension and silence and blank faces, at one of those bi-annual Beckettian conferences, this one of all places in Monte Carlo, one of the least sympathetic places in Europe except for the extraordinary beauty of the sea and coast. Even my (and Beckett's) close friend Ruby Cohn, the doyenne of Beckett intellects who tromped up the hill every morning with me, consequently avoided the subject of my 10-minute paper.[6] It occurred to me that, good or bad, the blank incomprehension wasn't just due to what might've been a bad paper (it is reproduced herein) but was due to its aberrance, and it is that which I've for whatever reasons always had as an impetus, an internal necessity. The aberrance is in taking issue with what, and how, aesthetic subjects (i.e. our presence as much as the works') and objects (the works' presence as much as ours) are equally engaged in, namely political critique. Their being viewed, being heard: our *being* through that. And vice versa.

The alternative is endless academicism. These essays, then, whatever else they might be, good, bad, indifferent, are I think – to be honest, I know, or think I know, or better, hope to know by now – not that.

The politics of the reader/viewer/listener, how you as subject are placed in relation to the other, the 'it' that is the ostensible subject of whatever it is you are dealing with, is for me in all these essays of importance, as the motive force for the writing, antagonistic or not. It is both subjective and, to my mind, political in the extreme. If one cannot practice a politics of writing that struggles with the conventions of what was in the sixties and seventies called dominant practices, or dominant ideologies, then there is no struggle at all. Then we have quietism, at best, and collaboration with power at worst. This makes for the overuse of the term 'career'.

There are some essays on painting in this collection, stunning works by Gerard Richter, Andy Warhol, Thérèse Oulton, and these come out of the need to write about what is so unwritable about: abstract art, if it can be called that, nothing being abstract without being concrete.[7] Abstract doesn't mean pure form, as neither pure, nor form as such, exists. It is always

---

6   Consequently i.e. *with persistence*, also meaning the entirely different *thereafter*.

7   And equally nothing being purely, or airlessly, abstract other than the derivative meanderings of abstracted.

against that which the seen also refers to for one, the painting determining those references, those meanings, those positions the viewer is put in position by the work to take. It's complex and hard to articulate, both a process and an impossibility, but that doesn't cover it, I don't think. Intensely taken by Oulton's work (writing of her first one person show, in 1984) – I can still now feel that in the writing. "Fugitive Theses" created an extreme stir and caused quite some public anger. In spite of what's been said in this introduction so far, I was truly shocked at the furious, rather nasty responses in some quarters. One good poet on BBC radio was in such a fury he critiqued the essay on an arts program, didn't speak of the paintings he was meant to be reviewing (hardly my intention), then quoted a long paragraph to prove the horridness of my prose. I still remember hearing it with the artist and a friend or two, aghast equally at his hysteria and bewildered only by how the writing sounded when read so beautifully aloud. It wasn't meant to be that but was that.

How beauty inveigles itself! In any case, other essays about art include two on Gerhard Richter's powerful paintings which are essays – whatever else they are – seen as aberrant (which they are) to the norms of writing by the best-known others who write on him. Nor have such others – to my amazement – brought out any, let alone the precise, Brechtian strategies his work incorporates. Brecht, mind you, whose extraordinary theoretical output, apart from the wonderful poems, lyrics and plays, was acutely evident – if not the cultural given – in East Germany since the War. The piece "Endless Finalities" from 1993 for the *Parkett* issue on Richter's work – dealing with the concept and reality of material substance – was immediately taken up by him for reprinting a month later – last minute, with some haste – in his three volume French/German/English catalogue raisonné. The essay "The Polemics of Paint", commissioned on his insistence for the book/catalogue *Richter in the Nineties*, which became, perversely, art book of the year for *Art Journal*.[8] Can't think of any other institutional compliments, but to have had one is nice.[9]

Personal relationships with artists for me have *always* come after my writing, so it was never a matter of getting approval for supposed insights from the voice of the artist, as why then should anyone bother writing on aesthetics, on painting, one can just end up as so many do, finding justification in quotes from the artist in the first place. This has been anathema to me from day one. The friendships with the three painters came later.

Thus the same held for the Warhol book begun in 1969. I had for other reasons gone to the original Factory in November 1967 and sat around watching rough footage from his 25-hour film ★★★★ and chatting a bit, taking some Rollei black and white and Leica colour pictures in the near gloom. It was only long after the book came out (January 1971), going back to visit New York after 1975, i.e. after a largely self-imposed exile during Vietnam, that seeing Warhol once every year or two (for at most half an hour, though we seemed to like one another) began. In any case, one impetus to writing aesthetics were Warhol's brilliant, crucial, works in film *and* painting. His art is of such resonance and depth, I've never *not* thought of it for any considerable period. In 1966 I had written a pedestrian essay (thus not reprinted) on "The Closeup in Godard and Warhol", thankfully such a dull title never occurring to me again.

Writing about art began at Munich University in 1966/67,[10] Ludwig-Maximilian-Universität to give it its proper name. Signing up for what I thought was a normal class on Hegel's

---

8 Published by the CAA, an association of college art history teachers in the United States.

9 Some years ago a director of the gallery recounted with some hilarity that Richter's request was at first met by them with a sense of shock, additionally being hardly of help in the social or economic circulation of his artworks.

10 Hence the start date in the title of this volume, though the piece was not published, whilst other – earlier ones – were. The 1966-2016 title just seems more sympa than say 1964-2016 or 1970-2016!

aesthetics, only on the first day to realize it was a doctoral seminar with twelve Hegelians. Each of us, during the semester, had to speak a 45-60 minute paper. Mine was "James Rosenquist's pop-painting of the (Vietnam napalm bomber) *F-111* in relation to Hegel's *Aesthetics* via Dewey's *Art as Experience*". Hard to believe now that this occurred. The support given by the other members of the 'proseminar' as it was called, in the face of this, was amazing. Of course I barely passed with the necessary 'Note Drei' (3) (1 being best, 5 failure). Writing about art was also inflected by one of the other seminars, on early 20th century art historian Heinrich Wölfflin's *Classic Art*. At the time I didn't realize this university was the epicentre of Wölfflin studies, and had been for fifty years. I loved his way of describing things. Have forgotten just about every particular, except his amazing structural analyses which were so vivid they didn't semiotically kill a work but gave it resonance beyond – or better through – that inhering in the respective paintings. The third proseminar there in 1966 was theatre directing at the Kammerspiele, and I quickly realized I couldn't find a reason to move an actor from point A to point B, so ended the dream of being a theatre director. This coincided with notes towards my first experimental film. But aesthetics for me, I am trying to outline, were never separately either film, or painting, or theatre, or anything else separable from polemics, from theory, ... and I hope some of this comes through in the sixteen essays chosen for this book. I don't want to mix genres, but keeping them separate doesn't deny what they have in common for me: to write, pure and simple.

Second Draft

Willing to acknowledge in the texts there's less than meets the eye. This was to be the last line of the introduction, because the endless practice of writing since 1966 had/has within it the primary (material) pleasure of writing as such and the knowledge that practice does not make perfect, contrary to the first sentence of this introduction.

For me it seems that the driving force or libidinal need or just the way things are, in other words how it is when writing, on whatever 'subject', is the concept of oxymoron, the selfcontradictoriness within writing 'about' something, whether that obtains somehow within each paragraph, or each sentence, and sometimes even within a group of three or four words, or at rare moments, even within the use of one word.

How a word is used, so that it can ineluctably mean two or more things, within itself, not by positing such and such and *then* such and such (something else) thereafter. On the contrary, positing both within that word or phrase or group of two or three sentences, well that is something that came about only whilst writing over a long time. It begins to seem automatic as words flood through you and your mechanism (hand, eye, thoughts, etc.) not to add on more and more, not to amplify your resources or your ego. When one is writing theory and knows that theory and polemics are intricately linked – "no new idea appears in a void"[11] – one's defensiveness about subject-positions, beliefs, ideologies, politics, makes one libidinously involved in the writing itself, however attempting to articulate a position, simultaneously realizing during that process that one is in fact enabled by the (also self-)imposed endless meanings that words or phrases or sentences are made to mean. In other words, that within a polemic one is simultaneously articulating contradictory positions, yet realizing through the force of the writing and the editing-whilst-writing that one is producing a polemic and a theory. *That* means that whatever a piece, an essay, ends up being, or struggling to say or to impose, against other ideologies of representation (for example), one is, or I am, still producing a writing that 'admits' to the very possibility of those selfsame

---

11   Radical feminist Christine Delphy's phrase, during our ten-year friendship/correspondence, theoretically describing what was happening in my daily practice.

words meaning other things, or being used in such and such a way in relation to the previous and following sentences, *which could have been otherwise*. In any case, that's how I see it, or wish it to be true.

What I am getting at is to say that one's positions in the writing of a piece, say against sexual representation in film, or against narrative, exists within a writing in language that could have meant something other, thereby de-naturalizing the position, thereby not mimicking or reproducing the very positions one is in struggle against. In that sense form is content.[12]

This rather lengthy exposition (these last few paragraphs) is simply to say that writing itself leads to meanings and in that, its being, is language's own power to mean a number of things, to not be natural, or 'right', or more humane, or more beautiful, unless it is structured materially to allow the echoes of what it could have said but does not say, or does say in spite of having possibly almost not been said.

When in the late 1970s the cine-semiotician Christian Metz first saw an experimental film, my *Condition of Illusion* (1975), his infectious enthusiasm in seeing something that in some ways coincided and in others collided with his theoretical models until then attached to industrial, commercial, Hollywood cinema, it became a productive collision/collusion. After which, invited to show *Room Film 1973* to his doctoral class on the rue d'Ulm, sitting there with a 16mm projector and eight or nine of his group, meant a to them unknown temporal aesthetics was taking place (none of this has to do with whether the film is good or bad in whoever's view). The fact of that process, the film, forcing itself into an articulation (by him and them) meant that each time again one needs to find words that don't reify, and then replicate, what a work is attempting to undo.[13] An anecdotal

---

12   Only to do with certain political formalisms. See interview in *Rab-Rab*, No. 2, 2016.
13   Alain Reynaud, authority on Warburg's tableaux, longtime director of films at Centre Pompidou/Beaubourg, participant in that class, spoke of notes taken down

example for me of the cathexes of writing as such: at night in my flat on Holland Road in 1971 listening to some Stones album, I stopped and switched to 'just doing some typing' – words, phrases, a kind of dense monologue of poetic images barely holding together, 1000 words apropos of nothing ... had never done this before, nor since.[14] Being anything but an acolyte of William Burroughs, it seemed apropos to send the ensuing text to him on Duke Street St James's, not far away, and he responded by post. We'd had no previous connection. "It would be great as a film." He was thinking of his kind of film not my kind of film. But he recorded his reading of the text unbeknownst to me until recently when an acquaintance heard a piece of his called *Present Time Exercises* online, having been, it turns out, released as an LP already in 1986, and as a CD in 1998, *Break Through in Grey Room*. Within that cut-up text piece of his was the first line of my 'story', a line from the middle around 500 words in, and the last line "not far at all".[15] Apart from the temporal confusions, what interested me when I finally heard about this was that he was taking sentences out and recontextualizing them in a collision of semiotic memories, images, sounds: radio, air raid sirens, tv sets blaring, and his own subjective fumblings for sound which he recorded as "nothing there, there's nothing on the tape!" then finding a phrase from my text. One hears the clicking of on/off switches, click, rewind, click, etc., then a segment, then gone, nothing, other sounds, etc.

It struck me that this cut-up notion is the opposite of the one I've been trying to articulate and manage in my writings as shown in this collection: to put everything possible for each

---

when Metz spoke afterwards a week later about the work, notes I haven't managed to locate. Tangentially, and somewhat unfortunately, a Swiss journal has published sections of what Metz in a radio interview years later stated (approvingly) in relation to *Room Film 1973*, that it was the projection – duration, materiality – of blackness, which it is not.

14 I called it "Marcuse and Mick Dialectic".
15 How far is not far at all, in that it's the title of my 2015 film.

'subject' or each 'position' or each 'polemic' contradictorily within each phrase or paragraph, so it becomes a simultaneity of – ideological/political/personal – possibilities, that of a condensation of signifiers, *that* poetry: the German word *Verdichtung* meaning just that.[16]

But the insight isn't simply a belated acknowledgement of something I find in fact to be the only way to write theory of (any) value, whether by myself or anyone else, but rather another one: namely that one literally does not 'know' what one is doing whilst one is doing it if one is embedded within the politics of an aesthetic process.

At the same time the writing posited by me in this introduction is not totalizing, total, nor is it autonomous; the social use of language means one can battle for ideas philosophically inspite of and because of material disjunctions and impossibilities. To do that means to utilize what I guess could be called several discourses at once, probably the best one could hope to do, and for me more than enough to be getting on with. I hope some of these essays can be read by you in the present, through your presence, out of some adjacent aesthetic and political necessity. A different reader, a different subject. No, object.

Peter Gidal,
London, August 2015

---

16. When Deke Dusinberre in his *Screen* (1977) essay wrote of "Theory and Definition of Structural/Materialist Film", admittedly a mouthful, it argued the above case, yet to be honest, at that time I did not know in any real sense that that was what my writing was attempting. ("... that Gidal regards neither the 'voice' of the theoretician nor the 'eye' of the film-maker as a privileged or transcendent subject, but insists on their inscription – on all levels – as operative factors in theoretical and cinematic discourse.")

NOTES

a.

Q.E.D. (Quod Erat Demonstrandum)

Even for someone who loved Latin but failed miserably at it when at a German Gymnasium for a year, the self-referential redundancy of those three letters has always intrigued me. Tautology, whether in Marx (*Grundrisse*) or Spinoza (*The proof of the existence of God*) is fascinating. In the basement of the school for 750 students between thirteen and nineteen years of age (public in the non-British sense) was a thirty foot long eagle with a Swastika in its beak, beneath which unfolding lettering *Wir Werden Siegen (We Shall Conquer)*. Hard to pass Latin under those circumstances. I recall asking the director of the school when I was thirteen (1959) why that was still there, his reply was we haven't gotten around to whitewashing it. Brecht would've used that anecdote for a *Lehrstück* (Learning Play).

b.

As to writing about artworks.

Richter has already been discussed. With Warhol it was different. I wrote a small book, possibly the first to do with both films and paintings, and 'the other things', as the last chapter had it. Having submitted a one page idea to Studio Vista's editor David Herbert, who ran their whole wonderful series of paperbacks (co-published with Dutton in the States), I got a reply within days saying come in, let's talk. We did, he asked for the one page to be made a bit more specific into three pages, and the following week a contract was signed. I was still a graduate student at the Royal College of Art, hanging about doing very little, but loving it. My writing was still at a pretty simple stage. Yet it was through which I learned that practice makes, if not perfect, certainly for something in struggle in language.

Years later Warhol (I always refused to call him Andy) said

he loved the book and wanted so much for it to be signed. That kind of mixture of irony, sarcasm, and plain niceness has to be remembered too. After feeding me some asparagus leftovers and some indifferent red wine at the Factory (no longer the silver one which I went to only once) he would say something outrageous like, "Why don't you write for *Interview*?", knowing it was to me loathsome. Letting him know that, he'd say, "Oh yeah, sure, of course ..." and that would be that. What was extraordinary though was not only that Warhol stated, and it was true, "we're constantly working", meaning the (intellectual) machines of thought and practice, labour, never stop. He also could accept extreme political antagonism in writings both by myself, and prior to that, by his (and my) friend Gregory Battcock in *Arts Magazine*. Warhol's distancing devices and aesthetic strategies have been occasionally remarked upon. His work was perhaps Schklovskian in the end: "art has absolutely nothing to do with life", and this has to be understood complexly.

Warhol seemed genuinely excited one afternoon that I had letters from Samuel Beckett. And Beckett's generosity showed itself in my case when *Understanding Beckett: Monologue and Gesture* was rejected by Macmillan. It had taken me a good four years. He wrote, "it happens to us all."[17] That almost made up for the disappointment. Instead, I sat by the East River and ... put the book away for six months, went back to London, rewriting around fifty often very long lines, keeping 95% but cutting a crucial 5%. The book sounded entirely different. The original writing of the book had been commissioned against the grain by Stephen Heath. At the 1976 Edinburgh Film Festival psychoanalysis week, after reading out my "The Anti-Narrative (condensed version)", Stephen Heath had come up to me and said perhaps we can work together sometime. An elating thought. I'd attended his five two-hour morning seminars on Lacanian

---

17 For this and four other full letters from SB, see the forthcoming *The Letters of Samuel Beckett*, Vol. IV, Faber, 2017.

psychoanalysis that week and the extraordinary brilliance and beauty of his teaching had been literally breathtaking. We became fast friends. When together, we never spoke of narrative or psychoanalysis, we were curiously in sync on many things (not all). Heath's own idiosyncratically marvellous writings and lectures had a major impact in the 1970s, as did his translation (in *Tel Quel*, 1972) of twelve pages of Joyce's *Finnegans Wake*, which was not only a *tour de force* but was the only one since Beckett's twelve pages – as it so happened – fifty years earlier. The writing of a book on Beckett's work had initially been pushed on me for years by Jonathan Rosenbaum, Godard's favourite English language film critic, and it was also Rosenbaum who, by making quite a few subtle editing changes to the *Studio International* version of my "Theory and Definition of Structural/Materialist Film" (as published herein), helped get my anthology of texts on experimental film with that as the introduction published.

c.
Vacuum vs Pleasure and Instruction
All the above to show that one doesn't live or write or think or film or *be* in a vacuum. One fancies one is doing it alone, but one isn't. Whether it was at the London Film-Makers' Co-operative, from 1968 to 1975, or sitting in London writing, or anything else, the 'anecdotal' (ergo hidden in footnotes) is that without which the social results of the practice would not exist. But the practice of the practice, the writing has its own inner needs for me, always has (as Americans would say), always has done (as the English would say), and I hope only that the result chosen here is of 'pleasure and instruction' in the best sense. "From which both pleasure and instruction", Beckett wrote me of after the book finally came out ... but only twenty years later did I notice the irony of this, as one of the book's intentions stated on the back cover no less was to write of (formalist) Brecht versus (political) Beckett. And Brecht's favourite phrase, pleasure and instruction,

for his theatre work, was quoted from the shadows by ever alert Beckett. Last month (August 2015) reading, finally, Bertrand Russell's *History of Western Philosophy*, which is both endless fun and funny to boot, it turns out pleasure and instruction came straight from two millennia ago. *Verdichtung* (condensation) is the modus for so much. Q.E.D.

d.
Looking through these essays reminds me that as in the books there are many quotes, but thankfully never "as so and so says ..." to bolster a statement via an ulterior source, an infuriating academic habit, borne of (often understandable) feelings of inferiority. My use of quotes is often – so I tell myself – to place a contradiction to what is written, or is one of many which work as much against as with one another and have sometimes an uneasy relation to my text, yet not always. The now obviously unfortunate use in one or two essays of a wonderful Lenin quote on relativity (from *Materialism and Empirocriticism*, 1908) – for someone on the far left – though in the 1960s and 1970s that seemed apropos, and was in spite of one's knowledge of his mass killings, also quoting Rosa Luxemburg against Lenin's centralization, bureaucratization, and what can only be called his Stalinization of the party apparatus. Or another example: a quote by Wittgenstein precisely to intervene in what seemed conventional misreadings of his position, to make of him an empiricist, whereas the impossibility of knowing, perceiving a known, as the viewer is inseparable from the viewed, would enable a contrary – but not steadfast – philosophical position to erupt from the problematization of the conventional one. And so on. Such quoting inevitably and in spite of wanting to make all quotes as problematic as my own writing, partake of the ideology of a particular historical moment, and at that moment one (better said, I) fell – hopefully rarely – into quoting from readings some of which now might seem – are – unanswerable. (It turned

out there was/is a history to such use of quoting, whether in Brecht and Walter Benjamin, far more imaginatively in James Joyce (all 1920s/30s), but no less in *Tristram Shandy* (1767), Shakespeare (around 1600), and Spinoza (1650s). *The same but different.* (Different but the same would be conservative).)

e.
Perception versus knowledge.
Was in the mid-1970s going through stuff in the head neurotically, repetitively, various things, private, personal, intellectual, etc. ... and after thinking about it over and over, after about a year, whilst crossing a street thinking it through yet again, an insurmountable bunch of ideas, it got clarified as *perception versus knowledge*. That became a real breakthrough, and only some years later after theorizing it, writing it, feeling/thinking it as my own, an almost equal insight to find it has been a struggle since Sophocles, thus for centuries, millennia, a fundamental philosophical even theological problem(atic) ... which doesn't mean one has 'taken it' from another source with yellow magic marker in some anthology, nor does it mean one has invented, eureka, an idea out of the blue ... it means one struggles with an ongoing endlessly materially disturbing problem and ... so have others. It doesn't subtract from the force of the insight and importance of how it forms one's thinking thereafter about viewing, seeing, thinking, knowing, as well as about truth, beauty, etc. and questions of recognition/illusionism, narrative/anti-narrative, etc.

Whereas *pleasure and instruction* was Sophoclean, *perception versus knowledge* was anything but. As for him, what one sees is what one knows, even in the case of the future anterior: Oedipus' blinding/blindness *is* his sight/insight, which is his perception, which is (isn't) his knowledge.

Peter Gidal
London, October 2015

THEORY AND DEFINITION OF STRUCTURAL/MATERIALIST FILM
1975

Structural/Materialist Film

Structural/Materialist film attempts to be non-illusionist. The process of the film's making deals with devices that result in demystification or attempted demystification of the film process. But by 'deals with' I do not mean 'represents'. In other words, such films do not document various film procedures, which would place them in the same category as films which transparently document a narrative, a set of actions, etc. Documentation, through usage of the film medium as transparent, invisible, is exactly the same when the object being documented is some 'real event', some 'film procedural event', some 'story', etc. An avant-garde film defined by its development towards increased materialism and materialist function does not *represent*, or *document*, anything. The film produces certain relations between segments, between what the camera is aimed at and the way that 'image' is presented. The dialectic of the film is established in that space of tension between materialist flatness, grain, light, movement, and the supposed real reality that is represented. Thus a consequent attempted destruction of the illusion is a constant necessity.

In Structural/Materialist film, the in/film (not in/frame) and film/viewer material relations, and the relations of structure of the film are primary to any representational content. The structuring aspects and the attempt to decipher the structure and anticipate/recorrect it, to clarify and analyse the production-process of the given (that is, the specific image at any specific moment), is the root concern of Structural/Materialist film. The specific construct of each specific film is not the relevant point; one must beware not to let the construct, the shape take the place of the 'story' in narrative film. Then one would merely be substituting one hierarchy for another within the same system, a formalism for what is traditionally called content. This is an absolutely crucial point.[1]

Devices

Through usage of specific filmic devices such as repetition within duration one is forced to attempt to decipher the film's material and construct, and to decipher the precise transformations that each co/incide/nce of cinematic techniques produces. The attempt is primary to any specific shape, otherwise the discovery of shape (fetishizing shape or system) may become the theme, in fact, the narrative of the film. This is a crucial distinction for a dialectically materialist definition of structural film. That is why Structural/Materialist film in fact demands an orientation of definition completely in opposition to the generally used vague notions of 'Structural Film'.

---

1 The concept of structure's import *vis-à-vis* representational content's import led to the notion of shape taking precedence and confused the issue nearly irreparably. Slight shifts become major theoretical interventions which change the locus of meaning of the work being produced, and the axis along which it operates in time. This is not mere obsessive Talmudic or French academic (what analogue) preoccupation. It is not just a matter of "the cabalistic jargon of Jewish writers (of the fables of antiquity)". John Boswell, Vicar of Taunton, "On History", *A Method of Study or An Useful Library*, 1738.

  Althusser's concept of the most absolutely essential importance of the correct usage of the word bears remembering; the correct formulation is necessary to close the gap between advanced theoretical practice and the dominance of idealist speech. Louis Althusser, *Reading Capital*, 1965.

Production

Each film is a record (not a representation, not a reproduction) of its own making. *Pro*duction of relations (shot to shot, shot to image, grain to image, image dissolution to grain, etc.) is a basic function which is in direct opposition to *re*production of relations. Elsewhere in this essay I shall try to further elucidate this problematic of production versus reproduction. Suffice to say here that it is the core of meaning which differentiates illusionist from anti-illusionist film. When one states that each film is a record of its own making, this refers to shooting, editing, printing stages, or separations of these, dealt with specifically. Such film militates against dominant (narrative) cinema. Thus viewing such a film is at once viewing a film and viewing the 'coming into presence' of the film, i.e. the system of consciousness that produces the work, that is produced by, and in, it.

Represented 'Content'

Any represented content exists beneath the structure (or above it). There is this representational 'reality' one is aiming the camera at. This remains true even if for example the representational content is pared down to the filmstrip itself being pulled through the printer. That in fact isn't necessarily a paring down at all. The Structural/Materialist film must minimize the content in its overpowering, imagistically seductive sense, in an attempt to get through this miasmic area of 'experience' and proceed with film as film. Devices such as loops or seeming loops, as well as a whole series of technical possibilities, can, carefully constructed to operate in the correct manner, serve to veer the point of contact with the film past internal content. The content thus serves as a function upon which, time and time again, a film-maker works to bring forth the filmic event.[2]

The usage of the word content so far has been within the common usage, i.e. representational content. In fact, the real content is the form, form become content. Form is meant as: formal operation, not as composition. Also, form must be distinguished from style, otherwise it serves merely in its reactionary sense to mean formal*ism*, such as: this formal usage (e.g. Welles) versus that (e.g. Sternberg).

Film as Material

The assertion of film as material is, in fact, predicated upon representation, inasmuch as 'pure' empty acetate running through the projector gate without image (for example) merely sets off another level of abstract (or not) associations. Those associations, when instigated by such a device, are no more materialist or non-illusionist than any other associations. Thus the film event is by no means, through such a usage, necessarily demystified. 'Empty screen' is no less significatory than 'carefree happy smile'.[3] There are myriad possibilities for co/optation and integration of filmic procedures into the repertoire of meaning.

---

2   By the word *film-maker*, though, I do not mean to imply that the producer (same) is inserted as mythical figure, as shadow symbol of the 'real', as mirror. Anonymity is indeed prerequisite; but a superficial anonymity imitated into existence through e.g. 'coldness' (i.e. heavy atmospheric intervention) functions precisely as the opposite of its supposed intention. Anonymity must in fact be transformationally created, dialectically posited into the filmic eventiveness itself. That is, anonymity must be the result, at a specific instance; it too must be produced, rather than illustrated or obliquely poetically 'given'.

3   This is so because of: associativeness, symbolic reading, integration into the diegesis, subsumation to the dominant illusory system posited, displacement to a mere different level of fantasy-acceptance, poetic shock supportive of the primary story, etc. The signifier and the signified as arbitrary, as artifice, and as less than primary, is the arena in which production of 'meaning' must take place. Meaning at this stage must be seen to clearly obtain to Structural/Materialist reading. Yet by collaborating in the current usage of the term *reading* I separate myself from the bourgeois oppression of the dominance of the word while acknowledging its hegemony.

The Viewer

The mental activation of the viewer is necessary for the procedure of the film's existence. Each film is not only structural but also structuring. This is extremely important as each moment of film reality is not an atomistic, separate entity but rather a moment in a relativistic generative system wherein one can't *simply* break down the experience into elements. The viewer is forming an equal and possibly more or less opposite 'film' in her/his head, constantly anticipating, correcting, re-correcting ... constantly intervening in the arena of confrontation with the given reality, i.e. the isolated chosen area of each film's work, of each film's production.

Dominant Cinema

In dominant cinema, a film sets up (cardboard) characters (however deep their melodramas) and through identification and various reversals, climaxes, complications (usually in that order) one aligns oneself unconsciously with one or another or both or more characters. These internal connections between viewer and viewed are based on systems of identification which demand primarily a passive audience, a passive viewer, one who is *involved* in the meaning that word has taken on within film journalese, i.e. to be not involved, to get swept along through persuasive emotive devices employed by the film director. This system of cinematic functioning categorically rules out any dialectic. It is a cinematic functioning, it should be added, analogous on the part of the film director to that of the viewer, not to mention the producer, who is not a producer, who has no little investment in the staking out of the economics of such repression. What some of the more self-defined 'left wing' directors would rationalize in terms of dialectic are merely cover ups for identification, selling the same old wares, *viz* Antonioni and the much less talented

Bertolucci, Pasolini, Losey, not to mention committed right wing directors like Ford, Kazan, Bergman and Russell. Thus, if a character is somewhat more complex, or if the acting is of a higher order, or if the lighting cameraman does most of the work (as in most first-rate movies) then the director rationalizes the work which would seem to imply that he is as taken in by the fantasy as the viewer. Whether he is or not (there are few shes in such a position) is in fact irrelevant. The ideological position is the same.

Dialectic

There is a distinct difference between what can be termed the *ambiguity of an identification process*[4] and a *dialectic function-*

---

4 In the Japanese theatre, an actor holding a mask in front of his/her face, so the audience can see the 'real' face behind, is for all that no less identificatory, no less co-optable into the narrative structure and diegetic linearity. The essential grasping of this example is crucial to the basis for the whole theoreticization of the problem of narrative. So far all essays on narrative and narrative deconstruction have been mechanistic, derivative of dominant cinema's needs, in inverted form, with no break (epistemological or otherwise). The same goes for all attempts at narrative-deconstructive cinema. It is in order to point to the fact that illustration of a thesis (of deconstruction, or other) in (on) film denies duration, the basic cinematic structure. Illustration *mystifies filmic real relations*; the basic project then is thus illusionism, not deconstruction of representational codes, the latter being recuperated as the narrative is constituted (and not presented as such).

The latter statement should not be seen to imply naiveté on my part as to the frequent occurrence of so-called non-narrative film which in fact sets up an imagist illusionism, a set of ideological codifications equally manipulatory, undialectical, identificatory. The system of identification into the imagist code relies heavily on the usage of the imaginary referent, that which is referred to transparently, wherein the medium is not produced as opaque. This system of identification also relies heavily on the repression of the production of the signifier-as-arbitrary, that is, as the strictly ideologically posited coherence artificially manufactured between signifier and signified. As long as these relations are not studied and made to produce work, the illusionist project is not one step further out of its miasmic repressed state.

I must add: when stating that in identification real relations are mystified, I in no way refer to real *relations* in a positivist or empiricist manner.

ing. Ambiguity posits each individual viewer (or reader, listener, etc.) as subject. The subject, that is, who forms *the* interpretation. One becomes posited, formed, constituted, in fact, as the subject of the self-expression and self-representation through the mediation of a repressive ideological structure. That ideological structure is in this case narrative cinema, part of which is the process of identification. Ambiguity aligns itself as a concept (and therefore as a reality) with the concept of freedom and individualism. The two latter concepts are extremely rigidified in late capitalism. The individual also thus becomes posited as static, as essence, as ideal (or referring to the possibility of such). The individual becomes posited as unitary, 'free' view, centred in deep perspective space away from the screen, and invisibly solidified, ever-present. Our whole formation towards, and in, filmic enterprises is dominated by such ideological strangleholds.

Webster's 1961 *New Collegiate Dictionary*:

Empiricism: (1b) Practice of medicine founded on mere experience, without aid of science. (c) Quackery. (2) The philosophical theory attributing the origin of *all* knowledge to experience.

Empirical: Depending on experience or observation alone, without due regard to science and theory.

Positivism: A system of philosophy which excludes everything but natural phenomena or properties of knowable things, together with their relations of coexistence *and succession* (italics mine).

Positive: (3) Independent of changing circumstances or relations; opposed to relative and comparative.

"For objective dialectics the absolute is also to be found in the relative. The unity, the coincidence, identity, resultant force, of opposites, is conditional, temporary, transitory, and relative." Lenin, "On Dialectics", in *Materialism and Empirio-Criticism*, 1909.

"Feeling like a voyeur watching Warhol's pornographic *Couch* is precisely *not* to be in the position of a voyeur. It is precisely the *stare*, (and the seeming stare of *Wavelength*) that works to counter the identificatory process, though it does not of necessity smash it. And the word *subvert* has become too clichéd and ambiguous to be used effectively in this context. The ineffable stare presents the medium's presence, though positing a deep space centrepoint out from the screen, across from the objects of the film, particularly in *13 Most Beautiful Women* and parts of *Chelsea Girls*." Peter Gidal, London College of Printing Notes on Film, 1971.

Identification

The commercial cinema could not do without the mechanism of identification.[5] It is the cinema of consumption, in which the viewer is of necessity not a producer,[6] of ideas, of knowledge.

5   Aristotelian catharsis is inseparable from identification and the purging (whether this is a pseudo, i.e. unreal, concept or not) is inextricably bound to the latter's operations.
6   In reference to my own work, Michael Snow implies such a constant production rather than consumption. The example is apt because often what seems like (and is, in fact) an untheorized position is of the order of a theoretical supposition. Snow's words: "... your film (*Room Film 1973*) had to be worked at. I felt as if it were made by my father, as if it were made by a blind man. I feel that searching, tentative quality, that quality of trying to see." (MS, September 1973). This attempt at verbalization, loose as it is, in fact is stating theoretically clearly beneath the surface an aesthetic necessitating dialectic attempts at image arrestation, the necessity for production rather than consumption. "Sometimes the repeating shots would be clear, sometimes one couldn't tell if it was continuous." The constitution of the work, coming from the material relations of the work, but not mechanistically positioning (i.e. illustrating) itself tautologically, is at the base of the meaning of Snow's statement. Similarly, what seems an aesthete's formalist delight in light in Jonas Mekas' (*Village Voice*, 10 February 1975 and 29 October 1973) and to some extent Lucy Fischer's piece on my film are really attempts to bring to speech a problematic of the constitution of the filmic image opaquely through the agency of light, the whole problematic thus of image-constitution *through* something, a representation as a constitution rather than as a given, 'captured' transparently. This theoretically important difference is thus elucidated beneath the idealist mask which film prose in fact mostly is. Fischer is more analytical, less poetic, than Mekas. I quote only the former, the quote most apt to be diversionary *without meaning to be so*. "The rest of the film proceeds with an examination *of* a room and the way that light illumin*ates* the objects *within it*." Lucy Fischer, *SoHo Weekly News*, 16 January 1975, italics mine.

According to Lawrence Van Gelder in the *New York Times* (17 January 1975), "It (*Room Film 1973*) is a murky, granular journey *around* a room, *broken* by occasional *incursions* of light." The ideological concept of journey, a man's journey through a *given* universe, is somehow at the base of the writings on *Room Film 1973*. It is as if all film were (and I suspect this to be the case) still recuperated as some form of masked or not-so-masked documentary rather than a filmic articulation and constituting presence, a filmic production precisely in its operations on the level of the *problematics* of procedure and representation. That the pseudo-documentary is *the* unspoken gap in current film knowledge, in terms of theory, practice, and theoretical practice, I have hinted at elsewhere. ("Un cinéma matéraliste structurel", *Chroniques de l'art vivant*, No. 55, February 1975, as well as "5th Experimental Film Festival at Knokke/Heist, Belgium", *Studio International*, March/April 1975.) Past attentions given by me to critiques of my work made above examples (of a general malaise) closest at hand.

Capitalist consumption reifies not only the structures of the economic base but also the constructs of abstraction. Concepts, then, do not produce concepts; they become, instead, ensconced as static 'ideas' which function to maintain the ideological class war and its invisibility, the state apparatus in all its fields.

The mechanism of identification demands a passive audience, a passive mental posture in the face of a life unlived, a series of representations, a fantasy identified with for the sake of 90 minutes' illusion. And that 'fantasy' is often not *even* the insipid utopian romance of 'what should be' (Marcuse's justification for Goethe's poems) nor the so-called 'intervention' in bourgeois morality that at moments *may* be approached in de Sade, Lautréamont, Sacher-Masoch (never without intensely counterproductive repressions and paranoiac violence stimulating and appeasing the bourgeois' tastes and tolerances).

Identification is inseparable from the procedures of narrative, though not totally covered by it. The problematic centres on the question as to whether narrative is inherently authoritarian, manipulatory and mystificatory, or not. The fact that it requires identificatory procedures and a lack of distanciation to function, and the fact that its only possible functioning is at an illusionistic level, indicates that the problematic has a clear resolution. In that sense, it is more of a problem than a problematic. The ramifications of the essential, core question are very limited. Narrative is an illusionistic procedure, manipulatory, mystificatory, repressive. The repression is that of space, the distance between the viewer and the object, a repression of real space in favour of illusionist space. The repression is, equally importantly, of the in-film spaces, those perfectly constructed continuities. The repression is also that of time. The implied lengths of time suffer compressions formed by certain technical devices which operate in a codified manner, under specific laws, to repress (material) film time.

Narrative and Deconstruction

A further point on narrative: while the deconstruction of narrative as an academic exercise is not of vital import, it would be in any case a useful function towards expropriating the ownership of the codes of narrativity. Which means that the meanings formed by certain filmic operations could be analysed and no more be the privileged possession of the owners of the means of production, in this case, the means of production of meaning in film. Thus deconstruction exercises, in their limited way, are not irrelevant as sociological insight into certain filmic operations. Deconstruction exercises, maintained filmically (i.e. on film, in film) are direct translations from the written into film, and are thus filmically reactionary, though illustrative of certain ideas *about* film. The retranslation back into language (words) would seem to negate the necessity of narrative-deconstruction being undertaken on, or in, film, rather than in writing. This has now dawned, perhaps, on the overzealous graduates who wish to make statements about certain narrative usages.

Apart from work in deconstruction, there is also that film-work which is interpreted as deconstruction, works which have as their basic project an overhauling (not a criticizing and not a smashing) of narrative, such as the pseudo-narratives of Robbe-Grillet's appalling films, or Straub's post- (and sometimes pre-) Brechtian exercises in distanciation and reflection. (Even here the Brecht of the theatre is mistaken for the Brechtian theorizer).[7] Other examples are Dreyer's purist set-pieces of dramatics,

---

7   As to Brecht, there are some illuminating comments from his writings. "Science isn't so free of superstition. Where knowledge doesn't suffice, faith produces itself, and that is always superstition ... our lyricists didn't lose their voice because of the book *Capital* but in the face of Capital itself." "If Realism *isn't* defined purely formalistically (that which in the 90s was considered Realism, in the realm of the bourgeois novel) then much can be said against techniques like montage, interior monologue, or distancing (*Verfremdung*), only not from the point of view of Realism! ... as a technical means, the interior monologue (of Joyce) was rejected, one called it formalist. I never

straightforward identificatory narratives, the identification merely shifted from the psychological/emotional to the psychological/rationalistic. The identification into the narrative is into the thoughts, the ideas about the actions, the decisions, the *ratio*, instead of the melodramatic unthought motivations of characters propelled by unthought 'fear', 'desire', etc., as in most other films. An essay is urgently needed on the theme of narrative versus non-narrative form and on the inadequacy of the mechanistic deconstruction approach which ends up illustrating rather than being, which ends up static, time-denying, posited as exemplary rather than relative, contradictory, motored into filmic, durational transformation through dialectic procedures.

---

understood the reasoning. Just because Tolstoy would've done it differently isn't a reason to reject the way Joyce does it. The objections were constructed so superficially that one got the impression that if Joyce had put the same monologue (Molly Bloom's final one) in the psychoanalytical session, everything would've been all right."

"Realist, that means consciously influenced by reality, and consciously influencing reality ... the techniques of Joyce and Döblin are not simply waste products; if one eliminates their influence, instead of modifying it, one ends up merely with the influence of the epigones, such as the Hemingways. The works of Joyce and Döblin betray, in the largest sense, the world-historical contradictions into which the forces of production have fallen *vis-à-vis* the relations of production. In the works, productive forces are represented to a certain degree. Especially the socialist writers can learn valuable highly developed technical means (*Elemente*) from these documents of hopelessness (*Ausweglosigkeit*). *They* see the way out." "Perhaps our readers might just *not* feel that they've been given the *key* to events when they, seduced by many wiles (*Künste*) merely take part in (*beteiligen*) the soulful emotions of the heroes." Bertolt Brecht, "Über den Realismus" (1938-1940), *Gesammelte Werke*, Suhrkamp, 1967.

Brecht also, of course, wavered from the above views more often than not; though he fought against the formalist notions of Realism which the social(ist) realists conveniently sidetracked, he also wrote often of a "Realism directly from the standpoint of a class, unfolding the ruling viewpoints as the viewpoints of the ruling, and ... representing reality the way it is" (*die Realität wiedergeben*). Brecht's usage of the word representation, of modification, shan't be questioned at this point.

Correct class position and representation were linked for BB. For certain film-makers currently working, this is not only *not* a necessary link, it is a vital weak link. The whole platform between two ideological camps within film production rests, finally, on this opposition; it is the overdetermining aspect. The anti-illusionist project is determined, or not, at this juncture.

Art Movements

Two art movements had their special effects on the current avant-garde Structural/Materialist film, and on those structural films which are working in that direction. The art movements were: the aesthetics of Abstract Expressionism (though not necessarily the imagist results) and Minimalism (to include such work as Stella's).[8] A major problem erupts here: that of making visible the procedure, presenting such as opposed to annexing, using such. Throughout this essay, virtually every problem centres on the opposition between usage and presentation, incorporating versus foregrounding, etc. There exists also the problem of the 'sensitive' artist, ever-present *in* the final object, which can be one end, the means to which is an art which may record its own making. But the other end, and the division must be

---

8   "Stella's emotional and critical reaction at this time against what he considered rhetorical in the Abstract Expressionist posture was more marked than the gradual mutation of his style suggests. 'I think I had been badly affected by what could be called the romance of Abstract Expressionism', Stella recalls, 'particularly as it filtered out to places like Princeton and around the country, which was the idea of the artist as terrifically sensitive, everchanging, ever ambitious person – particularly as described in magazines like *Art News* and *Arts*, which I read religiously. It began to be kind of obvious and ... terrible, and you began to see through it ... I began to feel very strongly about finding a way that wasn't so wrapped up in the hullabaloo, or a way of working that you couldn't write about ... something that was stable, in a sense, something that wasn't constantly a record of your sensitivity, a record of flux.'" William Rubin, *Frank Stella*, MoMA, 1970.

"'I always get into arguments', he reported, 'with people who want to retain the 'old values' in painting - the 'humanistic' values that they always find on the canvas. If you pin them down, they always end up asserting that there is something there besides the paint on the canvas. My painting is based on the fact that only what can be seen is there ... If the painting were lean enough, accurate enough, or right enough, you would just be able to look at it. All I want anyone to get out of my paintings, and all I ever get out of them, is the fact that you can see the whole idea without any confusion ... What you see is what you see.'" (Ibid) I quote the above with full awareness that the statements broaden the parameters and raise as many confusions as they attempt to close up, yet in relation to the problematical, humanistic, ideology of process, Stella was more aware than most. And this his painting at its best is also clear on.

carefully analysed and researched with each case in question, is that of an art which is *not* an imagist creation, a decorative object (narrative or otherwise) separated from its means of production without a trace left. If the final work magically represses the procedures which in fact are there in the making, then that work is not a materialist work. This is a crucial point as to usage versus presentation. And in each work many factors are operating which produce either an overdetermination of the usage (i.e. repression) of the procedures, *or* an overdetermination of the presentedness of the procedures.

Jacques Derrida has clearly clarified what in fact is at stake in a work, in the procedure of constituting a work. His definition of *differance* (with an 'a') is useful precisely because it clarifies an aspect of work which previously was latent but not brought to speech, not adequately theorized and which therefore always fell back into the ideology of illusionism and unseen subject (the artist).

> We shall designate by the term *differance* the movement by which language or any code, any system of reference in general, becomes historically constituted as a fabric of differences ... *Differance* is what makes the movement of signification possible only if each element that is said to be 'present', appearing on the stage of presence, is related to something other than itself but retains the mark of a past element and already lets itself be hollowed out by the mark of its relation to a future element. This trace relates no less to what is called the future than to what is called the past, and it constitutes what is called the present by this very relation to what it is not, to what it absolutely is not; that is, not even to a past or a future considered as a modified present ... We ordinarily say that a sign is put in place of the thing itself, the present thing – 'thing' holding here for the sense as well as the referent. Signs represent the present in its absence; they take the place of the present. When we cannot take hold of or show the thing, let us say the present, the being

present, when the present does not present itself, *then* we signify, we go through the detour of signs."

Jacques Derrida, "Differance" (1967), *Speech and Phenomena*, Northwestern University Press, 1973[16b]

The aesthetics of Abstract Expressionism could in fact produce an imagist object which never separated itself from individualist psychological origins, whereas the 'same' aesthetic base could function in certain works as production itself *presented*, distanced. Such presentation of production functions in certain drawings of targets by Johns (for example), distancing the object as object, as created text, towards which the various marks added to each other, negating, erasing, produce further elaborations towards an as yet unfulfilled total surface.[9] (*Total* is used in the sense of at some point coming to a stop.) The essential locus is again the question of psychological orientation, that is, *identification*, whether into the 'fantastic' or the 'real' or the 'surreal', in opposition to stated notions of *distancing*. But it must be clarified that the distancing is *not* from some *wholly elaborated* fantastic, real or surreal, from which a distance is created. Rather, the text itself is elaborated and constituted in such a way that the whole work process of reading the marks necessitates a reading of differences and a dialecticization of the material procedures which produce the marking one is confronted with. The subject of the work is not the invisible artist symbolically inferred through the work's presence, but rather the whole foregrounded fabric of the complex system of markings itself.

What Stella may have verbalized correctly (see footnote 8) did not prevent his work from becoming exactly the Abstract Expressionist problem, the whole conglomeration of feelings, associations, seductions, representations, which an imagist work demands no matter how 'process' oriented the production

9 Michel Foucault in *Von der Subversion des Wissens*, in the interviews with Gilles Deleuze and Paulo Caruso, is particularly illuminating. (Hanser, 1974)

process itself was. Similarly the process of making a Welles or Fassbinder film is not in an adequate way the product. This is the root of the whole problem I am trying to get at. Some of Stella's early works could escape this abstract expressionist route, just as many of Johns' and Giacometti's works fail to avoid or solve that problem though some instances of their works do. Process as general definition is in fact vacuous. This vacuous definition is nevertheless filled, ideologically rigidified, in such a way that few works escape through the gap left, and those works are a conjuncture (happenstance or not) of a whole range of incidents and factors, co/incide/nces which enable this escape from the co/opting 'process' definition and concreteness. This 'escape' is not a displacement (which would therefore create a misunderstanding, or a theoretical gap, elsewhere) or a suppression, but an adequate solution of questions correctly posed in terms of materialist practice and theoretical embodiment. That doesn't mean the artist consciously verbalized the degrees and factors which had significance in the creation of the object that finds its way out, escaping the recuperative pseudo-freedom of the epithet 'process'. Stella's good intentions count for little, and *vice versa* for Klee's often naturalistic representational, evolutionist notions, radically countermanded by those works which form a conjuncture of structural disassociation, pared down 'simplicity' in terms of imagery and internal relations, formalized colour schemes and other factors, to realize (produce) works which function in a non-naturalized, textual presentedness. Non-naturalization means specifically that the works don't fit into the category of naturalness, whether this naturalness refers to the image-content (i.e. naturalness of the representation) or to what is natural *for painting*, what is allowable, what does not necessitate a reading but rather falls blindly into parameters of meaning consciously or unconsciously predefined.

Reading Duration

A materialist reading at one with the inscription of the work (which *is* the work) is enabled or forced: Klee's usage, in these cases, of the virtually unloaded or nearly empty signifier (Foucault cites them as 'completely empty signifiers') is possibly the dominant factor in the adequate presentation of materialist art practice in works such as *Alter Klang, Doppelzelt* (1923) etc.[10] Signifiers approaching emptiness means merely (!) that the image taken does not have a ready associative analogue, it is not a given symbol, metaphor or allegory; that which is signified by the signifier, that which is conjured up by the image given, is something formed by past connections but at a very low key, not a determining or overdetermining presence, merely a not highly charged moment of meaning. Thus, although this example is terrifyingly oversimplified, the edge of a leaf seen for a moment only, or only seen (in a film, for instance) slightly, related to other equally insignificant signifiers (within a context which allows them to operate as insignificant) does not necessarily lead to associations stronger than 'leaf', or 'another leaf quite similar' or 'room, leaf, not extremely emotional, no extreme existential *angst*, doubt, etc. A leaf. Not: a mere leaf, fluttering image or lonely fragility. Etc.' And that low level signifier in momentary interplay with other low level signifiers, foregrounds, brings forth a materialist (possibly) play of differences which don't have an overriding hierarchy of meaning, which don't determine the ideological reading, which don't direct into heavy associative symbolic realms. The actual relations between images, the handling, the appearance, the '*how* it is', etc., takes precedence over any of the 'associative' or 'internal' meanings. Thus is presented the *arbitrariness* of meaning imbibed in, for example, such an image-moment of a leaf. The unnaturalness, ungivenness, of

---

10 For a beginning though also insufficient piece of work on the above-mentioned, see my "Beckett & Others & Art: A System", *Studio International*, November 1974.

any possible meaning is posited. Such practice thereby counters precisely the ideological usages which are dominant; the usages which *give meaning* to images, things, signs, etc., meanings which are then posited as natural, as residing within. The whole idealist system is opposed by a materialist practice of the production of meaning, of the arbitrariness of the signifier. (Meaning is *made*.) And for this concept, this thought, the semiotic notions of signifier/signified are of tremendous import.

In film, duration as material piece of time is the basic unit. "Does a painting come into existence all at once? No, it's built up piece by piece, not different from a house. When a point becomes movement and line, it takes up time. Similarly, when a line pulls itself out into a plane. And the same when a flat plane becomes a three-dimensional enclosure. And the viewer, does he (she) respond to the work as a whole? Often yes, unfortunately." (Paul Klee, *Schöpferische Konfession*.) I am not positing direct cause and effect, or even direct analogue, between painting and film. Similarly, the effect, more specifically, of Abstract Expressionism and Minimalism on Structural/Materialist Film is not direct; some films were made before, during, or after essential works in painting, in photography, in film, in writing. Work by Hill-Adamson, Lumière, Vertov, Ruttman, Moholy-Nagy, Cameron, Klee, Kafka, Joyce, the Dadaists, Beckett lies at the root of much avant-garde practice this century.[11]

The problematic of reading duration when viewing a painting was important to Klee and others. Actual duration can only exist in film, in terms of the approximation towards a 1:1 relation between work and viewer (production time and 'reading' time). Vertov's *Man with a Movie Camera*, Eisenstein's *Strike*, Lumière's films, form a core of basic work in this field of research, the anti-illusionist project. As to structural music, Bach's preludes and fugues relate strongly to some of the work

---

11   Including Joyce's 'unreadable' but essential *Finnegans Wake* and Beckett's late works, *How It Is* (1964) and *Not I* (1973).

of Terry Riley, Steve Reich (*Stick Piece*), etc. More specific to film: 'real' time is more often than not utilized in the Structural/Materialist film in clearly defined segments or in the film as a whole, thus breaking from illusionistic time (substructured in codes of narrativity). The closing of the gap in space between viewer and viewed, and between the representation in one shot and another, is a basic repressive illusionist device. The implication of an unseen splice to integrate two shots also elides the function of editing, the function of producing, from material segments, a new complex relation. Instead, there is a seeming natural flow established, which suppresses all procedures of the editing stages. The concept of integration rather than disruption is predicated on a repression of the material relations specific to the film process, and this of course is not unconnected with the violence done to (eradicate) the adequate *presentation* of material relations in the sphere of ideology, of the image, of plastic representation, narrative mimesis, etc. Attempted in Structural/Materialist film is a non-hierarchical, cool, separate unfolding of a perceptual activity. That perceptual activity is *not* to be understood as relegating the primary function to the individual perceiver, who of course is embedded in ideological structures/strictures. The problematics of perception as a concept have yet to be delineated. Still, film is a perceptual activity (amongst others) and without perception and the relations attendant upon that process there is no film practice (or in any case not one that is non-idealistic, not one that is not mechanistically materialist).

Distance

Through the attempted non-hierarchical, cool, separate unfolding a distance(ing) is sought. This distance reinforces (rather than denying) the dialectic interaction of viewer with each film moment, necessary if it is not to pass into passiveness and needlessness. This interaction on the level of flesh and on the level of critical praxis is obvious. The real time element demands such a consciousness and will. I can here only hint at the deeper problematic within which the 'real time' 1:1 relation between viewer and viewed is located.

Aspects of Time

(1) 'Real time', that is, time present as it is for the filmmaker, denoted not connoted at the stage of shooting, editing, printing, projecting, and interrelations of these. Commonly, 'real time' is presented in single takes or film segments utilized for their actual duration (often after many viewings they separate themselves as such). (2) There is illusionistic time, time made to seem what it is not, as in conventional and in much, it must be said, Eisensteinian editing. Cutting from 10.15 London interior the lovers kiss, to midnight, near the lake, husband and wife murder each other, longshot. (Either implying a linear thread of events, with time compressed, or a simultaneity, with time compressed.) (3) The third 'example' is that of post-Newtonian time, Einsteinian time. There is here no absolute value other than that of the interaction of film moment and viewer. This relativistic time may but does not necessarily connect to 'real time'. The notion of 'real time' on its own fails to take account precisely of this relativistic nature of time, the absence of some universal clock, though for lack of a more precise definition 'real time' did serve its purpose *apropos* for example much of Warhol's filmwork (interrupted by splices and leader fogging).

Reflexiveness

Another matter which the investigation of Structural/Materialist film brings forth is the bearing it has on reflexiveness, which is inculcated by a film through certain procedures. Reflexiveness, or self-reflexiveness, or auto-reflexiveness, is a condition of self-consciousness which invigorates the procedure of filmic analysis *during* the film viewing event. Thus it is not merely a matter of reflection, or thinking, broadly taken. Reflexiveness, as a concept, can serve a meaning counterproductive to the direction Structural/Materialist film would give it.[12] It can, for example, serve as a decoy, an alibi, the opening up of individual interpretation. Such simulacra turn the ideological thrust of an issue towards radically reactionary paths, and bring one's work clearly to a point where each conceptual entity must be absolutely clearly defined and rigorously made clear, in order not to move down a blind alley. Without such rigour, one finds the illusionist, narrative, identificatory individualist mode of cinema is re-presented, re-instated without a battle, and the wearying struggle to define clearly and precisely becomes recuperated at the moment of least vigilance. A weak link in one's analysis of idealist, anti-materialist practices, can turn a whole body of work (in film, for example) to uselessness in affecting a forthcoming film's radically *retrograde* practice.

A film practice in which one watches oneself watching is reflexive; the act of self-perception, of consciousness *per se*, becomes one of the basic contexts of one's confrontation with work. The process of the production of *film-making*, and the filmic practice of filmviewing *as production*, become interlinked. 'Reflection' does ideological combat with self-consciousness, reflexiveness. To operate thusly is to break the dichotomy between feeling and thinking, or rather to break the illusion of their necessary separation and the illusion of their automatic oneness. The filmic enterprise, if such, presents consciousness of film to

---

12 Reflexiveness can be as much a diversionary tactic from the anti-illusionist project, as anything. Similarly, the concept of subversion, i.e. subverting the codes, subverting the meaning, is merely a rationalized annexation of precisely those codes and meanings, with attendant guilt contributing the enormous libidinous energy necessary for this repressive operation. The bourgeois academic cine-semiotician's simplistic usage of psychoanalysis is a ruse.

the self. The radical rejection of the *representation* of consciousness is a main concept.

Film cannot adequately represent consciousness any more than it adequately represents meaning; all are transparently, invisibly, encumbered by mystificatory systems and interventions which are distortions, repressions, selections, etc. That a film is not a window to life, to a set of meanings, to a pure state of image/meaning, ought to be self-understood. Thus the documenting of an act of film-making is as illusionist in practice as the documenting of a narrative action (fiction) (within certain codes, both). And consciousness is as encumbered by the illusionist devices of cinema, if one is attempting to document 'it', as anything else. Filmic reflexiveness is the presentation of consciousness to the self and consciousness of the way one deals with the material operations; filmic reflexiveness is forced through cinema's materialist operations of filmic practice.[13]

Self-consciousness, and consciousness *per se*, must in no way imply consciousness as deflecting onto a mythical subject; it must in no way imply transcendence or transcendent subjectivity; it does not set itself up in opposition to real relations, i.e. consciousness as knowledge in opposition to material relations as knowledge. One can see it in a schematic T form, the horizontal being the work upon which functions operate (the film plane), the vertical being 'consciousness', the line to the recipient as her/his necessary mode of inculcated dialectic operation.

---

13 The *self* posited here is situated in its self-alienation/distanciation, and this still refers to the concept, which must be fought, of self as centre (distanced though it be), self as unitary. This psychological centring of the self must be nullified in order to even begin to set up a concept of a dialectically posited, distanciated self. Merely to drop the usage of a word such as *self* does not fulfil the requirement of redefining the word. And the redefining must be done so that *self* is understood, not to be that unitary centre of knowledge, that 'I' through which the world is. For the 'I' does not form the world. Consciousness does not form the world. Material relations form the 'I'. The self is merely a clinical word for a cipher.

Technique

Access to involvement with technique is the formidable basis of all art which poses questions seriously, and which moves forward to new stages of development, the working through of contradiction in its practice. Thus technical innovation is itself ideologically conditioned; in many cases innovations and conceptual entities were not thought through inside a culture though the apparati and the actual scientific discoveries were already present. Or 'one crucial element' would wait 200 years to be discovered. The lag between the possibilities for innovatory technical practices (such as camera and photographic printing) and the realization of such practice (two centuries later)[14] is an ideological one. At the same time, when a new technical practice becomes operative, it bears directly on aesthetic practice (whether it produces that aesthetic practice or is produced by it is a complex matter).

Technique, which is often categorized as separate from aesthetic issues, is in fact inseparable; mass reproduction of photography had a considerable influence on the aesthetic possibilities of the mass-reproduction of photography, and vice versa. It seems virtually a circular argument, which makes it all the more uncanny that it is so often belied. The aesthetics of silk-screening as it is practiced (usage) by a Warhol has considerable relation to the technical fact of silkscreening *and* to the techniques made possible by certain *inventions* and their utilization at a certain period. In film, e.g. the flattening-out of space is possible through various devices of camera (usage) and this is an involvement with technique that is unavoidably present as the aesthetic basis of the work. In film, also, slow motion is a technical *invention*, inseparable from analytic work on representation. Thus involvement with technique refers to two phenomena:

---

14   Thomas Neumann, *Sozialgeschichte der Photographie*, Luchterhand, 1966.

(1) *Inventions* which make possible, fulfil, technical needs (and those technical needs are inseparable from the aesthetic which produces them and which they produce); (2) Aesthetic *usage*, inseparable from technical possibilities.

Theory and Practice

An important problem is the question of continuing and broadening advanced practice without elaborating distinct theory. The filmwork itself is an ideological practice, and in some cases a theoretical practice. Film Theory, if such exists, takes the form of written retrospective history which can function as a basis for its own practice (theoretical practice) and/or for the practice of film-making as it correlates to the theoretical embodied in it. (How it is how it is what it is.) Much formulation taking place at the moment deals with retrograde work, but this may be a step towards being equipped to deal adequately with Structural/Materialist film. Adequate work is indeed necessary in film-making and writing 'on' film. A semiotics that is right-wing is not the only one I can envisage, though little else is at the moment forthcoming. One can cite, in support of the above assertion, the lamentably reactionary, symbolic interpretation by Barthes of a series of Eisenstein stills. Such a position needs combating, but so too does Foucault's superb Marxist/Althusserian *interpretation* of, for example, Magritte's retrograde picture-puzzle-gimmicks. What we are stuck with is often advanced theoretical formulation, critically adapted to work which does not warrant such. This results in a *reading into* the work. For such a critical operation, the most reactionary work will suffice because, after all, one can read one's 'personal' list of wishful-thinking into virtually any film. Partaking of the primal scene and 'work on the signifier' seem to be the two most current malpractices.

> Left to itself, a spontaneous (technical) practice produces only the 'theory' it needs as a means to produce the ends assigned to it; this 'theory' is never more than the reflection of this end, uncriticized, unknown, in its means of realization; that is, it is a by-product of the reflection of the technical practice's end on its means. A 'theory' which does not question the end whose by-product it is remains a prisoner of this end and of the realities which have imposed it as an end. Examples of this are many of the branches of psychology, of sociology, and of Politics, of Economics, of Art, etc. ...
>
> Louis Althusser, *For Marx*, 1965

We have, among English advanced film-makers, work which utilizes traditional, transparent documentary film-making in an unthought manner, under the guise of Structural/Materialist operation. The usage, for example, of black leader to be cut into a film to be the *image of* the time when the camera motor was not running is a mystification of the most dangerous sort. The unthoughtness of such work can devise routes back to the apparent point of departure. One then ends up, through this repressive re-routing, at a stage prior to that of the anti-illusionist project. In fact, these mis-routings can lead further back, to the original point of aggression, the stimulus to one's film practice in the first place, i.e. the 'straight' documentary against which the anti-illusionist film project is working. In this example, black leader posits a direct representation of time, which it in fact is not. It posits a direct representation of an action, 'camera motor turned off', which it is not. Thus it is a representation which does not present itself. It posits itself as an image of something other than itself, which it in fact is not. It posits a gap between two 'realities', i.e. the preceding shot and the following shot, thus attempting to annihilate its *presence* (thus representing and repressing at the same time). Unquestioned in the above cited operation is the signifying area as well; no investigation, let alone intervention, is undertaken *apropos* that area. Thus the usage of black leader as posited in my example (a minute example merely hinted at here) instantiates an illusionist operation which is then covered, or masked.

The demarcations must be drawn all the more strictly when dealing with such work precisely because the rearguard revision it performs is seemingly not obvious. That some films do not in any way posit such rearguard work, though their makers cannot bring to adequate speech the verbalized transcription of their filmic method and practice, is in no way a contradiction in terms. The question of (artistic) intention comes up here, and whether or not that intention can be said to exist precisely by its presence in the work. More often than not, the non-verbalization of intention is not a sign of the non-translatability of the specific film practice into words, but rather a mere absence of *correct* verbalization, which does not deny in those cases the 'absolute' translatability into words of intention. In some few cases, indeed, this is not the case. The root of this question is the mechanistic, simplistic notion that without speech there is no production. It is obvious, nevertheless, that those intentions brought forth to speech are often not what is in fact operating as inscription in (and of) the work. It is the work one deals with; slight shifts in words, like slight shifts in filmwork operations, can radically alter the position and meaning. These slight shifts, which are in fact major shifts, exist in that untranslatability between the maker's intention as thought in speech, the maker's intention as unthought in speech though verbalizable, the maker's intention as unthought *at all*, the maker's intention as untranslatable into speech, though thought (i.e. "I know what I want to do, i.e. in advance and having gone through decision-making processes, but I don't know why i.e. can't say why") etc.

Suppressed in Anglo-Saxon structural and Structural/Materialist film is *any attempt* at theory. Advanced (mainly French) theory (not necessarily directly concerning film) is either not capable of dealing with film or else posits retrograde, illusionist,

post-Bazinian manifestations of such. With the (at best) nearly
total demise (flourishing) of New American Cinema[15] mainly

15 The reactionary basis of most American film-making has only been clarified recently,
and this through only the beginnings of analyses which work upon the mystificatory
and individualist aesthetics (ethics) of that movement. The English problematic as
I've stated is a pseudo-documentary production which does not question itself. (See
my text on Mike Dunford's *Still Life with Pear* in "5th Experimental Film Festival at
Knokke/Heist, Belgium", *Studio International*, March/April 1975.) "The European
film-makers certainly made a much stronger impression though without the presence
of clearly established masters. But that's a way of thinking which many of the Europeans reject ... It's difficult to pin down, but one senses an attitude towards film-making
not as the production of certain great works but as an on-going motive of artistic
work ... European film-makers are wary of the structure and ideology which might
create the conditions for cultural imperialism in the area of film-making. They are,
therefore, involved in a redefinition of the nature and function of film-making that
differs from those of the Americans who are making their way gradually toward
the centre of our own culture." P. Adams Sitney, talking with Annette Michelson, "A
Conversation on Knokke and the Independent Filmmaker", *Artforum*, Vol. 13, No. 9,
May 1975.

The spectre of romantic illusionism and mystique of the individual artist is the
reactionary concept of artist as god, artist as magician, artist as purveyor of beauty,
artist as fascist.

(A) The Film-maker. The film-maker makes the film. It is a source of constant
frustration that the illusion is so rigidly upheld that the film-maker produces not
(only) the film but him/her self in it. Reception of the film ought to be productive,
relational, not consumptive of the invisibly visible artist's character/persona. Even
if Peter Gidal films dark rooms what does it say about me except what it says
about itself, i.e. handheld consistency and repetitiveness presents procedures onto
'subject-matter', dehierarchicalizing it, presenting its arbitrariness as against an
essentialness; ... meaning is (ideologically) produced, not innate. Not a centreframe
steadyfocus annexation; ... constitution/deconstruction, deconstruction/constitution
of image through lightness, blackness, and annihilation as well through extremes of
such ... The film-maker is specifically not produced in the film, if the film operates
on a materialist anti-illusionist level, functioning as a practice, – film not literature,
dealing *with* illusionism, not inside it. Films that end up being adequate documentaries about the artist (subject's) concerns, transparently posit themselves against
anti-illusionist cinema.

(B) Illusion. A constant illusionist/anti-illusionist procedural operation is not
the same as a positing of illusion and questioning its 'reality' in the 'next' shot. True
deconstruction (for which the term is not usable) is simultaneous with construction
and vice versa.

(C) Narrative. Narrative is indeed a possible subcategory in the strategic investigation of illusion-systems; systems of representation, in the process of representation, through its resurgent romanticism, or (at worst) its continued operation as pseudo-narrative investigations, there remain the few English (one Canadian, one Austrian) Structural/Materialist film-makers, lamentably largely existing without the beginnings even of a theoretical/historical approach. Consequently, in most cases (at best) these films open up contradictions between theory (not necessarily of film) and the practice of film-making as it embodies theory i.e. *is theoretical*. That these contradictions are opened up by films which are largely 'unconsciously thought' on the film-makers' parts is another problem.

As to the theoretical practice of film theory, nothing at all seems to have been even begun. The lamentably derivative watered-down stuff regurgitated by the editors of *Screen* is merely importation from at most three Paris sources, which though at moments useful is not directed correctly, is not made to interact with avant-garde film practice in this country (or any other). Operating thusly in a vacuum as far as avant-garde cinema is concerned, it finds itself not coincidentally aligned with dominant cinema, with no production capacity of its own. The English film culture has not been studied, a film culture which has existed in the field of Structural/Materialist film since 1966. The works of the European avant-garde experimental film of the late fifties and the sixties have also not been studied. Thus at its most radical *Screen* switches from an analysis of John Ford or Orson Welles to 'reading' (literally reading words) and even seeing some Godard, Brecht and Straub, in all ideological blindness. Witness to this well-founded polemical statement is the total lack of knowledge shown in discussion with Laura Mulvey and Peter Wollen, when the following 'absurd' 'dialogue' took place (through no fault of PW & LM) in *Screen*, Autumn 1974:

> but filmically this study involves suspension of disbelief. It is this aspect, which is a central base for the whole narrativity-investigation, which is most consistently repressed. This repression overdetermines the whole 'study' of the codes of narrativity, and exposes its essentially reactionary state.

Screen Nevertheless, the importance of language and the way it is used in your film is very different from the kind of irrational, mystic overtones of the Anglo/Saxon avant-gardes, such as Sharits, Wieland, Frampton, and so on. I see your film as closer to a materialist conception of language such as e.g. modern French theories of writing.

Wollen That's an absolutely false characterization of those films. For instance, Hollis Frampton's *Zorns Lemma* (1971) is based on mathematical transformations in relation to the alphabet ...

Screen Which again comes out of mysticism and Kabbala.

Wollen But by that token Kabbalism is also very strong e.g. in Robbe-Grillet. I would say Kabbalism runs very strongly through all that French thought. You can see how, for instance, Jabès and Jewish thought feeds into Derrida. There is a very strong streak of Kabbalism in *Tel Quel* ... I see *Zorns Lemma* on the Straub side of the interface rather than the Brakhage side, though it does have a neoplatonist aspect concerning light.

Screen Maybe we should talk about that some other time.[16a]

16a (I thank Peter Wollen for having brought the issue up in the first place in the interview.) Without wanting to confuse matters I must add that the above diatribe isn't meant to imply that I subscribe to Mulvey's/Wollen's film or their views.

16b In addition, the issue is more complicated than it seems, because the inherent Kabbalistic influence on Derrida and *Tel Quel* (I read no French) to some degree certainly mitigates against a materialist praxis. Jabès' repetitiousness of 'the book', 'the word', etc., in a poem, does not erase the essential metaphysical stance which is elaborated precisely through his redundant symbolic schemata of circularity. But one can see the Jabès-Derrida connection, for example, in segments of the book *Elya* (1969, Gallimard; 1973 Tree Books, Berkeley): "Nothingness is our All. The sky is a repeat of its own absence on which the void bestows a relief of disintegrated constellations. So that there is nothing at the beginning, nothing at the end but a procedure caught in its hesitations and turns. The time the book first begins is a first time for being and things. All writing invites to an anterior reading of the word which the word urges and which we pursue to the frontiers of faded memory." Blanchot's exegesis supports the anti-materialism (and the metaphysical materialism) of Jabès' texts: "*Elya* is a meta-story (whose) breaks let the margins breathe ... the void becomes achievement ... thought shows through."

To add to their misfortune, *Screen*'s editors wrote an introduction, ending with the following statement: "The interview with PW & LM can be described as polemical in the sense that the ideas discussed in it as well as the film itself may appear totally aberrant when seen in the context of British film culture at the present time." Apart from the coy non-normative use of the word *aberrant*, the statement unmasks *Screen*'s editors' complete repression of the film culture existent. So years of study have brought the total repression of the film culture at present, and a weak, though obsessive, grasping at the British Film Institute's pantheon of heroes. Meanwhile, we are told by *Screen*'s editors: "... the purpose is not to provide a more correct or 'scientific' description than either the naive self-evident plot summary or the critical 'interpretation' can provide – on the contrary ... Heath's article (on Welles) is thus an extension of a tradition of work on the American narrative cinema exemplified by the *Cahiers du Cinema* study of *Young Mr. Lincoln* ..." (Ben Brewster, *Screen*, Spring 1975.)

Enough.[17]

---

[17] I have been advised by friends and acquaintances that it may be inapposite to attack *Screen*. I would be untruthful if I didn't admit to a wish to have the Journal of the Society for Education in Film and Television deal seriously with current film practice, avant-garde film. They do, after all, attempt at Marxist film theory. And yes, important translations have been made. Good intentions are not the issue. As I am a film-maker, writings such as this one put me in a dubious position *vis-à-vis* those who may at some stage be dealing with my work, even. Also, I've been told that any critique of *Screen* would more advisedly be calmer, rather than the form of my three-paragraph attack: *angry*. *Screen*'s attitude towards the avant-garde, so far, is mimicking the traditional attitude of criticism over the past 100 years towards contemporary art practices. It would have been rather useful in the past if there had been some critical work done, as the film-makers also would have found themselves, perhaps, reflecting upon their practice to a greater degree. Which can't be bad.

Structural/Materialist Film; End

Structural/Materialist films are at once object and procedure. Some are clearly, blatantly wholist, others work as obvious fragments, non-beginning-non-end film. Both rely upon an aesthetic that tries to create didactic works (learning not teaching, i.e. operational productions not reproductive representations). At the same time there is attempted avoidance of empiricism, and the mystic romanticism of higher sensibility individualism. This romantic base of much American structural film has been elucidated by P. Adams Sitney. Visionary film-making is precisely the post-Blakean mire that Structural/Materialism confronts, whether this confrontation is brought to speech or not. 'Unconsciously thought' processes define themselves in practice. One must go on after Warhol, not revert to a reinvigorated pre-Warholian stance; one ought to be, by now, tired of *express*ing the same old thing ... 'trying to express when there is nothing to *express*'. To ignore the ideological function of Sitney's exegesis of a "new romantic affirmation in recoiling against the tremendously crucial aesthetic attack that Warhol made" is precisely to be embedded in dominant ideology as located in the specific arena being discussed: film. (Sitney, *Film Culture*, Spring 1972.) The ideological direction of Sitney's arguments is not mentioned here as object of my criticism, as it coincides with the ideological weight of the works he discusses and therefore he becomes in fact the most adequate spokesman for and exegete of the films he deals with, with notable exceptions. (I shall also not attempt to elucidate the dominant ideology here in specific terms.) Structural film became merely another aesthetic mode, another formalism, in fact, with a vague set of rules and self-definitions yet without important function or meaning outside its mere differentiation *per se* from previous modes. I see Structural/Materialist film of course within a materialist function if it is to operate usefully. *Some* such works of Structural/Materialist film are the following:

> *Little Dog For Roger*, *Yes No Maybe Not* (Malcolm Le Grice)
> *Wavelength*, *Back and Forth*, *Central Region* (Michael Snow)
> *Trees in Autumn*, *TV*, *Szondi Test*, *Auf der Pfaueninsel* (Kurt Kren)
> *Diagonal* (William Raban)
> *Adebar*, *Schwechater* (Peter Kubelka)
> *Process Red*, *Zorns Lemma* (Hollis Frampton)
> The problematic *Erlanger Programme* (Roger Hammond)
> *Deck* (Gill Eatherley)
> *Film No. 1*, *Man with a Movie Camera* (David Crosswaite)
> *Word Movie*, 3 min section *Razor* in *Fluxfilms* (Paul Sharits)
> My own *Clouds*, *Hall*, *Room Film 1973*
> *Green Cut Gate* (Fred Drummond)

To make distinctions between works is a matter of clearly contextualizing the problematic, and each work's operation within it. Each work must be brought forth to clarity from the multilayered inscriptions that it *is*. Using the term Structural/Materialist is dangerous as well, as it refers to structural film. Equal emphasis must be put on the Materialist 'half' of the term (and a dialectical materialism, not a mechanistic materialism is necessary). The term structural film took as basic assumption the contexts of merely three or four works and devolved a thesis from them, works not all of more than minor importance. Perhaps the same can be said at this juncture of my definition of Structural/Materialist film. The 'theory' was meant for more than parochial definition of these (above) works.

One creates a work. One also creates, in varying degrees, a negation of past work, of historically constituted bases for tradition. The Structural/Materialist film and production of meaning in film, is the production of *film* itself, in its (thought or 'unthought') theoreticalness, and (thought or 'unthought') ideological intervention. To *crucially* intervene in film practice, the 'unthought' must be brought to knowledge, thought. The set of relations between film practice, theoretical practice and film as theory, can then be brought forth to operate in clarity.

*First published in Studio International,
November/December 1975.*

FURTHER FOOTNOTES
1976

I've never given a paper printed beforehand and will try not to deviate. All relates expressly to film theory and film-making by myself if not others though I notice others too – merely don't want to speak for those who speak for themselves.

Precisely the polemical aspect (of my "Theory and Definition of Structural/Materialist Film") opens up the theory to question its own end. In fact *if* it had been headed simply "Notes on Film" it would have had to have been seen as, if anything, *theory* disguised as polemic.

Parenthetically: those who say they can not understand it can not be answered; I suppose many people can understand it, four or five London film-makers have sworn so (!), someone in Manchester quietly working away on film, certain friends, students; ... some don't and those who don't at all I suspect would not understand at all the last issue of *Afterimage*, or the *TLS (Times Literary Supplement)*, which according to Sam Beckett not even farts could penetrate. I'm not asking for immediate comprehension of the turgidities of *Screen*. But as Mayakovsky said, "My poetry is of and for the people but it isn't for people who categorically refuse to think."

Great example, by the way, of critical/polemical work is Marx's *Critique of the Gotha Program*, but does it question itself? Meaning *totally*. No.

A danger is in seeing critical work as theoretical, and in seeing polemics as negating theory, and criticism *per se* as synthesizing, bridging ... that is, seeing criticism as some sort of theory merely because it 'objectively' analyses two modes then discusses both in relation etc. from an 'external' viewpoint. That precisely is where ideology hides.

I read recently, forget where, of Joyce's and Beckett's art of an end of a period or a style or an option or a school or a system. Artwork as an end not beginning, I like to think of *Room Film 1973* that way.

In fact (as to humility and/or comparing one's work and ideas with others, etc.) the whole operation from beginning to end has nothing to do with person, persona, personality, nor personableness.

The construction from where; how; ... art practice has to do with that. Mystificatory practice has to do with the repression of the presentation of the construction from where and how.

No attempted integration of art theories and definitions into film criticism that can be termed potentially serious if not interesting must be done in a way that does not allow for immediate re-emergence of precisely the object of necessary suppression.

In English: to speak of the subject's submergence in favour of materialist practice, in such a way as to assure its re-emergence in all ideological force, is retrograde but more it is a project which must be annihilated, not tolerated.

A major danger and a major trend is what can be called the repressive de-annihilation of the subject (after such a short time), thru largely co-optative cementing – of the 'new' reading of Freud (through Lacan) by certain people ostensibly 'interested in' film – *onto* film.

Ego psychology's death yet a new sustaining of the subject. How? Through deconstruction, which is a scholasticism at best an academic redundancy at worst, of what is least interesting as a cultural project but most amenable to 'a history', and an apologia for the way of the present. The sustenance, in other words, of dominant cinema and the sustenance of the concept, thus the concrete reality, of the subject, the individual creating ego etc., are not separable phenomena.

To continue (bearing in mind the bearing on Structural/Materialist film): as to Eugenio Donato's notes in the anthology *The Structuralist Controversy*:

Derrida's enterprise also reveals within our modern context the impossibility of drawing an essential line between literature [read e.g. filmwork/PG] and criticism. Literature can only be a denunciation of literature and is not therefore different in essence from criticism. If, as Derrida puts it, linguistic signs refer themselves only to other linguistic signs, if the linguistic reference of words is words, if texts refer to nothing but other texts, then, in Foucault's words, 'If interpretation can never accomplish itself, it is simply because there is nothing to interpret.' There is nothing to interpret, for each sign is in itself not the thing that offers itself to interpretation but interpretation of other signs. There is never a *thing-to-be-interpreted* which is not already a *thing-which-interprets*, so that a relationship of both violence and elucidation establishes itself with interpretation. Interpretation does not shed light on a matter that asks to be interpreted, that offers itself passively to interpretation, but it can only seize violently an interpretation that is already there, one which it must overturn, overthrow, shatter with the blows of a hammer – the reference here is, of course, to Nietzsche. Interpretation then is nothing but sedimenting one layer of language upon another to produce an *illusory depth* [my italics/PG] which gives us the temporary spectacle of things beyond words. Yet this momentary fixation is dependent always on re-establishing that very subject which we had begun by denouncing. To quote Foucault again, 'Interpretation will henceforth always be an interpretation by the 'who'. One does not interpret that which is signified but in the last analysis the one 'who' has laid down the interpretation. The principle of interpretation is nothing but the interpreter himself.'

The above lesson is learnable viewing *some* works by Klee, Giacometti, Warhol, reading and listening to some works by Beckett ... the post-Structuralists have learned a lot from their sources, and the labour on the word (and the concept) signifier merits relation to those sources. Structural/Materialist film is, so far, a 'blind' spot. I think the reason for this is in the main due to the difficulties of viewing works which present a critical and/or theoretical position as opposed to viewing works *into which* (such a) position can (or must) be read. Academics are happier with their love of interpretation of an object which can be appropriated, so that interpretation into the object can take place, a pseudo-penetration. More clinical I shan't be.

Lacan says, "The sign is something that represents something for somebody; but the signifier is something that represents a subject for another signifier ... the subject is always a fading thing that runs under the chain of signifiers." I must add that my kind of sloppy quoting bits here bits there, to bolster points made, is an obvious weakness and a strength: the quotes present themselves as borne of necessity as if points made (by me) don't stand up, don't have the critical backlog or rationale which would make them not need 'other' sources, or 'verifiable authority'. But also, co-incide-nces (not coincidences) exist that ought to be foregrounded, made clear and present. And that is my rationale. Another reason for using quotes is that I don't like paraphrasing, and where the ideas are so to speak imported from outside or accepted from without, I let them be clearly such. My hope is that the quotes operate as segments, a such, as opposed to a whole system.

Quotes always simplify, because (obviously) they are aimed at a point to be made and they extinguish (for a moment) the position given by the rest of the work available under same name. Thus for example the differences of position between Derrida, Foucault, Lacan, and Althusser, or Warhol, Godard, Brecht, Vertov and Eisenstein, on any one issue, let alone a number of issues, is elided (for a while). Which may or may not be a bad thing. Enough.

There is, in all the above, a political motivation on my part. The argument is for a truly materialist practice which is one of the presentation i.e. demystification of the material construction of the film, a dialectically constituted 'presentation', of film representation, film image, film moment, film meaning in temporalness etc.

New representations of old meanings,

Old representations of new meanings,

Old representations of old meanings ...

There remain new representations of new meanings, seemingly the only but only a seeming possibility: "tired of expressing when there is nothing to *express*." Representation of meaning *mean*s: Repressing the coming into being of meaning, the ideology of certain specific, concrete productions, as if image or connection or relation – meaning – just existed as a pure essence given automatically, naturally, not (definitely not) made produced constructed; i.e. the product is divorced from its necessary labour.

I won't elaborate now.

One can learn of dialectics in various ways, one must in fact. It is useful to study Marx and Lenin and Mao but not misguided to hear Monk's *Brilliant Corners* or study the decentred Pollocks (and only them), hear Karl Valentin's comic monologues which empty the word (in opposition to Joyce's project, or not?). S. Beckett's *Not I* as performed is essential. Brecht's quoting and stealing and refabricating is as well. But an idealist dialectics, always close at hand, ought to be vanquished. And the vanquishing of such is a constant a struggle. (Certainly for me it is.)

One can hardly present a reasoned and analytic position in one hour. By "one" I mean me.

The co-incide-nces between the mind at work at speech and the mind's other functions, can't be comprehended without speech (even if their formation (that of the other functions) takes place without it, or without consciousness of it, speech). Language after all is a dominant form of understanding. This paragraph is apropos the whole project of using words to deal with the filmsubject at hand.

M. Le Grice wrote a letter apropos the Film Issue of *Studio*

International, published in a recent issue, which bears on the matters that this paper is ostensibly about. I quote it in full:

> Publication of the last issue of *Studio Int.*, concentrating on avant-garde film in England and Europe, was a major event for the film-makers here. That it should be so remarkable is a measure of the lack of attention this work has received internationally. Of course, the issue provided much needed publicity for the artists discussed, but fortunately it worked at a much more significant level than that. As well as giving a brief history of European developments, and something of a scan of current work (absolutely necessary for a 'first' review), a number of the articles began to raise theoretical questions, fundamental to current film practice. Wollen and Gidal attacked these theoretical problems directly, and provided much discussion space in the 'gap' between them. For example, both raised a general issue of particular interest to me – that of narration. Wollen used my *L'arroseur arrosé* as an indication that the 'way into narrative cinema is surely not forbidden to the avant-garde filmmaker', whilst Gidal asserted that 'narrative is an illusionistic procedure, manipulatory, mystificatory, repressive', describing it as 'more of a problem than a problematic'. Though Gidal has not as yet made any *direct* comment on my last two films, I am not convinced that illusion, documentary and narrative are excluded as elements of the 'Structural/Materialist' problematic. Nor am I ready with Wollen to see my own recent work so simply as a 'way into narrative'. I am not even sure if these films constitute narratives. They certainly contain incidents of action, but the critical terminology surrounding narrative cinema is inadequate and any theory which has come out of the avant-garde to date has dismissed (rightly in most respects) narrative cinema. If my own films deal in any way with illusion, the representation of 'action' or narrative, they do so as a problematic from the base of photo-cine recording as an aspect of material process. What must be made clear is that they in no way signal a 'return' to identificatory narrative, a move

which would delight reactionary critics (in which category I do NOT place Wollen).

Steering away from my personal concerns, the nexus of the problem is quite deeply in the literary nature of commercial narrative cinema, and its system of criticism. Even the recent attempts to draw on semiology as a basis for analysis tend to continue the literary dominance over film criticism. Both C. S. Peirce and Ferdinand de Saussure, who were independently the originators of semiology, saw it as a general study which would include linguistics. But as Barthes has noted (quoted by Burgin on page 42 of the July/August 'Photography' issue of *Studio*) we should face the possibility that this proposition be inverted and that semiology become a part of linguistics. As semiology has drawn on and modified concepts developed almost exclusively by linguistics this inversion is largely an established fact.

Having it both ways. Far from dismissing the semiological direction of Metz and Eco, much of what they have developed is thought provoking and certainly the most developed system of film analysis available to us in a very bleak field. Without Gidal's vitriol about *Screen* (whom he admits have been responsible for making most of the material available here) I completely agree with his view that the critical application of the Metzian method to films like *Touch of Evil* lends artistic credence to works which are aesthetically and politically reactionary, by implication making stylistic consistency and virtuoso intricacy an artistic *raison d'être*. But the flaw is not simply that of application to the 'wrong' films. Both Metz and, it seems, Eco (whose work is less available to the English reader) have stumbled over, and failed to resolve adequately, some basic problems concerning the distinction between film and language (in the strictly linguistic sense). For example, the question of what can be considered as equivalents between the identified elements of the linguistic code (like the phoneme for instance) and those of the cinematic image, is not satisfactorily tackled. Some of the many confusions at this fundamental level are illustrated by Metz's unbelievably simplistic flaw in his categorization (basic to his concept) of 'four signifying substances' making up the total perceptual materiality of the film. These are listed as: the moving photographic image, recorded noise, recorded music, and recorded phonetic sound. How is it that the 'sound track' which is after all simply recorded (or concrete) audio signal, warrants three categories at this stage of analysis, whilst the 'moving photographic image' equally unified as recorded (or concrete) visual signal, is not similarly subdivided as separate 'substances'? (Metz's later addition of graphic titles, etc., as a fifth 'substance' does not answer this criticism.)

There is no space here to trace the consequences of the lack of analysis of the material substances of the 'picture' track, nor the fundamental problematic of all recording media – the perceptual resemblance between the replayed record and the thing recorded. Metz, though sensing the problem, glosses over too quickly to develop a 'quasi linguistic' filmic system. One consequence being that factors of fundamental signification, like duration and time/space construct as plastic experience, and the behaviour (trajectory and viewpoint) of the camera/observer are relegated to half grasped (if at all) issues of 'stylistic code'. It is only when these factors are shifted from the periphery to the centre of the system of signification that the reactionary nature of films like *Touch of Evil* will become clear. It will be of equal value to avant-garde film practice to see that factors of 'form' and 'structure' are themselves significatory, eliminating the falsely posited impasse of essentialism (Wollen article previous issue). Much more theoretical work needs to be done on examining signification in the fields which have to date been denoted as the 'plastic' concerns of cinema, and on formal strategies and filmic procedures."

On a small point I beg to differ: just as dangerous as the *raison d'être* of stylistic consistency (*vis-à-vis* reactionary cinema) is the *raison d'être* of stylistic inconsistency. Now to the question of the "impasse of essentialism (Wollen article previous issue)".

The dualistic arguments of Wollen which see "anti-illusionist, anti-realist film: ironically (having) ended up with many preoccupations in common with its worst enemies" don't move us forward. Certainly Wollen realizes that there are certain filmic devices, and there are certain literary devices, and certainly there are differences between the two. Stating that is in *no* way seeking an essentialism, a soul of cinematic ontology. It is analysing the material of which 'film' is made. The reasons for this are in no way to make films 'about' film (or films about love, or films about the right political line to take (though there is one)).

The reason for this analysis of the material of which film is made (material in the broadest sense) is precisely to facilitate investigation of the ideological properties thereof. To investigate the *how* of representation, to work on the way representation works. (If one did not realize though, at some point, that one of the material bases of film was representation as such, and 'decided' (more specifically), that film (for some reason, essentialist or otherwise) *ought to tell stories*, then one's ideological position would be at another scene. And any scientific investigation would also be located at a different site. If one 'decided' (for some reason, essentialist or otherwise) that in fact, for example, a message was what a medium *ought* to be transparently telling, or documenting, then again we'd be at a different site of work. Obviously film is amenable to a variety of uses.)

By the way, the building of bridges I feel is a danger and a detour. We, instead, need a clear delineation of differences, of areas of separation.

(Essentialism would mean that if film is at its best, if film's real base, is in the telling of narratives, then film ought to be doing that. Illusionism would come in as a secondary preoccupation. I find it hard to understand that Wollen would seem to ascribe (such an) essentialism to me, for example. I have probably misunderstood him. The clear delineation of differences needs to apply precisely on such an issue.)

Much, I must add, that Wollen states, is perfectly correct, as is much that Le Grice states, as is hopefully *some* of what I state.

> Don't wait to be hunted to hide.
> Samuel Beckett

> Now it is still difficult 'somehow' to think in 'non-subject-oriented' visuality. But that's no tragedy – *ça viendra!* (it'll come).
> Sergei Eisenstein, Notes for the film *Kapital*

One of three talks given at the London Film-Makers' Co-operative seminar programme "Theory of Avant-Garde Film Practice" on 11 February 1976. The others were by Malcolm Le Grice and Peter Wollen.

PROBLEMS 'RELATING TO' WARHOL'S 'STILL LIFE 1976'
1978

Andy Warhol's *Still Life 1976* measures 72 x 86 inches, or approximately 6 x 7 feet. It consists of acrylic pigment painted and silkscreened onto canvas. In some sections the acrylic lies underneath the silkscreened hammer-and-sickle image; in others it is painted on top and in sections (largely) separate from the silkscreened image. The basic colours are red and black (with gradations from light grey to solid black).

The image is a reproduction of the real. That is to say, here, a hammer, given as such, a sickle, given as such, reproduced – re-imaged. The referent for this image, this painting, is a hammer from a hardware store, and a sickle from same. The signified, on the other hand, is a rather more complex matter. Obviously Communism is the concept signified by a hammer and sickle, but that is by adducing a *system* from the specific to the general. What I mean is that Communism is signified by a hammer and sickle when hammer-and-sickle is a general concept, when it is *no longer* the specificity of such a hammer and such a sickle, as here reproduced.

Moving from the specific to the general is the first step toward social meaning (the abstract). It is also the first step toward the theoretical: taking a momentary perception and moving that toward knowledge. Only when the immediate, specific perception is abstracted – only when it is constructed with a view *to* a possible knowledge or as a possible position in social meaning, in a social space of operation – can one move on *from* the ideology of spontaneity which sees meaning as residing only in immediate perception (the empiricist fallacy).

Meaning is not only always constructed; it is always already constructed. So it isn't just a matter, then, of consuming meaning, but of re-placing it as a pregiven construction in ideology. This is not to say that meaning can somehow escape the ideological, but, on the contrary, that meanings must be placed and seen *in* their ideological locations without the repressive mechanism which would give them a timelessness, an essence-of-truth value, outside their specific historical construction – outside their specific ideological moment ... *in the interests of* (someone).

Every meaning is in the interests of. Every value is created *toward* something. Every immediate perception is the effect of something else: thus the emphasis on effect (without denying affect). To see an image, to accept (or not accept) a meaning, *as if not produced as a specific effect* but as a happenstance, is to deny the positioning of each signifier – each image, in this case – inside a chain of transformations, transformations which, each in their turn, effect, and are effects of, a process of meaning-construction. The point I am thus getting at is that the concept Communism is already a *specific* effect of transformation from the general image hammer and sickle, of a process of meaning-making and relativization which (re-)moves this specific reproduction of a specific hammer and sickle into hammer-and-sickle. This (re-)move, I am also positing, is a step (though one only) from perception (the immediately physiological) to knowledge (knowledge here *not* meant to signify mere scientific knowing of that which is represented, i.e. that it is such and such a hammer, such and such a sickle, in such and such a formal arrangement), but knowledge of the (necessary) processes and structurings involved to create (produce) a certain determinate effect, the certain determinate meaning which is created (produced) by 'the image'.

To backtrack, and as to formal arrangement: without getting into a polemic on formalism (the meaning of which has radically changed since Russian Formalism), the form of the piece must be designated. And I am also here avoiding for the moment the form of the form, and the form of the content, and the content of the content, and the content of the form. I am speaking, more simply, of what we generally mean by the formal arrangement: how the hammer and sickle are set up for the first step of the process of reproduction into a photographic image. The hammer is standing 'on its head', the weight thus (from our knowledge of the physical laws of the real) in a noncontradictory position. We know such a hammer could in our lives be placed that way (on a table, on the floor, etc.). The sickle, on the other hand, is in an impossible position. It is in impossible balance, held at one end by nothing and at the other end by the unseen, out of frame. There is nothing within the image to give it a rationale for its physical positioning. It would fall over except that the frame edge allows precisely for the absent presence of a stabilizer, something to allow for the physical impossibility of the seen.

Thus offscreen space (as frequently in Warhol's films) is, firstly, given in its very absence; it is, secondly, given as both problematic and nonproblematic. The offscreen space is given as nonproblematic because it allows for the possibility of a rationalizing *inside* the reproduction (the 'real'), i.e. for the possibility that the image of the sickle is 'true', i.e. the documentation of a true state of physical position. The offscreen space, on the other hand, is given as problematic because there is no evidence of it. The right frame edge functions as the limit of the knowable, without clues as to the probability of such suppositions as given above. Thus the balancing of the sickle is within a construct of our not yet knowing of such information being possibly present (in absence). This creates an obvious tension *vis-à-vis* the real, *vis-à-vis* the possibility of documentary truth in the reproduction that is given in this image. Its constructedness is foregrounded, its procedure of construction – of nongivenness – is foregrounded. We are presented with certain forms, or signifiers; they are presented rather than used. This differentiation between presentation and usage is fundamental in an art which is aiming toward a materialism.

There is one other 'possibility'. The sickle could, by leaning against the hammer, hold itself and the formal arrangement adequately. In that case, the right frame cutoff would not play the conflictual role which I've outlined, but instead the hammer's position would be 'out of sync' or 'unreal' – outside the necessary convention of a first stage of acceptable veracity, of duplication. It would imply a weightlessness of the sickle *vis-à-vis* the hammer which our possibly incorrect 'knowledge' from the real would belie; precisely what can be called an antidocumentary tension would thereby be created, one that, in other words, questions the legitimacy of what we perceive in terms of the categories of what we know. This antagonism, this contradiction, propels thought through the workings of the mechanisms which (this) painting, this image, is. Thus it is placed – and we are placed – inside a materialist procedure that disallows the simple apprehension/consumption of the meanings of one set of images (this specific painting's) as if they were covered, cohesive, and closed by another (imaginary) set of images – the referents in the 'world'.

Already what constitutes 'the image' here, in the 6 by 7 foot painting called *Still Life 1976*, is a mechanism, an apparatus, a series of constructions in certain interests. The 'material' which goes to make up such an image is given as construction, not the happenstance 'capturing' of the real. The concept of the real is thus censored and not given its usual seamless, unproblematic reproduction and availability.

The whole series of constructions I have so far spoken of is built, of course, on the fact that the reproduction here of hammer and sickle is not simply such; it is constantly, in our viewing of the image, not such, but a reproduction inseparable from *the painted* – the acrylic application (through brush, or whatever) onto, and under, 'the image'. For without that basis there would be simply (simply!) a photograph (colour or not), and the foregrounding of the work's constructedness would obviously give way to merely photographic veracity or the photographic documentation of an (however balanced or unbalanced) object or series of objects which then becomes the ostensible subject of a picture.

To get back to the painting: the image of hammer and sickle is inseparable in two ways from painting's material: the image of hammer and the image of sickle, in themselves, are painted under, over and added to, thus not acknowledging, for instance, a privilege of the part that is purely photographic reproduction to hold onto the image as 'its'. What I am getting at is that the ownership of the meaning is thereby separated from that of the strict photographic reproduction. The hegemony of the 'true document' and the meanings that come with it are combated by disallowing 'hammer' to mean 'photograph of hammer' or 'sickle' to mean 'photograph of sickle'. Hammer instead is given to mean and to be produced as 'hammer-as-constructed.' and sickle, similarly. And thus the acrylic 'outlines' – the forms which in the end *include* the photographic reproduction of objects in the real but are not limited by them and are not fulfilled by them – are 'the real'. The real is thus now redefined as the material operation which constructs the processes of meaning and image in and for this specific reproduction *Still Life 1976*.

Now the 'next' step: the shadows. They might seem to be the shadows of the objects given, in such and such a figuration. But these shadows give themselves away (although there is no proof) as the specific effects of several light sources, conflicting positions for light outside of the deep-space frame 'in' which 'the objects' (in the first instance) are situated. One light source is set low, creating the shadow as sized greater than the object (a device common in Expressionist cinema, *Nosferatu* being one example); one light source is set high, creating the broad horizontal shadows that fill the lower right-hand area of the picture. In fact, the arrangement is more complex than these two light source descriptions suggest. The low left light would produce the tall shadow of the hammer handle, the left high light and the right high light would produce the horizontal shadow filling the lower right of the picture; the right medium-level light would produce the sickle's shadow slightly below the strictly photographic sickle. Together, these shadows create an *other* image set, one which takes the deep space of the reproduction of the 'original' hammer and sickle as photographed, and flattens that out *into a painting*, procedurally transforming that *into* something, breaking it, rupturing the surrounding space, breaking the coherent singularity of the final image we are constantly set up for (in this case, this one) and that is set up for us. Because we are not constructed in a single, unquestioned space as viewer-subjects. And the painting is even, in its final form, never really given its 'final form' as a final form of anything other than its own material construction, thus repeatedly *negating* concepts like 'final', with their attendant meanings: the finished, the complete, holding meaning, binding itself cohesively to a teleology which, retrospectively, we can retrace as having been reached.

Let me explain. Shadows give themselves as the specific effects of light sources, light sources in this case outside the frame yet producing these effects inside the frame or reproduction. Conventionally, one is located, as viewer, in identification with a singular position inside ideology, the imaginary. That is to say: the all-knowing/viewing subject has complete unfragmented knowledge, in immediacy, of the real – the subject who creates the world through consciousness: "I think therefore I am, therefore it is." This unquestioned solidity of the viewing subject (posited as a male inside a patriarchy) as all-seeing/knowing, in a superior position that permits apprehending in immediate perception, is an ideological construct that denies precisely the ideological pattern otherwise being constructed. Such a mode of consumption is inculcated exemplarily in antimaterialist work by the unceasing attempt to affirm the passive consumer of (pre-)given meanings, the undivided viewer who makes up (determinately) his 'own' mind. These meanings are never given as determinate effects, but are taken as symptoms without cause, as givens, religiously. This, given, additionally, as the male, the rational, the maker of meaning – as opposed to the hysterical, 'emotional', labile other (the female) – is inseparable from such an ideology of viewing, and meaning-consumption. The repression of the specific values created, of the fact of exchange, of an economy of meaning and an economics of reproduction, of a teleology: all this is in certain interests, interests that are repressive not only of desire but also of a politics (of representation, the real, the psychoanalytic subject, the formation of textual and contextual meaning). And it works on behalf of the power to hold you in a position of consumption and to abolish for you the process of specific productions and constructions having the end *in sight* of changing such power relations. This confirms the established positions for the viewer-subject, the collapsing of perception and knowledge, the visions of unified, uncontradictory, complete phallic centres, in a constant regression into (infantile) fixations/fantasies at the expense of the alternative.

To return to the painting: in identification with the position from which this hammer's and this sickle's shadow can be seen one is constantly shifting from right to left and back, and from normal height to a 'higher', more theatrical, beam and a lower, uncomfortable, grounded one. The left low light would produce the tall shadow of the hammer handle; the left high light and the right high light, as mentioned already, would produce the horizontal shadow filling the lower right of the picture; the right medium level light would produce the sickle's shadow slightly below the strictly photographic sickle: these series of shadows in their material inseparability 'in' the picture, disallow an easy reading of the (merely) variously differently placed possible light sources inferred. Instead we are placed into a specifically constant shifting through the elicitation of a constant lack of knowledge, a constant unsureness, a constant ungivenness as to final cause, although always each effect is given as the determinate effect of a cause, never just given pure and simple. Thus the way the total image is constructed in *Still Life 1976* forces the viewer into a constant shifting of identificatory subject-position.

By denying fulfilment, the mechanism of constant unease in an identification into something other (the imaginary, that which is not there but is phantasmed to be there for one or to be 'in') militates precisely *against* the repression of the time and the space of a piece. It militates against the repression of distance, within the picture, of its various relations, and between you and it as well. These distances cause specific, determinate effects, rather than evoking a unitary whole that could be identified into, as if the finished picture were mere stand-in for a character or a position.

This picture is, thus, unlike so many others, not an analogue for some characterization of emotions or expressivity, which is then, in its turn, a double for a person(ality), for a series of humanizations and anthropomorphisms that lend themselves to being identified *into*. The whole concept of identification is problematic, as that force which impels a movement *from* one's position in a social space of social meanings or a political space *to* and *into* a different human residence – another body or another figure – where the phantasms and fantasies, the realities of one's projections, are enacted. Such projection-into is merely the obverse of introjection, that taking into oneself of pregiven meanings, positions, politics from the outside (introjecting the Laws of the Family, for example). The system of identification which ultimately reproduces the dominant codes of meaning and behaviour, of sex position or of other 'values', is the basic support structure for precisely the telling of the (patriarchal) story, that recurrent search for the origin of truth, the Word, the Law, Power. Holding 'oneself' in identifications and resisting breaks in them is precisely the apparatus of dominance, in which most cultural production operates (and some operates *on* it and some *against* it). Thus, the mechanism of producing constant unease in identification, of allowing no secure place for such, and of inculcated resistances and breaks, is at least an attempt at impossibility or an antagonism. The next step, of course, is to produce anti- and non-identificatory works, combating the structure of identification as a 'necessary' system.

Here the viewer is always in relation to a difficult text, in attempting to grasp the cause of its effects. But those causes are always outside; they are never given in 'clarity', even in their absence, and are not even closely *opaque*, precisely because the picture is a mechanism which propels the viewer into an analytical transformation that disallows an easy mechanistic reading back toward a retrospectively clear evolutionary beginning. Beginning is instead a denied, abrogated, final causality. The individual creator is absented from (this) text which is, then, like history, "a process without a subject" (Althusser). It is important to grasp this radical anti-humanism without falling into a mechanistic materialism that would see such painting as merely illustration of certain techniques, and also without falling into an idealism which would see such a painting as representing a full meaning and a full cohesive position 'inside' the 'consciousness' of an essential viewer.

The title, too, ought not to be forgotten: *Still Life 1976*. Not *Opus* this or that, not *Abstract* this or that, not *Hammer and Sickle*, even, but 'still life'. A series of interpretations, all of them evident, could be offered here. Here are just some: a resolute determination to link this painting with 'painting' in general, in which 'Still Life' (dead life: *nature mort*) is the convention. Or 'still', with its attendant meaning: 'yet', 'persisting', 'in the face of'. And the date '1976' within the title, giving it its historical time, rather than an eternal 'timeless' metaphor, in which to find its context.

I have refrained from discussing any other Warhol paintings or films. I have not wanted, for instance, to consider those usages which unite them and those which do not, or to analyse, say, the way Warhol's silkscreen technique differs radically from others (as it does). For the time being, I have not sought to speak of his work in the context of the work in the years 1960-1978. I have instead merely wanted to isolate beginning interests in relation to one painting.

First published in Artforum, May 1978. Reprinted by kind permission of Artforum.

THE ANTI-NARRATIVE
1979

Recently an unnamed Marxist feminist was quoted in *The Times* as saying there can be no breakthrough for women until the essentially male (as constructed in patriarchy) linear narrative patterns are smashed.[1] But the dominance of transparency as an ideology, as a political reality, as an economy, functioning on many levels, must be smashed for the culturally induced processes of men's and women's identifications to be smashed as well. We must learn to manage without the reproduction of identifications through, for example, familial structures, without the reproduction of identification *through structures of representation*, familial orientation and biologism being merely the birthplace of such modes for the individuated self. In fact, to speak broadly, dominant ideology places transparency and representation/illusionism at the centre of oppressive structuring in society. Thus we must not manage the way we've managed so far.

My arguments have been directed all along against reproduction in any form, though the so-called ultraleftism[2] (existent, though not totalistically, in the non-bourgeois feminism of the radical feminists, and unfortunately hardly at all amongst men as yet) of 'being against all reproduction' betrays itself as existing problematically, as has been pointed out for example *vis-à-vis* my filmworks, which in fact *use* 'the materials of reproduction

---

[1] This construction is not transhistorical: the construction onto and through the biological difference neither determining it nor determined by it. See Monique Plaza, "'Phallomorphic Power' and the Psychology of 'Woman'", *Ideology and Consciousness*, No. 4, Autumn 1978, and Christine Delphy, *The Main Enemy* (1970), trans. Women's Research and Resources Centre, 1977, for particularly useful positions.

[2] See Note I below.

not held into the terms of a representation'.[3] My theoretical position has always acknowledged this crucial difference, but the necessity of this acknowledgement magnifies the misfortune of being positioned ideologically, inside and through a practice of *re*production, when an end to such practice is what's sought. The concept of reproduction speaks of the empirical, the 'real' 'outside knowledge' – it just so happens that watching an apple fall off a tree does not teach Einsteinian physics, nor does looking at a factory teach capitalism – and the disability to distance oneself from that enough even to posit another way, one which no longer reproduces, one which disallows precisely the need for such. Not to reproduce is either to consume or produce (or both)[4] and in idealist construction against consumption, which stems from an ahistorical humanism we can well do without (but can't), reproduction becomes valorised and reified – as if it's somehow evil to consume and good not to.

Thus, notions of style become dominant, wherein style is understood as the holding of a specific form for a picture, an image of, a reproduction. One film-maker, Godard, reproduces the real with or through one style, another, Vertov, does so dissimilarly. But the lessons the learners would learn from this are precisely those of naturalism: the image speaks of reality or truth. Pre-Brechtian 'realism' asserts itself, and of course not

3   Stephen Heath, in transcript discussion between Stephen Heath and Peter Gidal, Cambridge, 1977. The problem here is that one is not in a position pragmatically not to reproduce but it is, however, a viable theoretical position. "Nobody said anything about femininity and masculinity when those first two damaged cells threw in their chips together. How did we hit on the idea of sexual reproduction after getting by for so long with populations of soloist reproducers, who flourished for thousands of years. Probably by accident, and a very long shot at that." J. M. Smith, *The Evolution of Sex,* Cambridge University Press, 1977.

4   "A transitional stage between capitalism and socialism is defined, at least structurally, by the fact that there is no longer generalised commodity production; that the means of production are no longer commodities; that they have therefore, by definition, lost their character as capital ..." Ernest Mandel, "The Nature of the Soviet State", *New Left Review*, No. 108, March-April 1978.

innocently.⁵ It reasserts itself in the current 'theoretical' debate in *Screen* and without, in a huge blockage, an immense work of reaction, giving fetishistic significance to Steenbeck-analysis, whilst of course denying it constantly, to 'the' relation of the signifier to the signified, inferring somehow that a film can, or can attempt to, intervene in socio-political reality, to the extent that it becomes a decoy for political work on another level. Ultimately the old bourgeois sociological literary reading of meaning, whether in literature, theatre, music, film, whatever, reaches hardly surprising conclusions: the viewer makes meaning (one step from the notion that consciousness produces the material relations of concrete reality, as opposed to Marx's notion of consciousness as product, as determinate effect of social relations and relations of production).⁶

Slowly, the anti-feminist so-called Marxists do their work, to a point at which idealism is entrenched in the name of everything but itself. Such work relates to the matter of reproduction, because if production is repressed and reproduction valorised,

5   "As to Peter Wollen's piece, "'Ontology' and 'Materialism' in Film" (*Screen*, Spring 1976, Vol. 17, No. 1): to state that 'any post-Brechtian sense of materialism (must) be concerned with the significance of what is represented, itself located in the material world and in history', is to hark back to notions of given significance, found when searched for, true reality as merely exhumed. It is to see, for example, in Straub/Huillet's *History Lessons*, in the car scenes, 'reality as it is', reality as given not constructed, not as ideological (on, through, by, and for, etc.). This is far from work on the signifier. The route of significance is the route of the pre-given, which is the route of subjective interpretation of necessity felt to be correct by *each* interpreter."
Peter Gidal, Letter, *Screen*, Vol. 17, No. 2, Summer 1976.

6   "Consumption produces production in two ways: (1) because a product becomes a real product only through consumption. For example, a dress becomes a real dress only in the act of being worn; a house which is uninhabited is in fact no real house; in other words, a product, as distinct from a mere natural object, proves itself as such, becomes a product only in consumption. Only by destroying the product does consumption give it the finishing touch; for the product is a product not because it is materialised activity, but only as an object for the active subject; (2) because consumption creates the need for new production ..." Marx, *Preface and Introduction to A Contribution to the Critique of Political Economy* (1859), Foreign Languages Press, 1976.

we can have no history, nothing new (as opposed to Althusser's "Something New") ... nothing old, as redundancy not repetition is here the key (as opposed to Beckett's *Lessness*).

An aside: I take issue with the notion of deconstruction for the very reason that it reinvigorates narrativity, within whatever 'more perfect' definition of diegesis is come up with, imaginary space, mental space, fictive space, rememorated space of action ... narrative space. Yet this is an incorrect notion, to my mind, of diegesis, which in fact should be seen as separable from narrative. A recent position that there can be non-diegetic film (as opposed to non-narrative film) seems a reformulation of a form of idealism. (It is also terribly naïve as to avant-garde cinema, specifically avant-garde cinema in England. The same naiveté holds irony to have a radical function, is incredulous at its easy recuperability, and sees ironic displacement as another way of saying deconstruction without admitting to such silliness). Such idealism would be to state for example "Illusion of depth disappears and we enter the realm of the non-diegetic". In its broadest determinations, it is clear that diegesis resides in every representation, and to suppose for example that *Arnulf Rainer* is a non-diegetic film is wishful 'thinking', a search for some purity of threshold beyond which presumably the air is clear not murky. What must though be stated clearly is that the existence of diegesis in no way of necessity presupposes the existence of narrative.[7]

7   "For also, and even first of all, through its procedures of denotation, the cinema is a specific language. The concept of diegesis is as important for the film semiologist as the idea of art. The word is derived from the Greek 'narration', and was used particularly to designate one of the obligatory parts of judiciary discourse, the recital of facts. The term was introduced into the framework of the cinema by Étienne Souriau. It designates the film's represented instance ... that is to say, the sum of the film's denotation: the narration itself, but also the fictional space and time dimensions implied in and by the narrative, and consequently the characters, the landscapes, the events, and other narrative elements, in so far as they are considered in their denotated aspect." Christian Metz, *Film Language*, Oxford University Press, 1974. Narrative in the end would have to be defined as story, inferable or otherwise from (effect/affect of) the given, although the problem arises of the ideology of

This is crucial.[8]

A related interruption:

... open question as to whether work/pleasure in film 'viewing' (a difficult concept in itself) equals the (or a) gratification of desire. For Wittgenstein film was the acting out of wish fulfilment/dream (as indeed the dream *per se* was for Freud), and therefore bound to end up with the gratification of desire. Film without a happy ending was (for him) a misunderstanding of the cinema, whether ontologically or cinema-as-constituted, whether descriptive or prescriptive. The question is, can the non-narrative film bring this gratification, this optimistic search, this annihilation of the real which is other and certainly *not* (t)here for gratification (and certainly not for the experience *of* gratification either) ... The traps laid by and inherent in dominant discourses recuperate avant-garde film which relies yet again and again on work on the signified, (and so-called 'work on the signifier') – films which, like *Man with a Movie Camera*, an unfortunate model these past ten years if ever there was one,

---

reading a text, in which viewers 'automatically' are placed in positions for themselves which do not necessarily have anything to do with the text/process/procedure/meanings in question.

8   To make some connections with my filmpractice, what follows are my notes for *Silent Partner* (1977):

    absence/presence (onscreen/offscreen)
    sound sources and synchronicity
    gender
    rememoration/reduplication/repetition
    beginning/end
    'extradiegetic'
    non-oneness (no-oneness) within/without
    documentary/fictive
    from meaning to use
    process/in-process/how it is (s/he)
    inculcated arrestation *attempts*, by definition unsuccessful: the signifier remains: unnaturalised, meaningless, unauthored, anonymous, arbitrary, in combat, specific, historical, in operation, in process, precise.
    (September 1977)

give the illusion of concretising social reality or (even) dialecticising it. Contemporary social formations cannot be adequately given *through* cinema ... and the present assumption that the ideological nature of social constructions (of 'society') can be the problematic around and through which a film operates, is incorrect. That any problematics *external to* cinema's *representations* of the social, economic, sexual, political can be somehow portrayed, dialectically or otherwise, or even operated upon and through in cinema, in relation (some how) to social practice of the extra-cinematic (i.e. all the rest of life including non-cinematic codes) is useful for academic(s') hope(s) but nothing else. Trying to bring back a hopefulness, a last-ditch attempt to fight, for example, the hideous insights of Freud which lead to nothing like such. (And none of the above to imply autonomy to (a) discourse.)

Of course ideology of representations exists, and to reproduce a certain image of, for example, a naked woman is to do precisely such – reproducing in its similarness to 'the real' the ideological representation and the image's meaning (the denotation/the signified) for men and women. That being *held* is to a figure, and if anything I would have thought the absence of (the) body/figure(s) in (the) film would demand a re-call outside the film – such a voice, not a representation of, for instance, woman's voice *inside*. Political power, thus, not voice – a Brechtian realism outside (but through, in the real sense) representation.

Recent valorising of certain representations of women, ones which are again and again so close to the mystery, the secret, the unknown, 'yet' at the same time motherhood, the feminine, and the emotional as to make one wince at the representations and even more at the lack of superego amongst those producing and feeding on them. As no concrete historical materialist analysis or practice has existed for those who play with these images, we find ourselves confronted with profoundly reactionary archetypes covered by verbiage ostensibly denying this fact but in fact revelling in it. Examples could be found in different ways in the films of The Berwick Street Collective, Godard, The London Women's Film Group, Oshima, Comolli, Akerman, Mulvey/Wollen, Le Grice, etcetera. Women need/men want; women feel/men think; women's visages betray/men's control (mind); men are tough/women soft (lighting plays its part here) *and the opposite:* lines in men's faces signify thought/in women's: ugliness; etcetera. Statements which should really be spewed out as reactionary (but aren't) are condescendingly accepted and reproduced as advanced texts. Film journals ostensibly dealing with advanced film practice are finding easy material after some slack years. This is a dangerous political event within film practice, and its long-term effects are being skilfully repressed in exchange for short-term opportunism.[9]

The project must be the distance between knowledge and perception, my project since 1966, but it is one which (due to misreadings by many of Marxist texts as to science and knowledge) is constantly subjected to denial. Similarly, some have claimed my films suppress a knowledge of the imaginary of the image by asserting the objectivity of the images and the rationality of our relation to them ... Those who think this way do not realise that one is in ideology *and* one does ideological combat. One can know of being in process, one can know of constructions operative in image formation/transformation: one does not know, one 'misses' or 'misrecognises' one's position, one's relation, one's bindings/fractures against *that*. ('It' is where I 'am' not.) A film can inculcate positionings which force attempts – moment to moment attempts – at knowledge, attempts at delineating precisely the perception of distance between perception and (absent) knowledge. The apprehension of the functioning of that distance is a position in knowledge. One has to remember the unconscious doesn't get excavated at

---

9   See Note II, below.

all; it is constantly operative, for example through repression, but it is of no avail to call on the unconscious as a position against knowledge in the name of non-suppression of the imaginary. That is why it is important to fight against 'the objectivity of the images and the rationality of our relation to them', *not* in the name of a position which seems current: the subjectivity of the images and the irrationality of our relation to them. Such a position might otherwise get close to attributing to the unconscious all the characteristics of the known yet out of control, out of sight. It isn't either universal unknowingness *or* conscious knowledge, depending on one's political position on/in film. Were one to accept 'it' as the unconscious, one wouldn't use 'it' as an argument against knowledge, against materiality and materialism, in the guise of being against rationalism. Stating the term in terms of the latter would close the case. A materialist isn't a rationalist isn't 'against' the unconscious (which by the way is a process).

What is not needed is 'a different narrative', 'at the limit of fictions of unity' (Stephen Heath), 'an enigma, contradictory': The notion of 'the limit' is both a Barthesian and Metzian notion, one which in fact refuses the necessity of denial, in terms of enactment, if not its mechanism *per se*, and finds pleasure in solidifying limits even in their occasional or constant so-called transgression. Stephen Heath's recent work seems at times to have criticised this position, though still more often than not indulging it.

A move away from dominant forms of expression is necessary because dominant forms of expression means *current* dominant forms of expression, which are ones of transparency, invisibility, in which the mechanism, the apparatus, the construction is not such, does not exist. A move away from dominant forms is thus not a matter of anti-manipulation, or deconstruction of certain codes in the sense of explication-after-the-fact, but of *film-as-projected*, as anti-illusionist, remembering that a mechanistic finality to this is not achievable; but attempted anti-illusionist practice through consequent/consistent materialist practice wherein the process is the film, the procedure: construction of production of the film, its effects, of an image of the real, of production of the real (this real).

The attempt at meaninglessness is precisely the non-givenness of meaning,[10] the undermining of determinate meaning, the latter being always and necessarily ideologically produced and arbitrary, and to be given as such (for example, for ideological battle). Somehow the audience mustn't be mentioned: not that Structural/Materialist (or any) film needs no audience, but the audience isn't the 'answer'; the fact that Freud wasn't read in France until recently doesn't mean that the French don't have infantile sexuality. The fact that Lenin loved Gorki and hated Majakovsky, who was loved for a time by Stalin, and that the masses loved Gorki as well, doesn't prove anything about the political efficacy in the revolutionary sense of any of the above-mentioned. Radek's vehemence against Joyce and Trotsky, *and* his death at Stalin's 'hands', says little about the latter's relation to work on the signifier.

It is no more than illusion to assume that most fantasy enacted is not fascist.

Lacan's 'delerium is an act of interpretation' is itself a problem, in that the placing of the subject can be unconscious and (nevertheless) remain unproblematic. A curious idealism, this unconscious wavy-swaying of the spectator-tress (subject) which if 'found' to be 'heterogeneous', somehow suffices for

---

10 "The possibility of contemplation offered by photographs is recouped and even radically undercut in *Film Print* (Gidal, 1974) by the continually moving picture ... when meaning does seem to emerge (it) is immediately displaced by denial of the space ... The suppression of meaning-production as a cinematic process is a structuring feature of the film ... The repetitions, the radical refusal of semioticity (denial of the codes of dominant cinema but also the codicity of structural film itself) and the unfixed nature of the space articulated by the film, all serve to operate against the kind of closure associated with a defined and homogeneous film space." Annette Kuhn, *Perspectives on British Avant-Garde Film*, Hayward Gallery / Arts Council of Great Britain, 1977.

'contradictoriness', 'production not consumption', etcetera, ultimately by way of the redundancy *being is being* opposed to a metaphysic of knowing. But there are other possibilities: "What is interesting here is to grasp the extent to which narration is, in our imaginary of film, as important as, and in fact, more important than, narrative: film, that imaginary has it, must be representative *for*, in order, directed towards something for someone (narrative as the common ground of film and spectator). Thus with *Condition of Illusion* the power of the response against the film to find an order of narration, a direction; 'against the film', since what such a response has to ignore, impossible in the experience of the film, is once again, the repetition, the disturbing return of the signifier across the signs of any narration." (Stephen Heath)[11] This position, a momentary realisation of the position of narrativity in Structural/Materialist film, asserting itself only through the displeasure of the battle against voyeurism, superiority, and its sustenance through lack of pleasure, is not easy for anyone to uphold. Which is why I insist work, not play; process of construction not Steenbeck analysis; meaningless: neither production *of* anything (meaning, etc.) *by* anything, in the common spontaneous sense of empirical non-historical production of the spectator, as he/she is sitting in front of *a*

---

11   Stephen Heath, "Repetition Time: Notes Around Structural/Materialist Film", *Wide Angle*, Vol. 2, No. 3, 1978. Another problem arises, of which Heath's closing in this article is emblematic: after 4,000 words to the contrary, the penultimate paragraph restates the way *Condition of Illusion* operates, as a threat which forces repression – the re-statement is not of *Condition of Illusion*'s threat, but of the (illusory) closure of, and by, the threat which Heath has been at such pains throughout to analyse differently. See my letter, *Wide Angle*, Vol. 2, No. 4, 1978. 'Everything ok' seems to be the need here, in contrast to Heath's usual habit of not closing up his articles with final answers when it comes to Oshima, Welles, Narrative Space, Akerman. Closured reactionary films of ideological effacement of process, contradiction, are spoken of without closure – the threat is repressed anyway in the works – and the exhumation through academic interpretation only a bare shadow of the threat implied by other work: Structural/Materialist film. That there's a desire *vis-à-vis* the signifier in Structural/Materialist film forcing such closing-up is the (not my) conclusion. Threat, Paranoia, *Answers* (sic).

screen ... (in every sense).

As deconstruction-analysis is still the predominant form for so-called materialists, so-called Marxists, so-called theoreticians in various journals of so-called contemporary film, some further notes on the subject: notions of deconstruction, as well as of films which "address themselves *to* ... politico-ideological practices"[12] (or whatever) still refers to the identification (to be identified with) space ... the necessary mechanism for the subject whether identifying with him/her/itself, primarily, with unseen narrator, with character, position, story, narration, physical or psychoanalytic space of action or inaction, etcetera. We must, thus, do battle with the Brecht whom we are constantly, correctly, quoted to back up theories of suspension-before-identification, suspension-during-identification. It leads to ideas such as: distanciation from the characters can come to constitute a very special kind of intimacy, which completely misunderstands/destroys the complexity and radicalness of distanciation-practice. Psychological motivation and the backtracking to points of origin imbue such arguments as well.[13]

There is also, then, the problem as to the 'breakdown' of

12 Paul Willemen, "Notes on Subjectivity, On Reading 'Subjectivity Under Siege'", *Screen*, Vol. 19, No. 1, Spring 1978.

13 (a) Attitude Theatre Company's production of Brecht's *The Measures Taken* (2 December 1978, Cockpit Theatre, London) is exemplary in this respect. Also see, on the political context and tendency of this play in 1930, Peter Horn, "Truth is Concrete: Brecht's *The Measures Taken* and the question of party discipline", *Brecht Jahrbuch*, Suhrkamp, 1978.
(b) "Never in my life, except in my sleep, have I committed unconscious acts." Karl Radek, 1937 (Moscow Trials against the Trotskyists), *Prozessbericht über die Strafsache des sowjetfeindlichen trotzkistischen Zentrums: Vollständiger Stenographischer Bericht*, Moscow, 1937.
(c) "And yet the establishing of these frameworks does not in the least weaken the striking diversity of the images that come and fit into them." Lacan, Migault, Lévy-Valensi, "Inspired Writing: Schizography", *This Quarter*, Paris, 1932.
(d) "On the panels was developed the story corresponding to the divisions. With strange pleasure I imagined myself walking on this disc-time-space and reading the story before me. The freedom to begin where I liked, for instance to start off from

specific signifiers and signifieds rather than of process of production of signification, thus presuming a deconstruction of specific reality through film, or a meaning that, when all is said and done, exudes from the screen (whether this is posited as dialectical or not hardly matters). The fundamental problem is this, of the final communication that is constantly being sought, with ever increasing verbal strategies of reformulation. Whether this meaning is then deconstructed somehow or other also hardly matters in terms of the operation and process of film that is being effaced. Something is not about social practice merely because it is a social practice. The production of diegesis, of the effects of a film text, is a social production; that does not relate in any way to being *of necessity* about the constitution of social productions. There is a fundamental difference between usage of codes, systems, theories, film processes, and the presentation of such.

To mimic the modes of dominant cinema and then 'refuse' them or use them as a standard against which to measure is not necessarily any more progressive (usually less, if that's possible) than using the strategies and propaganda, the sexism and the fascism, of the ruling classes 'with a difference', 'at the edge'. "Fascinating seductiveness and enormous voyeuristic pleasures"[14] are afforded in certain interests, no matter how much *ex post facto* writing submerges this politics. Correlated to this mimicking of the modes of dominant cinema is the reintegration (or attempts at such) of narrative, in the cause of 'rich' productions which stimulate curiosity about dramatic fiction's intensity, passionate irony, and so on. This cannot be disavowed by presuming an effect which transforms, somehow inverts, the power of the system

---

the dream in October 1946 and, having gone all the way round, to land a few months earlier in front of the objects, in front of my trowel. To find the bearing of each fact on the disc meant a great deal to me. But the panels are still empty: I do not know the value of words or their relationship with each other well enough to be able to fill them in." Alberto Giacometti, "The Dream, The Sphinx, and The Death of T.", *X*, Vol. 1, No. 1, November, 1959.

14 Willemen, *Max Ophuls*, National Film Theatre Programme Booklet, September 1978.

of representation, transparency, at one threshold or another of consciousness. It all seems like the sadism of the masochist: screen's juncture.

So we must get 'back' to work on the signifier and process of production, the inscribed oneness of diegesis with process of its production. And that is a social reality, if such a concept must be used to justify the obviously *political* of such work.

> By denying fulfilment, the mechanism of constant unease (in an identification into something *other*, that which is not there but phantasmed to be there for one, to be 'in'), militates *against* the repression of the time and the space 'of' a painting. It militates against the repression of distance, within the picture, of its various relations, and between you and it as well. These distances cause specific, determinate effects, rather than evoking a unitary whole that could be identified into, as if the finished picture were a mere stand-in for a character or a position. This picture, thus, unlike so many others, is not an analogue for some characterisation of emotions or expressivity, which is then, in its turn, a double for a person(ality), for a series of humanisations and anthropomorphisms that lend themselves to being identified *into*. The whole concept of identification is problematic, as that force which impels a movement from one's position in a social space of social meanings or a political space *to* and *into* a different human residence – another body or another figure – where the phantasms and fantasies, the realities of one's projections, are enacted. Such projection-into is merely the obverse of introjection, that taking into oneself of 'pregiven' meanings, positions, politics from the outside (introjecting the 'laws of the family', for example). The system of identification which ultimately reproduces the dominant codes of meaning and behaviour, of sex position or of other 'values', is the basic support structure for the telling of the (patriarchal) story, that recurrent search for the origin of truth, the word, the law, power. Holding 'oneself' in identifications and resisting breaks (whether

conscious or unconscious) is precisely the apparatus of dominance, in which most cultural production operates (*and* some operates on it and some against it). Thus the mechanism of producing constant unease in identification, of allowing no secure place for such, and of inculcated resistances and breaks, is at least an attempt at impossibility or an antagonism.

The next step, of course, is to produce anti- and non-identificatory works, combating the structure of identification as a 'necessary' system.[15] Here the viewer is always in relation to a difficult text, in attempting to grasp the cause of its effects. But those causes are always outside, they are never given in clarity, even in their absence, and are not even closely opaque, because the picture is a mechanism which propels the viewer into an analytical transformation that disallows an easy, mechanistic, reading back towards a retrospectively clear evolutionary beginning. Beginning is instead a denied, abrogated, final causality. The individual creator is absented from (this) text, which is then, like history, "a process without a subject" (Althusser). It is important to grasp this radical anti-humanism ...[16]

Realism itself could be invoked. An attempted Marxist notion of realism was sometimes spoken of by Brecht, as being that of the constructedness of artifice of internal relations, of contradictions producing consciousness (though singularly unsuccessful

---

15   Here the thrill of passionate contradiction is lost: for, distance to and resistance to the manipulations of phantasy's *ideological* level disallows that constant stirring, so loved, that pleasure/pain syndrome which oppresses (politically and otherwise). To repress the 'automatic', 'spontaneous' indulgences of sexist desire is, to repress (in unpleasure and pain) those excesses liberating only to those already in power (class-power, sex power, etcetera). Fear of loss which comes with such is also constant *threat* of loss, and paranoia is constantly re-instituted in that critical moment. There is *then* constant contradictory movement, play, dispersal, of the subject, which is a hysterical stasis: oppression. In addition, it's a bad exchange: long term pain for pain of less duration (given as enthusiasm).

16   Peter Gidal, "Some Problems 'Relating to' Andy Warhol's *Still Life 1976*, Artforum, Vol. 16, No. 9, May 1978.

in most of his plays, Therese Giehse's readings[17] are quite another matter, extraordinarily so). The term consciousness is not meant to mean consciousness as subjective or unique, but as residing obviously in individuals as *products*. The perception-training concept, which the word consciousness sometimes implies, of some theories of film practice is alien to my theory, unless *any* mention of effect on viewer implicitly connotes such. Of course training, pedagogy, education on codificatory modes of representation, etcetera, is necessary. The mechanistic notion of all the work being done up on screen (a displaced form, therefore, of an *it*, available, merely veiled, an 'apprehendable reality', 'pregnant') is dangerous but no less so than a concept of a pure un-ideological existential(ist) viewer who 'freely' perceives and learns from each confrontation with the screen. When I use words like 'dangerous', or 'combat', I really mean (for dangerous) misdirected, ideological-without-admission, mystificatory, idealist (even though ideological is here simplistically misused), and (for combat) 'work must be done on', 'contradictions worked through and motoring practice', etcetera. Using language isn't often (or always) easy.

An interjection from some notes of March 1974:

> One cannot, in film for example transcend the real; but also cannot transcend it then destroy it; that destruction is otherwise the destruction of an adequate representation. Thus the whole concept of adequate representation would be re-introducing itself this way.[18] This thus would be to not take into account that film is

17 "Ein Bertolt Brecht Abend" (A Bertolt Brecht Evening), mit Therese Giehse, Deutsche Grammophon Gesellschaft, Literarisches Archiv, 168093-4.
18 As to misunderstanding of adequate representation: "For Marxists interested in Africa, for example, there is a particularly fascinating question related to this problematic: the exact definition of what African society was at the time of the colonial occupation ... they [according to whom Marxism is inapplicable in Africa] fail to understand the historical process ... they fail to understand development,

not the adequate representation of anything. Positing a reality in history (allowing for associations by the viewer and/or within the film), then destroying it, would be film as metaphor rather than as material. I must (must I?) reiterate yet again that by material I do not mean a *material: signification* opposition. It is not a matter of "substance over signification" or "signification over substance"; it is a matter of constructedness and process, as I have tried to state and make clear since 1967.[19] Yet there is a real difficulty here: obviously material is such; non-contradictoriness and therefore non-productiveness (that which is labour-denying) is inseparable from such a concept *if* it does not simultaneously mean material as intervention and artifice, *how* it functions as a construct. It would be film as symbolic (as in: symbol of), destruction of specific historical reality after symbolic positing of it, instead of positing a film-time and film-space which does not allow for an adequate-seeming

---

taking mere snapshots from one moment of evolution. But the snapshot, although sometimes blurred, is not always inaccurate." Ernest Mandel, "On the Nature of the Soviet State", *New Left Review*, No. 108, March-April 1978.

19 Mick Eaton in the last issue of *Screen* misunderstands my practice in this respect. More importantly, from a theoretical standpoint, than this little misunderstanding (which happens a lot because people read and pick out one or two quotes still heavily laden with idealist formulation, something I've tried to remedy these last seven years) is his conflation of writing and film. "Obviously one of the polemics of Gidal's extremely polemical piece is a rejection of the kind of analysis Sitney made of Structural film, seen in terms of consciousness ... and to instate materialism in a dialectical rather than a mechanical sense; it is disputable whether he does in fact achieve that aim." The article then speaks of theorisation, then of filmpractice, and then about the 'Structural/Materialist aesthetic' *per se*. Thus, with the best of intentions, Eaton conflates writings with film and then proves one with the other, proving neither. In addition he takes up the notion that my theorisation of duration, as well as the way duration operates in my films, "can lead to a retreat from editing". This is incorrect. I also hope no one by now anymore has the desire to quote my silly phrase "watching oneself watching" which I stole from Brecht, Freud, and Mao, but shouldn't have. Same goes for "presentation of consciousness" "to the self" wherein was meant not a content of consciousness nor any structure of consciousness but act and process, and, additionally, not the presentation but the miserable failure of the attempted presentation. The idealistic metaphysic of the self as I posited it was not yet expunged by 1974, when I wrote "Theory and Definition of Structural/Materialist Film".

representation, one in which moment-to-moment difference, simultaneous construction/deconstruction, disallows a projection into that space as real, thus an un-holding of image. The internality of that space would have to be compressed in its articulation (precisely not an articulation).

It is an idealist metaphysic to imply there is the world in a film (however much however long) though to present an inadequate representation (or a reproduction never held into the terms of a representation, which amounts to the same thing[20]) at all times is a physic of film upon something that can *not* be though it *seems to be adequately* (re)constructed in the mind from the information given (constructed in the mind, with effacement of that process of construction, it always can be). The historical moment is the film-moment each moment. There is no history *in*, as opposed to *of*, a representation itself, of anything, but there is in the relations to it/through it/produced/motored effected, affected, and infected by it ... that profilmic object that is seen in the viewfinder is not necessarily an (essentialist) metaphor, nor carrier of history, nor transcendental. It is the *specific* present, remembering the nonexistence of real presence in the Derridean definition. Nevertheless, that which is held in the viewfinder is a signifier and a carrier of signification.

There is another problem with 'the real'. That is of the imaginary presence of the film-maker within an absent narrative referred to for example by, supposedly, the unsteady camera (opposed to the supposed objectivity of the still frame and the concomitant absence of the subject (film-maker/filmviewer) magically posited, centrally located, in a 'knowledge', full in its individualistic apprehension, and intimately conspiratorial position within the imaginary space-depth of the film. Now, increasingly, in many films and writings, that imaginary referent (the subject

---

20 Phrase added August 1978.

mentioned above) posited within the space, is propounded in a decoded form; previously 'she' or 'he' was militated against (though theoretically constituted as existent). These two attitudes towards the absent/ present subject observer are not the only possible ones, and they are certainly the most reactionary. This is especially so when these propounded presences are inserted into, and help constitute, the 'social reality'; and one step from there and we have 'historical materialism', magically produced from what others call merely 'history', and others still, 'memory', or others still 'social reality, or fiction, filmed'. For many reasons the concept *process* has become demeaned mainly due to mechanistic and idealist formulations. It mustn't be expunged from our labour on theory (nor from theories of labour).

The insertion of 'social reality' by Straub/Huillet, the essentialist abstractions of *Tom, Tom, the Piper's Son*, the ambiguous documentary realism of *Unsere Afrikareise*, must be studied without the echoes of the search for the real. Telling stories is as old as ... so what. Racism and sexism are not exactly inventions of individualist, romantic intellectuals and members of editorial boards and collectives. Narrative is of course enormously seductive, even more so in the guise of not being such, but that only (re)proves the dominance of certain modes which we are all presumably aware of.

"You either identify with it or *it* becomes the object of libido." (Freud: two choices[21]). Or else (third choice), phantasy as the one means of *replacing* object-libido (Lou Andreas-Salomé's 'solution'). This must relate to a 'distrust concerning every form of enthusiasm', which has been my theoretical position since 1964, though the concrete practice of and in that *theoretical* is another matter. Wittgenstein was right about dominant cinema when he stated that film without a happy ending was a misunderstanding of film. The question remains: can non-narrative film bring this

---

21 Sigmund Freud, *The Ego and the Id* (1923), Hogarth Press, 1974.

gratification, this optimistic search, this annihilation of the real (yes, the Lacanian real) precisely which is other and certainly not there for gratification. (Though it is also not other.)

The hook, if film needs it, is no more a 'hook' as in the narrative wherein resolution, etc., is needed and wanted. (These two concepts by the way, are crucially different, determining, on the one hand, the ideological and phantasy, and on the other, the material and historical. Which is not to say one is ever *in* the Lacanian symbolic and *out* of (though out of) the imaginary. No actual separability is implied in terms of mechanism, though in terms of enactment there are definite separabilities, effects). As to resolution being needed or wanted, as Patricia Mellencamp has written:

> The End spirals back to the Beginning and a series of other presumably new beginnings. By effacing the presence of the metaphor ... those re-presentations (in dominant cinema) reproduce the subject within that construct, denying a materialist definition which accords the spectator the 'coming into presence of the Film'... the work, that is produced by and in it. The cover-up of classical narrative in the guise that what is being received is different, additive rather than repetitive, a concealment of the return of the same.[22]

The hook could be defined, for non-narrative film, as that which is of interest *per se* because unknown, that which one has not seen, that which is (not) other. Thus an interest in a film which does not somehow necessarily bind the subject-position into a complicity, even a supposedly fragmented, jagged, gapped and gap-filled (as in punctuation) one. Not to be bound into such a complicity would be the radical opposite of for example Barthes' supposition and seduction: "Through the Tower [Eiffel] men exercise that great function of the imagination, which is their

22 Patricia Mellencamp, "Reflections: Mirror Mirror on the Wall", unpublished paper delivered at Purdue Film Conference, Indiana, April 1978.

freedom since no history however bleak has been able to take that away from them."²³ Here, thus, the ideological hook against non-narrative, against a practice that does not reproduce identification. And Barthes' influence goes further, and is always already there in the ready acceptance of that which is:

> ... an oedipal pleasure, to denude, to know, to learn the origin and the end, if it is true that every narrative, every unveiling of the truth, is a staging of the (absent, hidden, or hypostatised) father ... which would explain the solidarity of narrative forms, of family structures, of prohibition of nudity, all collected in our culture in the myth of Noah's sons covering his nakedness ...

and

> This is a very subtle and nearly untenable status for discourse: narrative is dismantled yet the story is still readable; never have the two edges of the seam been clearer and more tenuous ... never has the pleasure been better offered (to the reader) – if at least he [sic] appreciates controlled discontinuities, fake conformities, and indirect destructions. In addition to the success which can be here attributed to an author there is also here a pleasure of performance; the feat to sustain the mimesis of language [language imitating itself, akin to Metz's transcendental viewer identifying with him/her self] the source of immense pleasures, in a fashion so radically ambiguous (ambiguous to the root).²⁴

This position, radically decadent, and reproductive of patriarchal hetero- and homosexual sexism 'to the root', takes us back to that battle against reproduction so abhorred by all the mothers and fathers in film theory.

To return to the question of identification. If identifying itself

23 Roland Barthes, "The Tour Eiffel", *Via*, Vol. 2, University of Pennsylvania, 1973.
24 Roland Barthes, *Pleasure of the Text* (1973), Hill and Wang, 1975.

brings pleasure or forms or forces the viewing then it is simplistic to conceptually oppose it to identification. One attempts to identify everything, during viewing, but that does not of itself offer a validity to the project of such viewing, because although identifying is a first step towards identification, it has to be crucially separated from it, otherwise there would be nothing by definition that is non-narrative (which is a position some recently seem to be holding). The moment of identification is the moment of the establishment of illusionism, and the collapsing of the two terms is a necessary one, otherwise we have theoretical models of illusionist projection without identification, or identification as separable from illusionist space, both concepts being untenable. Knowing one is in the Odeon is of no matter: it is psychoanalytic identification we are speaking of, not the actual suspension of disbelief in a noncontradictory manner posited by some (though for some of the latter see *Driver* and *Coma*). Unbelief, the persistence of belief in the architectural Odeon qua Odeon, in simultaneous existence along with identification-structures, in no way necessarily produces some kind of contradictory 'relevant-ambiguity' stance (were such a stance conceivable). What it produces is simply (complex or not) identification, an illusionist practice within an architectonics uneffaced. This kind of 'relevant ambiguity' stance is one (another one) upon which the whole narrative structure builds its meanings. To speak of the knowledge of the Odeon would be automatically (and empirically/mechanistically) to clear a whole terrain and colonise it for 'narrative as contradictory'. In this sense, narrativisation is a detour, another manner of attempting to repress the power of the signified and its predominance and therefore givenness in ideological narrative usages. Narrativisation consistently 'fails' to work against the reproduction of the signified, thus allowing for stasis, unity, holding, under whatever rubric. The emptying of meaning is what comes up against most resistance yet that emptying of meaning, that making of meaninglessness which is the construction and constructedness of signification presented, is formed from a defensive resistance against the reproduction of meaning; the latter which is the reproduction of dominant ideological meaning, the representation. This is the area where political does not mean aestheticising politics, as it does in 'avant-garde political documentaries' and in much Godard or in 'political, avant-garde documentaries'.[25]

The desire for satisfaction in/of the full figure is the desire of the satisfaction through narrative, and no amount of 'constant slippage, constant contradiction' (metaphysically turning into some quality) within the narrative (or the narrativisational) film can efface that desire (amongst those who desire it). This is the impossible dream of those who find new radicalisms time and time again (in no time) in dominant or un-dominant narrative cinema, for whom individualism (and individualism's voice and image) cannot be finally annihilated as it must be.[26]

What had considerable import on my methodology was that ... by mere accident I leafed through.
    Marx, letter to Engels

We don't yet know what we have to imagine, and it first has to be determined what we would call a life that corresponds to ours under the new circumstances.
    Wittgenstein, *Remarks on Colour*

---

[25] "Photography has come to be defined as a subcategory of nostalgia and/or art. With portraits of people, we always have the possible cliché rationale of 'that's how it is' but never 'how it is how it is'. Thus the cliché becomes solidified, and the myth is conceived and perpetuated through that usage. The frame through which you view the image is just that, and the image just that, but the two together a difference, the crux in fact of that difference resting precisely in such pseudo-documentary's dichotomous nature, when a parallel to 'nature' is attempted (constructed). That is the basis of the problematic." Peter Gidal, "Photo Collection", *Studio International*, July/August 1975.

[26] In relation to a strategy of hypersubjectivity as distanciation-process, a recent publication, *Stories* by Jane Warrick, must be cited as important.

NOTE I

After all, ultra-left once meant leftism, meant storming the Winter Palace before the Bolshevik Party was ready, setting up the Commune before Marx and Engels were ready (and before the correct time, but placing a meaning though not a persistent politics, that was ideologically progressive), before Marx and Engels thought it the right time or line, though full support *then*. Rosa Luxemburg's separatist women's groups, as separate but within the Communist Party, were castigated by Lenin (to Clara Zetkin, and to Inessa Armand, his feminist mistress). By ultra-leftism I mean, what Lenin castigated as 'leftism' in *'Left-Wing' Communism, an Infantile Disorder* (Foreign Languages Press, Peking 1975) from which though, the following: "As far as I have been able to familiarise myself with the newspapers of the 'Left' Communists and with those of the Communists in general in Germany, I find that the former have the advantage of being better able to carry on agitation among the masses than the latter. I have repeatedly observed something similar to this in the history of the Bolshevik Party, though on a smaller scale ... For instance, in 1907-08 the 'Left' Bolsheviks on certain occasions and in certain places carried on more successful agitation among the masses than we did. This may be partly due to the fact that at a revolutionary moment, or at a time when revolutionary recollections are still fresh, it is easier to approach the masses with tactics of 'mere' agitation." (op. cit.) A problem arises because the 'non-Left' (i.e. non-ultraleft, in modern prose) is usually a 'Right' Communism (op. cit.), as exemplified in the French C.P.'s current national-chauvinism e.g. with regard to the wine produce of Spain and Portugal and those whose labour produces it: current slogan plastered around Southern France, "Keep Them Out of the EEC with Their Cheap Wine". This, aligned with humanism/stalinism in its moral self-congratulation, is the elitism of left and right populism alike.

> Lenin never depicted his opponents on the Left as enemies to be struck down or to be driven out of the Party. Not only did he call on

them to work with him at the peak of the hierarchy, he explicitly endorsed certain points of their programme, especially the striving to proletarianise the cadres of party and state. In November 1920, for example, while accusing the members of the Workers Opposition of becoming 'an opposition for the sake of opposition', Lenin admitted, somewhat in contradiction to this, that 'the opposition which exists, not only in Moscow but throughout Russia, reveals many tendencies that are absolutely healthy, *necessary*, and inevitable at the time of the Party's natural [sic] growth.'

Marcel Liebman, *Leninism under Lenin*, 1975

Furthermore:

After 1921, however, when Leftism assumed a more virulent form, leading to actions that were all the more adventuristic in that they were out of line with the general evolution of the situation in Germany, Lenin undertook a vigorous campaign against it. The Third Congress of the Comintern was the scene of a grand attack. Nevertheless, after savaging the Leftist leaders, some of whom, such as Béla Kun, were living in exile from their own countries, Lenin hastened to send them a letter in which he said, 'It is quite natural for émigrés frequently to adopt attitudes which are 'too leftist', ...' and expressed his sympathy with such 'fine, loyal, dedicated and worthy revolutionaries.'

Lenin, quoted in Liebman, op. cit.

One last quote from same source:

Lenin had just written his unsparing attack on Leftism. But then, in September 1920, the action begun by the workers of Turin at the end of August took on a wider scope, leading to the occupation of various factories. Even though these actions failed to develop further, the country did not return to normality – the crisis persisted. It was in these conditions that Lenin wrote to the Italian

Communists that, 'in the present day conditions in Italy one should *lean to the left*. To successfully accomplish the revolution and safeguard it, the Italian party must take a definite step to the left ...'

Lenin, quoted in Liebman, op. cit.

None of the above should be seen to be an attempted validation of anarcho-adventurist Leftism which both denies mass organisation and theory.

NOTE II

Such opprobrium is not to imply that any one is outside sexism, although the status as oppressor is not the same 'status' as oppressed. Nevertheless, overt and unquestioned reproduction of sexist ideology is not the same as work against it. Similarly with racism and capitalism. Using polemics to such an extent reproduces that which you're ostensibly criticising because it makes it so impossible to reach that goal that it can be dismissed as idealistic, allowing one to never take a stand, to deny the political, avoiding thereby any problematisation. Similarly, constant problematisation or 'working through' is not such if not accompanied by a political stand against (dominant) ideological mode, an antagonism (though all this nevertheless takes place in ideology, one is never outside).

I agree with Judith Williamson's position in its specificity:

> ... supporting Laura Mulvey as an independent film-maker, which I do, is quite different from 'agreeing with' her film. *Riddles of the Sphinx*'s very title suggests the sort of Mystery of Woman which is precisely a *male* view of women. This mysteriousness is set up in the 'stones' section with blurry shots of the Sphinx accompanied by electronic music: it almost has the aura of a Turkish Delight advertisement, 'full of Eastern Promise'. This use of the Sphinx can be seen as part of a strategy intended to evoke mystery and an image of inscrutable womanhood, as a preliminary to their 'deconstruction'

with the later role of the Sphinx as a speaking subject: 'she' is given a voice. But this involves a fundamental misconception: you don't dispel a myth by trying to make it speak, or reject an image by giving it a voice with which to deny itself. The film undercuts its own strategy, by not recognising that the power of an image of Female Mystery is so strong that it functions in the most traditional way and is *too strong to be undercut by anything later in the film* – even if this were intended.

The Sphinx on the screen traverses time and space to imply that there are eternal qualities of women ... the necessity that women *ask* the questions becomes confused with the idea that women *are* the question. The Sphinx's riddle is herself. *'She'* is the eternal puzzle, unable to question actual oppression because, like real women, 'she' is not located socially but removed from history and used as a symbol, *something women have had enough of*. To assume that such a symbol 'does not have a meaning but does have meaning within the shifting contexts set up for it by the film's discourse' and to see the text as only 'producing meanings' ignores the dangers of *re*-using, *re*-presenting existing social meanings.

> Judith Williamson, "Two or Three Things We Know About Ourselves: A Critique of *Riddles of the Sphinx* and *Three Women*", unpublished, 1977.[27]

The makers of *Riddles* seem to think that aiming, or swivelling, a camera at someone talking rather generally and simply about housework is 'dealing with the signified, problematising it', housework and its meanings (or, even, problematising the relation of signifier to signified). Supposedly problematising the signified without specific political context is formalism at its most decadent. For films, nevertheless, which persist in *not* learning that the ideological position of the representation is overdetermining, the *signifier*, the *signified*, and the relation of the two, would have to be problematised, inasmuch as this is possible. Leaving

27 Since published in Judith Williamson, *Consuming Passions: The Dynamics of Popular Culture*, Marion Boyars, 1986.

the means of representation, i.e. the *filmic* articulation, *un*-problematised, for example, in Godard/Gorin's *Letter to Jane*, whilst maintaining the myth of 'working on the signified' (the photograph from Vietnam, in this case) sets the theoretical table for socialist realism/capitalist realism. In the *practice of film* problematising the filmic articulatory mechanisms, the means of representation, the technique, is necessary to effect a problematisation of the signified. Nevertheless, the privileging of the signified has a history so broad that an opportunistic film will find immediate 'spontaneous' space in the dominant ideology's academic subsector, the resuscitators of Welles, Sirk, Hitchcock, Ford, etcetera.

Thus: either the playing around of decadent formalism and keeping 'open' possible political positions and meanings, or capitalist realism, held in to (or by) the representation's overdetermination, therefore reproducing dominant ideology's dominant mode, dominant meaning(s). It is an idealism, a voluntarism, to assume the photographic signified ('the aesthetics and politics of the photographic signified') can be always and necessarily problematised; transhistoricism asserts itself here, the way it similarly does in Wollen/Mulvey's latest script referring to a woman's menstrual period as 'the usual feminine problem', thereby overdetermining through that specificity, at this conjuncture, any possible stylistic or 'anti-code' manner of its imagined filmic representation, unless concepts like deconstruction and irony remain in force. What I'm saying politically is that if one holds, though I do not, that it is possible to problematise any image or referent then at least one should use politically left-wing rather than right-wing models, antisexist not sexist stereotypes, to work through productively, materially, dialectically, historically.

First published in Screen, Summer 1979. In the original publication, the article was followed by an afterword by Stephen Heath.

TECHNOLOGY AND IDEOLOGY IN/THROUGH/AND AVANT-GARDE FILM: AN INSTANCE
1980

> Though, in one sense, our family was certainly a simple machine ... it had all the honour and advantages of a complex one.
> *Tristram Shandy*

Since 1966, members of the London Film-Makers' Co-operative have thought it necessary to have equipment at hand in order to allow for the making of films. Whatever ideologies of 'spontaneity' can be read through this, the fact of the matter is that equipment was bought and built to that end. Malcolm Le Grice built some machinery and, together with David Curtis, persuaded one person to give money to assemble and buy more. The sum was not in excess of £3000. Stated rationale: expense; concepts like 'non-alienated labour' were current. The Co-op thus ended up with a 16mm printer and a 16mm developer, as well as editing equipment, viewer, rewinds, lenses, grading strips, etc. A film-maker could shoot footage and see it in negative and then in positive within a few hours in black and white, within a couple of days in colour. The control of the process by the individual was not an individualism. It was the possibility of having access into and thereby through and thereby onto the possible processes of representation. A freeze frame in a final film is no longer within the context of eternity/infinity when you have been holding a strip of original master material while the print stock noisily continues through the printer constantly copying the 'same' image. The metaphysic of silence and stillness was, if not annihilated, certainly lessened considerably. Such knowledge could be gained by one person working with one machine. No ethic of petit bourgeois handworker. No aesthetic of individual genius. You sit there with a machine and you are process, no more or less than the machine, because the handling is necessary yet does not cause an effect – quite a different matter from painting for example – which somehow seems 'higher' or 'greater' or 'separable'. The effect and the cause are in direct relation, even though transformations take place at each 'stage'. These transformations, in that they are operable and operative within the process, are seeable as relations: acts have effects. On the other hand, this kind of procedure does not give rise to a bland empiricism or, worse, positivism, because each move in process can or can not be transformed through chance, through random event, through unknown machinations ("What had considerable impact on my methodology was that ... by mere accident I leafed through ...", Marx). These 'unknowns' have specific determinate effects, which thus matter and are of matter, but what was important was that there could develop in this practice of cinema no aesthetic/ethic of mechanistic or idealist causality.

The spontaneous, untheorised practice of film (when it was this, often it was unspontaneous, theorised) at this stage of the Co-op was a concrete social production, one which involved determinate modes, relations, etc. Later these operations will have to be taken up and analysed. At this point, suffice it to say that such a practice made for the possibility of films which, through the context of their production, already disallowed a position of imaginary knowledge for the spectator, equally disallowing for the spectator a position – identified with the camera/film-maker – of superiority. The context of some of the work done as well as the processes which the films betrayed (during viewing, film-as-projected) forced the viewer into a position of attempting a relation to the production, even if a contradictory one. Signification as problematic function; the apparatus as a whole as difficult, ungiven, laborious ("value only exists when someone receives it"[1]); images as (re)produced, the image being an image of an image, something learnt some years later through other routes by those more theoretically inclined (and often 'forgotten' by many of the film-makers).

When you loop a strip of master film material (threading) onto a printer and attempt to pull it through in order to 'see' how the reproduction will appear if the original is *not* led through automatically on the sprocket-wheel, you are attempting to set up a difference between image and its reproduction. If, then, because of the mechanism (the machine *per se*), occasionally, the sprocket-wheel catches the sprockets of the master material which you are trying to pull through freely and the result – within 24 hours – is screened moments wherein the illusion of real-time-represented (movement at 24 frames per second) is worked against 'the rest' of the material which was slipped through and which (therefore) blurred betraying hardly a three-dimensionally-acceptable movement at all, *then* you have set up a contradictory representation: holding and not holding a series of reproductions into (the) terms of (a) representation.[2] Thus the final film section (as illustration here I am speaking of one segment) works in and on the terms of representation as they 'necessitate' opacity, clarity, an identifying of *what is*, for what it means. At a second

---

[1] Christine Delphy, *The Main Enemy* (1970), trans. Women's Research and Resources Centre, 1977.

[2] "In *Condition of Illusion* what is not achieved is the stabilisation of reproduction into the terms of a representation: effectively, the materials of reproduction that are engaged by the film are not stabilised into representation, the photograph given precisely as a holdable moment (why else a photograph if not for that?). The distinction between reproduction and representation is important, though difficult. In a sense, all the films of yours that I have seen are full of the materials of reproduction held off of – not fixed into – representation. Duration and narrative thus come apart, narrative being exactly fixing, stabilisation. In the phrase 'reproduction of reality', reality itself means a specific set of reproduced reproducible representations, positions, stabilities, clarities – representation is a series of positions for the spectator in relation to a certain clarity of position and meaning ..." Stephen Heath, in conversation, Cambridge, 1976.

level, each frame as visual impetus or stimulus is a signifier and works (in clusters) on the viewer, and the differences there have determinate effects. Thus, spontaneous or not, work with one possible operation through one aspect of one machine at the London Film-Makers' Co-operative in, say, 1969 could yield a specific kind of work on representation that another system of technology could not. This is one of a great number of possible specific examples leading to the general. Commercial laboratory processing could not yield this kind of work on/in film, regardless of whether or not theorisation had reached a point of desiring such a work. The ideology of this spontaneous-or-not practice is another matter: we know, of course, that unequal development allows for all sorts of overdeterminations (determinations in the last instance not withstanding). The ideological implications of such work could 'go' several ways, some of which I have hinted they did not go. The abstract expressionist ethic had worn off by this time in London, if not in the United States, and held little attraction for those working in the Co-op in the manner described. The film-makers at this time, 1966-69, were mostly ex-art students, aware of Pollock, de Kooning, Giacometti, certainly aware also of Rauschenberg, Malevich, Warhol, Moholy-Nagy, aware of modernism and Kafka and *Tristram Shandy* and greyness and urban lower middle-class income; they were aware of the Campaign for Nuclear Disarmament and British socialism which left less room for utopia than did American and European left-movements; they were aware of Hollywood and *cinema vérité* and Godard and surrealism and underground cinema.[3]

My point is that the ideological implications of such a technological practice were ones which had importance for the context of making the work, the context for viewing the works (and the commercial dominant cinema as well), the context for

3   For treatment of problems of influence, see Peter Gidal and Malcolm Le Grice, "Letters from Gidal and Le Grice", *Millennium Film Journal*, No. 2, Spring/Summer 1978.

rejecting the past painterly ideologies, the context for intervention in dominant modes of discourse not in the profilmic but in the filmic, in duration, and its non-suppression, problematising the imaginary, realigning continuity in dominant narrative in such a way that continuity and contiguity were two crucially different concepts and constructs, and so on. The concrete and the abstract became *one* for the film-makers who handled materials; an image of 'reality' with its signification became no longer purely an abstract, a meaning, a symbol, a metaphor, a literariness ... and no longer a concrete, a documentation, a kitchen-sink/coal-board cinema of realism; the reinvigoration of, for example, Bazinianism was built *out* at this stage. As too were various positions for the viewer, since the context for the obvious manipulation of continuity of space and time, the perspective illusion of the lens, was materially attacked: cuts were made and procedures effected which no longer permitted such continuity. Or, when readings overdetermined the inscriptions, as they often do, at least a difficulty was organised as to the unconscious flow via rhythmic linearity making that difficult. Superimpositions of negative and positive and positive on positive were made which so densened the 'image' that a flatness (only, at most) was produced, not a new dark catholic space of depth (as in Bresson's *Mouchette*) but a heavy grey flatness disallowing a safe distance from the screen surface and a secure cohesive subject-position, viewpoint; a situating, unidentified. Bindings were surely there, psychoanalytic and otherwise, but the secure binding of positionality was not as holdable, not 'as' sutured.

The fact that work at the Co-op was in conditions of non-subsidy and so without pay may or may not have been an impetus to some but again the technology was not given as given, rather as barely there, and then only with the utmost work. It was necessary for the film-makers to work the machinery, and not only to keep it working but, in the process, to build more machinery in order to allow for more production: (i) for more people, out of socialist principles of access and a base for a practice rather than just a spontaneous utilisation; (ii) for more adequate experimentation (no matter if that 'experimentation' was in some minds an unquestioned good, in other minds a play, a game, a learning, in others still a necessity for cinema, in others yet the necessity for one kind of cinema to do battle with another; these schemes are precisely that, and in no one could one of four possibilities be isolated, though two perhaps ...).

So work had to be done by those involved and work was done: building a cinema, projecting, cleaning, writing about films. Thus already, based on the material necessity for an audience, a critical context had to be developed. If you want an audience to see your films (no matter how that *want* is defined), you need to write about the works *in advance*. So certain critical work was done in those – and other – interests, further elaborating the 'machine' called the Co-op, that *apparatus* of experimental film (the term fits precisely). It now became impossible to separate the critical context in which the films were seen and presented from the further work and the retrospective thought about the works and the capacities of specific machines, together with the capacities of the film-makers, were inseparable from the capacities of the social space to allow, to a certain degree, a certain social practice to take place. This social practice, namely Co-op films in London, was thus processed through and into and from an ideological space and a theoretical ideology soon to be recognised as such.

What are the interests of a machine (if we are not to get anthropomorphic, not to mention anthropomorphised)? The interests are in continued functioning: when working with a machine such as a printer, you invest in the machine an interest to continue functioning; you invest the machine with your notion of continued operability, its necessity for continued functioning within the parameters given it by its structures as apparatus in the interests of performing whatever function it is made to perform – printing a film, for instance, holding a strip of film in place to avoid a blur which undermines narrative continuity. The machine is thus placed within the realm of technical functioning, within which it stays: its fixations and those of the operators are coterminal. You have the same teleology for it as you think it has by definition. So that when the machine is kept up to standard, kept running, and you then wish to experiment, the experimentation takes place within these parameters, unless something goes wrong or conscious force is permitted, for some reason. It is that area which allows for determinate effects such as the aforementioned example of a strip of film sliding through off the claw, catching by mistake. Another example would be receiving a certain film stock for which neutral-density filter does not have the desired effect. Another again would be developing positive as negative (and/or finding out that the two require the same process, within limits). Yet another would be the fact that when shooting light through a very dark shot, an iris effect takes place, a circle of light which expands or contracts as the scene may become lighter or darker. So that on a dark (technically: thick, as in thick negative, opposed to light, thin negative) master material getting darker, with enormous amounts of light being shot through in order to 'get' an image (the original darkness being, or not, another 'error' possibly: not 'enough' light), you end up with a constantly stutteringly changing iris-effect. This circle of light, when the image reaches a certain point of 'acceptable' (normal) lightness, opens up so wide that in effect it is no longer an iris 'on top of' – or through – an image but enlarges to become in effect coincident with the rectangle of the frame: that is, it disappears (in fact, it is a much larger iris, so large that it allows for the film frame rectangle to exist within *its* unseen parameters). This change of iris effect as materially given as determined by quantity of light makes for a relation of viewable image that forces an interrelation to be made from this inscription; an interrelation of quantity of light and shape of representation (or, at first, shape of reproduction). I am writing here merely about one shot, one usage, one procedure, one possibility, one aspect of technique, as far as such can be isolated descriptively, as a part of the apparatus experimental cinema.

The machine's technical functioning and continued technical functioning is subsumed by the parameters the film-maker has given for that specific and particular machine, and finally, of course, by the machine 'itself'. Now with the example above, the film-maker could decide to make this function one which integrates into a film at a different level of light, thus necessitating filters which could dissolve the iris-effect sooner, or later. The film-maker may see as an effect of this effect that to construct a film from higher or lower density stock would in one case or another be beneficial to a given aim or desire, which may seem to be ('spontaneously') satisfied without a reason formulated to him or herself. This would then necessitate a control of the speeds of the printer, speed and light being contiguous principles in cinematographic reproduction. Thus relation is set up to the speed of the machine and this question becomes 'possible'. The example is a schema for the 'simple' process of the kind of decision which names as 'smooth running' or 'efficient operation' of a machine those particulars which assert themselves through the process of the machine itself. The technical functioning and the standards by which experimentation is possible become at once the limits, within which proficiency and its ideology maintain, and become the limits which can be broadened as in such an example, a broadening which makes one machine out of another. And this process is one which is essentially given in the kind of social practice which the London Film-Makers' Co-operative workshop was, and is. It is through such positioning of the machine that the positioning of the meanings of the film works over the last ten years was seen by those who worked around, through and in the Co-op; it is this which is the context again for the film work and its meanings, though it does not – obviously

– enclose them. The 'interests' of the machine, which I hesitantly spoke of, should now be clearer: they assert themselves precisely as the re-mechanisation of certain technical possibilities and the meanings given through them, disallowing 'the machine' its status as fascistic giver of meaning, constantly militating against the process as dominant overdetermining of meaning repressive of the social practice of cinematics.

Where does the *camera* come into all this? Certainly, it is not used *for*, or *toward*. It, in fact, *is* the seduction for viewing the way the erotic object vague hidden but there *is*. But how? Via the scopophilic pleasure imbibed in through possibilities of looking (being seen or not being seen, gaze broken or not broken, etc.), in any case resistible, recuperable, and hence a false location of the problematic. Thus the focus on the view-*through* (keyhole), the focus on voyeurism as placed *either* in the category of not-being aware (conscious) of watching the forbidden, feeling 'like' a voyeur (in that case *not* being one), *or* of necessarily being aware but doing it anyway, resisting that awareness, allowing the drive its fulfilment precisely in its unlawfulness, though of course sanctioned to the point of legal/social *measures not being taken*. The camera is taken up in that space of definition of voyeurism or its undecidedness, and the machine for recording (in the first instance) sets in motion a series of further operations which position themselves dialectically: each film-making act in relation to each other, only in relation to each other. Various inscriptions result, again inseparably from the positionings and arrestation-attempts inculcated by such. For example, a splice is not 'splice', nor is it 'a splice'; the conscious(ness) implied thereby – of pure knowledge versus materialist dialectic – is false: a splice differs and differs its meaning(s) when, for instance, it is an inscription, one of many, upon: a series of frame(d) close-ups, a long-shot preceding a close-up, an out-of-focus long-shot at first inseparable from a close-up due to its out-of-focusness, an in-focus close-up at first inseparable from a 'cloudy' long-shot (whether of an object, a space, or whatever), and so on. Such matters orientate the cohesive positioning of the subject-viewer via the constant imaginary; such matters materialise differently the function and the degree – or lack of it – of fetishization of the splice (mark) itself, for example. Also bear in mind here that a splice-mark is an image, a reproduction, a photographic image, as is every cinematic device given through projection of film through a projector. This is not an ontological inference but rather a description, an effect, a determinate effect of a photo-chemical process. Some seem acutely unaware of this. 'Similarly', certain effects of certain cinema-technological operations have certain meanings, though neither the technology nor the effects nor the meanings (nor anything else) are ontological (and if anything were, it would have to be avoided – voided – the way biologism has to be, no matter what the state of any proof happens to be at any time).[4]

Metz has written:

> that which is the object of this study: various optical effects obtained by the appropriate manipulations, the sum of which constitutes *visual*, but not *photographic*, material. A 'wipe' or a 'fade' are visible things, but they are not images or representations of a given object. A 'blurred focus' or 'accelerated motion' are not photographs in themselves, but modifications of photographs. 'The visible material of transitions', to quote Étienne Souriau, is always extradiegetic. Whereas the images of films have objects for referents, the optical effects have, in some fashion, the images themselves, or at least those images to which they are contiguous in the succession, as referents.[5]

---

[4] See my letter on ontology in *Screen*, Vol. 17, No. 2, Summer 1976; and on Structural/Materialism, my letter in *Afterimage*, No. 7, Summer 1978.

[5] Christian Metz, "Trucage et cinéma", *Essais sur la signification au cinéma II*, Klincksieck, 1972; trans. "Trucage and the Film", *Critical Inquiry*, Vol. 3, No. 4, 1977.

On the wrongness of which the following remarks need to be made:

1. Optical effects *are* photographic inscriptions;
2. The status of "given object" is to be severely questioned, to say the least; there is no difference of photographic status whether it be a 'blurred image' or 'an object';
3. "Modifications of photographs" fails to see *photographs* as processes and not transparencies;
4. "The visible material of transitions" is a highly questionable material in anything other than the most conventional commercial narrative film, so it must be remembered that Metz is not writing about *film* but about a specific kind of film, and we are forced to reject prescriptiveness in the form of descriptiveness;
5. "The visible material of transitions is always extradiegetic" – if diegesis is the imaginary space and *time* of the film representation – is not true in most films: conventional commercial narrative, Structural/Materialist, New American Cinema, Old French Surrealism, what have you;
6. The last sentence quoted, on optical effects and their referents, is true only for the most crudely conventional films, is untrue of most avant-garde films of interest.

With regard to all this, look at a film, *Spot the Microdot* (Malcolm Le Grice, 1970), to name one of dozens.

At the same time, however, it is important to combat the simplistic misreading of avant-garde film practice's historical relation to technological development. Avant-garde film practice in England since 1966 has not in the main been determined by technological development, so that, for example, optical printers, quality of film stock, computers, advanced colour processing all have nothing to do with the experimental work done over the last ten years. This is first of all because such materials were indeed not available, and also because the (materialist) beginnings of a practice (as it stemmed from its relation to various other social practices) did not privilege consumption on that level as its implicit or explicit ideological form. The lesson of various art forms, for instance, was read as *not* coincident with capitalist expansion. As it happened, for economic reasons, specifically, East German Orwo film stock was often used, at a cost of approximately £1 per 400 feet (11 minutes) of black-and-white negative, one-tenth the cost of Kodak film. This fast 400 ASA stock obviously does not allow as much detail, hence larger grain due to lower resolution of the image (or the less controllable temperature in the developing process at the Co-op). Though Orwo's range is the same as Kodak's, for all Co-op workshop processes the black-to-white spectrum (range in fact) is more muted (grey!). The cause for this is imprecise development (over or under) or imprecise exposure (over or under) resulting in reduced contrast. Thus lighting must be on a more sophisticated level to achieve contrast, if this is desirable (which means merely that the objects one filmed, or the people, had to be correctly measured for reflected light – a simple still-camera light-meter sufficed). There is another fact here though as well: not only did Co-op members use technologically less advanced means, in addition 'technologically advanced means' refers in many cases to *less* sophisticated materials, less precision, less room for manoeuvre. In other words, the *Siege of Lucknow* photograph (Salt Print) of 120 years ago has a fine grain image which is 'unobtainable' now through 'normal' (namely much smaller) cameras and, therefore camera-negative sizes, or with 'normal' camera lenses. Similarly the average photographic paper cannot manage anything near the fine grain quality of a Woodburytype of 100 years ago (see, for example, Thomson and Smith's, *Street Life in London*, 1877), fades quicker, is less resistant to moisture, etc. Another example, Technicolor, no longer used for motion pictures, employed three black-and-white negatives that were then dyed, which allowed virtually no fading; the more modern process uses film material that is itself dyed whatever colours are wanted, thus producing negative fading. In photographic reproduction, to give yet another example, gravure is, for economic reasons, hardly utilised, thereby denying the production of finer resolution and – in perception terms, though not in physical, photochemical process terms – greater depth of field.

So in many cases 'technological advance' is synonymous with democratisation, which means in this practice greater crudity, less possibility, less advance. Or rather, advance is defined as everyone having a camera without a handground lens or one that matches its possibilities, printing on paper that is extremely limited and limiting in possibility and in its solution, and so on. This is not to push for elitist 'quality' as opposed to democratisation; it is to show the uneven development of both in various cases, depending obviously in the last, and often in the first, instance on the economic interests at work. The four categories mentioned – optical printing, advanced colour processing, film stock quality, computers – do, of course, come under the heading 'technological advance'; simply, that 'advance' is redefined in the cases of film stock qualities and processing.

A parallel in the United States would be the work of Warhol which abnegated certain technological refinements in the interests of non-mystification of materiality, and as a distancing device/operation, which enabled a beginning again: experimentation through the practice instead of an idealist 'moving forward' from one practice, cinema, to another, technology *per se* (which is not to say that technology *per se* exists). For us, the project was one of the inseparability of the technology from the ideological and the inseparability of both from representations/constructings. By inseparability one is referring here not to any singularity or univocality or to some amorphous conglomerate but to integrated practices which figure on, in and through one another.

Pages from Peter Gidal's notebooks.

Above: Television broadcast of Samuel Beckett's *Ghost Trio*, 1977.
Photographs: Peter Gidal

Right: Peter Gidal, *Film Print*, 1973-74. 16mm film strip.

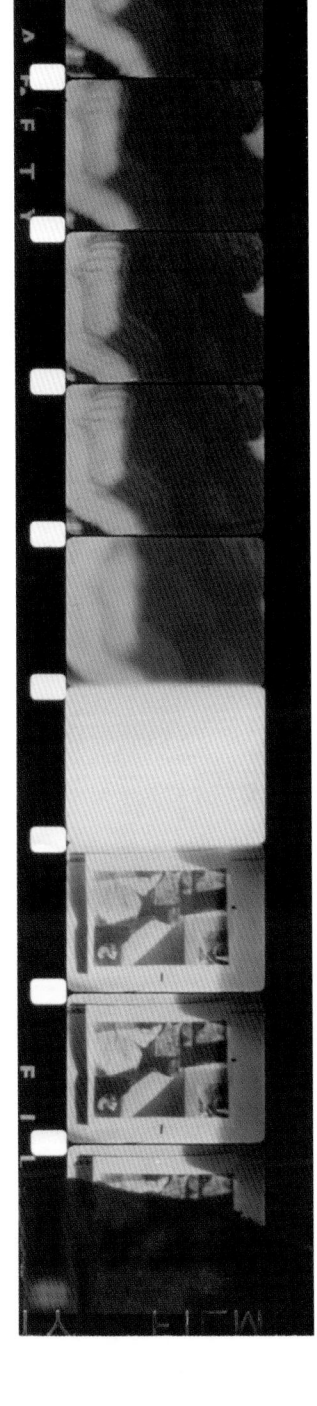

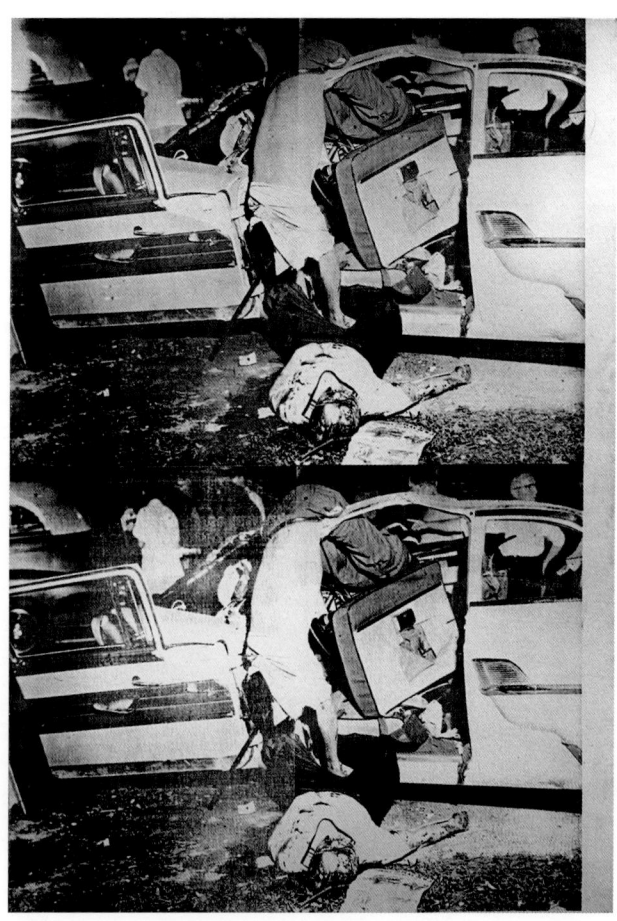

Andy Warhol, *Saturday Disaster*, 1964.
Acrylic and silkscreen on canvas, 119 x 82 inches.
Rose Art Museum, Brandeis University, Waltham, Massachusetts, Gevirtz-Mnuchin Purchase Fund.
© 2015 The Andy Warhol Foundation for the Visual Arts, Inc. / Artists Rights Society (ARS), New York and DACS, London.

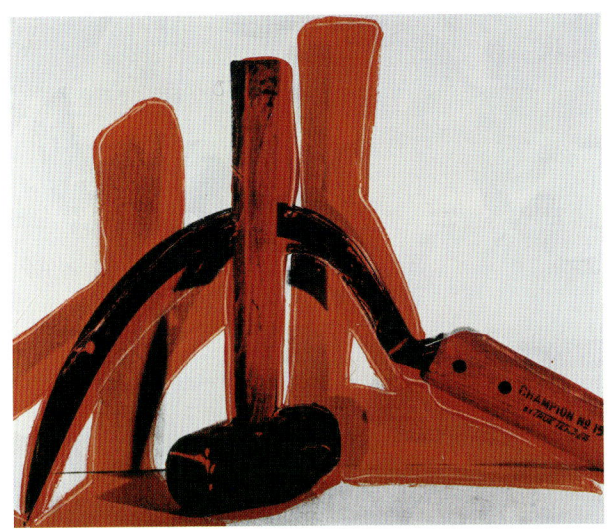

Andy Warhol, *Still Life*, 1976.
Acrylic and silkscreen on canvas, 72 x 68 inches.

Metropolitan Museum of Art, New York, Gift of Richard and Peggy Danziger, 1986. © 2015 The Andy Warhol Foundation for the Visual Arts, Inc. / Artists Rights Society (ARS), New York and DACS, London. © Photo SCALA, Florence.

Andy Warhol, *Blow Job*, 1964. 16mm film still.

© 2015 The Andy Warhol Museum, Pittsburgh, PA, a museum of Carnegie Institute. All rights reserved.

Flare-Out
(Peter Gidal, 16mm, colour, 1992, 20mins)

Sound: unrecognition unidentified, in time, you hear?

Image: recognition identified, out of time in time; not *not knowing* the unknown but not knowing the *known*, no trace of 'no trace of any thing'. E.g. grain: is grain silver, black & white, or colour? Is silver black & white or colour? You see?

Peter Gidal, London, February 1992

Copyright Peter Gidal 1992

Financed by the Arts Council of Great Britain

Distribution: London Filmmakers' Coop, 42 Gloucester Avenue, London NW1
Telephone: 071 586 4806   Facsimile: 071 483 0068

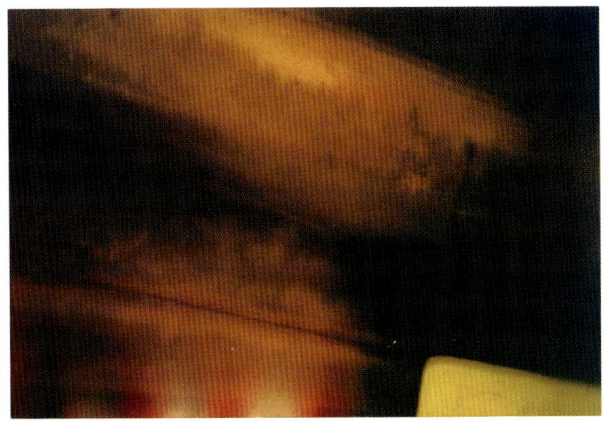

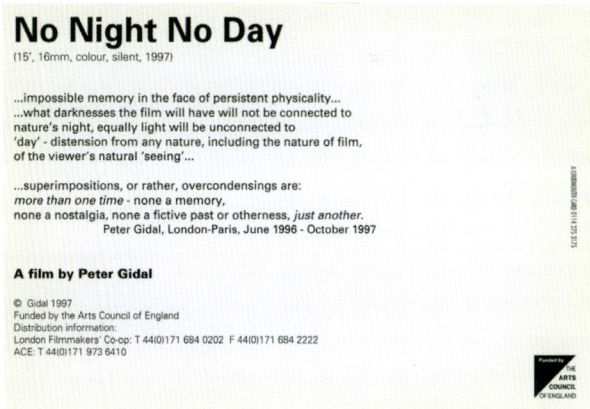

Arts Council postcards announcing the release of Peter Gidal's films
Flare Out (1992) and *No Night No Day* (1997).

Thérèse Oulton, *The Heart of the Matter*, 1984.
Oil on canvas, 242 x 228.5 cm.
© 2016 Thérèse Oulton.

Thérèse Oulton, *Marking Time*, 1994.
Oil on canvas, 213 x 233 cm.

© 2016 Thérèse Oulton.

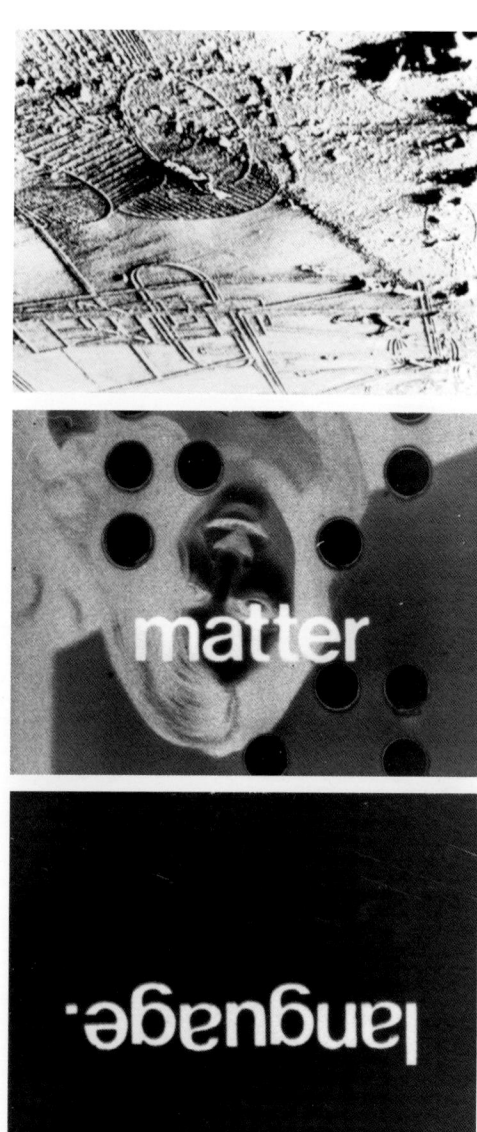

Peter Gidal, *Upside Down Feature*, 1967-72. 16mm film stills.

Peter Gidal, *Volcano*, 2003. 16mm film still.

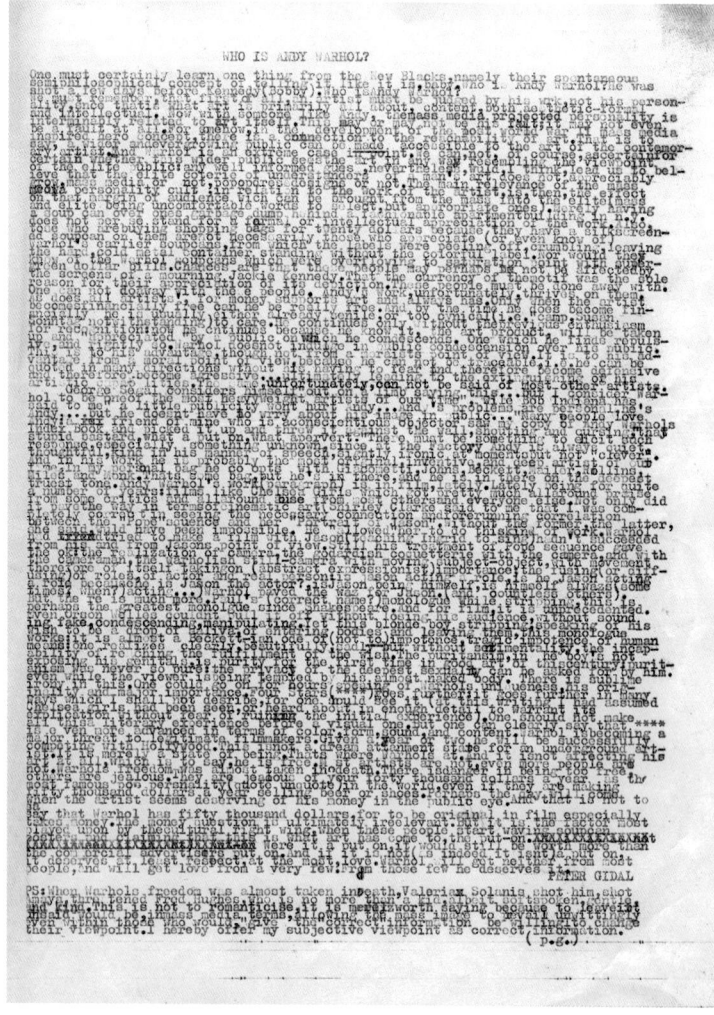

Peter Gidal, *Who is Andy Warhol?*, c. 1969/70.
Printed Roneo copy of RCA Newsheet.

END:YES NO MAYBE ET CETERA or ~~[struck through]~~ MARCUSE AND MICK DIALECTIC

Joe Boys went to the beachhead with Gorilla-Mary.
Beuys said:"Hey max,that's the kind of whaling I haven't done
since my first pre-teen b-day party,and whaam!that really sends
me,daddi-o"(i should explain that mailer says the "o" after
"daddy"in the late fifties implied an attitude towards the male
as mr.vagina,therefore the "o"added.In any case,mailer having
made his bucks sucking the minds of the jewish intelligentsia,
Joe Boys was still stickin' it out at the beach(head)with
Jello-Mary,tits wobbling inside her hot-pants dress-suit,
I mean the kind of tits Bellmer would put into asshole and
out the other end,all firm and in-shape,you bet.Telephone-fairy
couldn't take the brown sugar that the sand resembled,so,
having waylaid his last lady-lay,having sprung his last sing-song
from the mind's eye of melon-tree lemons,he split.And fast.
The whales kept comin', though,like wild horses,onto the
not-anymore-so-forlorn beach,i t was more like a magritte
without the magritte,complete stasis in motion,you know,sort
of a nothing but with lots of WHAAAM!MaX B. flew down for the
weekends,the sway was waylaid by Beuys' dream.A dream which
neither Freud nor Jung couldx analyse,but they tried,dearie,
I tell youu,they tried.Max B.and Boy's dream colided,coincided,
glided into one,you know sort of orgasm-at-the-same-time,did
you come well too,dear?(Hemingway would say and spit onto
Madrid's shit-steaming airport lounge and order another Jack
Daniels.)Well,The dream of Max B.-Boys was made to order for
the 5o dollar an hour analysts,like Bettelheim,jiving jived
his way thru auschwitz in the hope of making a book,you know,
keeping going telling himself"beyond this point i will not go".
So he told us about all the jews who ate shit to get a nazi's
cap and gown.Very Visconti.And now he's jewbaiting ~~[struck]~~ only   just-born
the jews are the niggers,and the niggers are the ~~[struck]~~. Anyway,
Bettelheim andother such 5o bucks an hour analysts had dreams
made to order,and this Max.B-one was one,times one.The dmam
was about the meeting between waveman and caveman,and
lingo-ringo and rango-laingo were angels watching,breating deeply-
deep white pelvis-mickey was choking on his own slimy spam-machine-
-made wild,wild horseshit. Down on Dukestreet burroughs and
fuckerdaddy were having it off in the 5th floor elevator
pondering the sighs and sights while deep down near the earth
of seasperm and whaleflight the frungians were jiving to the
tune of buckytoothed money,pentagonism,and just plain blues.
And nothing helped,for the pepsipkles were all stolen and melted,
pelted with clay of pre-frontals and you-know-what,you betcha,
skalps a la carte blanche.Noir.Et cetera.Not rouge,you betcha.
Haha.Back to the dream it wasnt really one but once thought
perhaps it was,for you know i tried to treat you rite but
well after all i want tits you want prick what to do but change
eachother into eachother,and then we're back where we started.
The dream was something like that I guess,perhaps,let's do some
thing,some sweet thing,after we'll die, the Rolls is waitin,for
that pie-in-the-sky near the nam,nambo sambo,oh fuckit,you know
what i mean.Sontag does.She was there.Or was it montag(no)
after the previous-last war,nice car to drive,i'd say,if your
souls on gin and tonic. Which it ain't.Or if so,Max B.would
try to exchange that tonic for another,the other being one
of a kind,the kind only you and you alone would have the nerve-gas
to ask for,let alone drink(precluding no-one,dog-o!).Don't
forget that,because I've come and gone all these ways,yeah,
youve got,nasty boots(and no's knife was twice as spiced,with
well hey hey naturally,hitchhiked-H;yeah). Get on your knees and
pray.The silver wig has fallen.Mindfucker's lost his mind.
And my bread is not eadible,in any form,live or dead.The choice
was mine,was yours,and know that I felt free then but now,the
whales are comin' all over the sugar-sand seashore,and I just
drown,a little further off the edge of minds' eyes,but not
far.Not far at all.No.

                            Peter Gidal ~~[struck]~~

Peter Gidal, *Marcuse and Mick Dialectic*, 1971.
Typed manuscript.

Above: Gerhard Richter, *Abstract Painting 810-4*, 1994.
Oil on canvas, 200 x 200 cm.
© 2016 Gerhard Richter.

Top Right: Gerhard Richter, *Abstract Painting 724-4*, 1990.
Oil on canvas, 92 x 126 cm.
© 2016 Gerhard Richter.

Bottom Right: Gerhard Richter, *Abstract Painting 800-1*, 1994.
Oil on canvas, 46 x 51 cm.
© 2016 Gerhard Richter.

Photograph of the original publication of *Against Metaphor*.
Fascicle Books, 1998.

The point is not to humanise technology in the guise of an attack: technology does not present itself to certain functions through ideological 'need'. There is no reason, that is, to assume that the lens as the most perfect example of the reproduction of Renaissance perspective was invented at the right time because of technology's embodiment of ideology. This may have been the case, of course, but it need not have been. Similarly, the camera as possibility for reproduction: an invention that 'could' have been made 200 years earlier as all but one of the 'elements' existed. It waited out its time. But not necessarily. We must not let the 'ideological' (pure and simple) become overdetermining at the expense of – amongst other categories – the economic in the last instance. A further danger is that of seeing technology as the embodiment of ideological subject positions (for example, Renaissance space for the subject viewer), a technicism which then labels as idealist constitutive productions which combat that placement of the subject-position. If the final arbiter of materialism is the current technology, we are inside an opportunism (in the Leninist sense) and an effective relation called sublimation; but in the interests of which class? Of what kind of power relations? Of what kind of sexed positioning? Of what kind of materialism? For a materialist analysis and position, it is thus important not to privilege the technology, the instruments for the production of meaning (or meaninglessness). Which is not to say that inventions just happen, happen on a neutral ground; it is to say that there are a complex of determinations and that, whatever these determinations and whatever the conjuncture and the specific effects/affects, we are still never in a position of finality – neutrality – and ultimate reason. To historicise inventions, even in the interests of combating bourgeois science, is to give a teleology to technology's ideology, to biologise and humanise a social practice (technological advancement) and forget that ideology is not simply presented and not simply represented. Otherwise, technology would be a simple matter, a reflection of a certain ideology: for example, the positioning of the male subject in capitalism, in *his* space, is obviously not the only positioning achievable with or without technology, with reference to the cinematic apparatus; there is uneven development. A 10:1 zoom lens on an Arriflex camera can, through a certain labour, formulate a fragmented, uncohesive subject position; a pinhole in a Rice Krispies box can, through a certain labour, formulate pure Renaissance perspective solidity and transparency.

Several problems arise in connection with the practice at the London Film-Makers' Co-op as here described:

1. An ideology of process was evident in the procedures of work and relating to a fetishisation of process, finding its way into the profilmic discourse, let alone the intervention on the filmic. Hence one can oppose, at an initial stage, the fetishisation of work/process/technique to the concept of necessary labour, processing something into something else (other). *Process* must be brought back into the vocabulary minus its fetish meaning.
2. In the same way, *material* must not be understood as vulgar materialism merely because of the pragmatism its utilisation as a concept in some beginnings implies. The machine seen for what it is/does: function ... factory ... in process ... not mechanistic ... a materialist process ... no other work form capable at that stage – 1966-76 – of producing work on and in and through representation. This was opposed to Godard's aestheticisation of the political combined with a romantic/fascistic individualism, a seductive criss-crossing of cultural and other language/image possibilities. Our production attempted to rest on other matters.
3. *Duration* in printing/projecting technically shows aspects of (non) discontinuity, producing the machine as the whole apparatus rather than its opposite: the specific fetish. The inability to deal with de-signifying works or semioticity

denying works arrives at a pseudo-apparatus close to Stalin's 'efficiency' through concepts such as 'deconstruction' (alienation from, and recuperation to, the machine in its mechanistic form) and 'popular memory' representations. Mechanistic repetition – for example, loops – produced contradictoriness through duration, the mechanism producing itself as separate from the profilmic; not a metacinema but a force of separation and difference referring to just that.

4. There is no film which *subverts* the real, that which is; the (a) placing of the viewer in contradiction in that case being confused with a (the) placing of the viewer in a totalised and totalising apprehension of (seeming) knowledge, or, equally in keeping with the dominance of what *is*, the placing of the viewer in a position of ambiguity, each 'moment' a *frisson* of desire to 'figure out', precisely, what is happening and why, with the answers always present even if not duly – unduly – given. That which is, the material real, is only subvertable by another material real, not by any material image of a material real. Film which subverts the real is idealist, *because it cannot*. One real subverted by another can be revolution, but different social practices are collapsed if one thinks film subverts life *as opposed to ideological conflict* (a conflict exactly of positions in knowledge, through knowledge). Surely a non-obsessive in life is not radically criticised by the image of an obsessive in the cinema.[6]

5. As to *anti-humanism*, necessary even when not evident as a conscious concept to film-makers (theory often lags behind practice): the machine as a critique of humanism, (a) durable and unendurable, (b) ineffable stare. The latter is machinistic, as in other cases, within another techno-historical space, the non-stare is machinistic – Rodchenko's

---

[6] "I've seen *Wavelength*, now show me something that has some signifieds; enough of the signifier", Julia Kristeva, in conversation, New York, 1976.

disavowal[7] of naval perspective so the machine-isticness is linked to the non-normativeness of the code, the persistence away from, in difference to, another, not merely defined by some 'connection' to machine or to a specific machine-analog (machine-like, machine-likeness). Which is why the machineness is present in *Chelsea Girls* and *13 Most Beautiful Women* (both by Warhol) and not in automat photographs (for instance). The anti-humanism also of the de-bodied, de-sexed, towards an uneasy consumption forcing production, as inculcated (meaning, in fact, active viewing: constant dialectic, constant repositioning, resituating; with 'situating' understood not as some idealist 'newness' for the subject, from moment to moment or otherwise, but as a replacement, a newness and originality nevertheless).

6. The difficulty of identifying space as inhabited by certain techniques/images is only of interest if the identification, as in Structural/Materialist avant-garde film, of the techniques/usages is of equal difficulty; otherwise, it is always a meta-language and a fetishisation of whatever (of whatever: process, image-making, subject position, the look, the naturalisation of sound, etc.). Avant-garde does not mean good conscience films relying on signifieds, nor crypto-melodramas 'in a different' light such as *Tom, Tom, the Piper's Son* (Jacobs), *Thank You Jesus for the Eternal Present* (Landow), *Straits of Magellan* (Frampton), *Rameau's Nephew by Diderot (Thanx to Dennis Young) by Wilma Schoen* (Snow), *Epileptic Seizure Comparison* (Sharits) and other *men*, nor landscape films whose mimesis and solidity as text and therefore also as viewer-situating is justified as a literalness.

7. There is a further difficulty with *process*. 'Process' was a term used by certain London film-makers around 1966-69 with reference to one another's works and to the overall interests

---

7   Cf. Rosalinde Sartorti and Henning Rogge, *Sowjetische Fotografie 1928-1932*, Hanser Verlag, 1975.

which they felt their films represented. But 'process' can imply the artist-subject and this was criticised in the early seventies with an emphasis on the material trace and the notion of inscriptions of such. The question arose as to the artist-subject implied, for example, through hand-held shaky camera movements (lighting, angle, distance, speed, and so on, not to mention profilmic event, were equally determinants, were discussed as such); the question as to these camera-movements was that of the positioning of the artist 'behind', present in its (determinately his) absence. The 'answer' to this 'question' was that *de-subjectivisation* was possible through, for example, repetitions and retake working on similar or same profilmic material – the notion of a series of camera-functions and editing-functions which would de-subjectivise the resultant projected film-segment's procedure. This would then undermine or negate the ideal (idealist) viewer's ideal subject-centre outside the film-trace's inscription. The project embarked upon through this critique was to make of the procedural a system wherein the viewer does not find him or her 'self' (the gaze, trapped[8]), it was to disallow *identification into procedure* the way Abstract-Expressionism (and Expressionism) so often did not (identification is a concept which could never exclude structures of self-identification). The answer, though, tended towards a mechanistic materialism when its implications were not fully grasped: privileged status was given to the inscription *on* – in – the film-image (rectangle), thereby lionising the trace (explicitly) and subscribing to crude distanciation and perceptual positivism (implicitly). Such distanciation and reliance on the privileged place for the image (deconstructed or not) was also inseparable from a reliance on meaning as given, the signified as solidified in capitalist patriarchy,

---

8   A current myth is that every gaze is broken by the return of the look, the look back, and that every film has to be a trap for the gaze.

only to be 'questioned' through the reproductions presented (a metaphysical intervention) or through the mode of the reproduction's presentation (another metaphysic). 'Deconstruction' turns out to be juxtaposition and the 'non-denial of history' and the 'social spaces of meaning' turn out to be fixations on metaphor. The overdetermination by social meaning of everything else refuses materialist practice the indulgence in setting up, figuring an image, a sequence, and then somehow contradicting, deconstructing, repositioning it. What finally had to be learnt was that neither the process with the concomitant subject-creator established nor the framed inscription of trace 'out there' would suffice. Process would have to be repossessed for and in materialism, which it then was. So would subject, structure, perception, economy, sexuality, art, ...

First published in The Cinematic Apparatus (eds. Teresa de Lauretis and Stephen Heath), Macmillan, 1980. In that book, the text was followed by a transcript of a discussion between Jean-Louis Comolli, Sandy Flitterman, Peter Gidal, Christian Metz, Laura Mulvey and Maureen Turim.

SAMUEL BECKETT'S 'GHOST TRIO'
1981

Ghost Trio was written expressly for television by Samuel Beckett in 1976 and recorded by the B.B.C. in October of that year. It was published in the United States (Grove Press) and in England (Faber and Faber). The British publication, which first appeared in the *Journal of Beckett Studies* for Winter 1976, includes revisions made during the broadcast-recording; hence, the British texts are, finally, based on both the writing and the tele-recording. As *Ghost Trio* was written as a tele-play; it has not been otherwise performed, and it will not be. The Male Figure is played by Ronald Pickup, the Female Voice is played by Billie Whitelaw. No name is given for the boy who plays the boy, in any printed text. The production was directed by Donald McWhinnie, under the constant supervision of Beckett, who also directed a German television production of the play. A trilingual publication of this, and various other recent pieces, was brought out by Suhrkamp, in Frankfurt, as *Stücke und Bruchstücke*; that edition also includes Beckett's work notes and instructions for various performances, outlines, drawings of precise movement structures, etc. – all in all, a more useful publication.

As to *Ghost Trio*, a conventional description to start:

The play itself is conceived within three frames, each containing another frame and another world like a Chinese box. The outer frame is that of the television screen itself, the rectangular shape of which gives the play its most striking visual aspect other than the human figure. The voice of the woman announcer operates on this plane, explaining what is seen in the second frame, that of the visual narrative. The third plane is interior, that of the inside of the mind of the protagonist and of the music that comes from a small cassette recorder, Beethoven's "Ghost Trio", Op. 70, No. 1. The announcer's voice tells the viewer that hers is a faint voice that will not be lowered or raised and that the predominant colour of their picture should be shades of grey. She describes three of the rectangular objects that can be seen, a door, a window and a pallet or simple bed on the floor, all of which are the same rectangular shape. (...) There are also three other rectangular objects not described, the cassette-recorder, the stool on which the man sits, and a mirror. (...) There are also three other rectangular shapes shown and mentioned: a section of floor, a section of wall, and another view of the pallet, this time resting against the wall. (...) The narrator also describes the sole inhabitant of the room, a man. The man is immersed in listening to three musicians playing a trio, the sound emanating from inside a cassette-recorder, and he is observed from outside the television set by the television audience and by the narrator, (...) he is also listening for another sound, for "her" to come. What he sees, after twice opening the door and window, and looking in the mirror, is a surprise to him. The steps coming down the passage, the imperious knocks of a stick, are no surprise to him. (...) It is the boy who comes, dripping from the rain, who indicates, smiling and negative, and retires down the passageway (...) we are told by the narrator that the light never changes, never dims, that the room contains no shadow.[1]

In quoting the description, I have left out as much symbolic interpretation as possible, although exegetes of Beckett's work always thrive on seeing his work as some kind of pre-text, autobiographical or otherwise, as if the work were there to illustrate some notion of Beckett about his personal relation to rooms, knocking, boys, mirrors, doors, tape recorder, waiting, the number three, and so on. Also, an intense humanism is always inferred (or interfered), which may indulge whatever writer is writing, but which has nothing to do with the work at hand. As

---

[1] John Calder (Beckett's publisher), in *The Journal of Beckett Studies*, No. 1, Winter 1976.

if saying good things about the human condition were in any way akin to political action, for example, or as if a written or performed work were not a *work*, with such and such relations of production, of meaning (and meaninglessness) as opposed to some sort of preexistent truth that is somehow given back, reproduced (adequately) to be consumed into 'life'. Thus, there is a constant search for (a) symbol, ironically 'forgetting' Beckett's often quoted statements to the effect that if he had wanted to say such and such, he would have.

I am not, here, attempting to use the author (authority) for verification. It just happens that his theoretical position on his texts is more advanced than that of most critic-academics. Hence the many attempts in *his* speech, on the subject of his work, *not* to see it as imbricated with symbolism, anthropomorphism and, ultimately, a message of humanism. A common problem: "Kafka's radical critique of humanism was one of the things that made him unintelligible to a Marxist author like Lukács. When it comes to revealing the ties between humanism and upper-class ideology, the Marxist 'demystifiers' are as timid as Freud."[2] Of course, the Marxists referred to are precisely those who *cannot* cope with humanism and its demystification, whereas writings by, for instance, Louis Althusser advance a materialist critique of humanism.[3]

On with *Ghost Trio*. In most works by Beckett, the subject is charged with hyperconsciousness, the subject being the (heard) narrator, or the (seen or heard) protagonist, or the viewer in her/his identification with one or another of the former. In *Ghost Trio* – which had originally been entitled *TRYST* – to repeat, an act is narrated by a woman's voice. Through being narrated while the enactment is produced, the act, whatever it is, initially undermines any view of itself that would allow for a naturalism

---

2 Marthe Robert, *From Oedipus to Moses: Freud's Jewish Identity*, Anchor, 1976.

3 Louis Althusser, *Essays in Self-Criticism*, trans. Grahame Locke, New Left Books, 1976.

or a suspension of disbelief. The fact, in other words, of a narrator overtly narrating a series of actions renders problematic, at this first stage, certain identifications into the imaginary space and time of those actions. When the scene begins with, "Mine is a faint voice. Kindly tune accordingly," we are given to believe in one fiction only: not the fiction of the enacted, but the fiction of the enacting, the voice of the woman speaking constituting that enacting. The *words*, thus, are the reality of the scene – the words, her words, the signifiers. Hence a convention within signification – within a play, a film, a television play, and so on – is countered from the start. The images – that series of actions seen conventionally as the necessary producers of meaning – are here given as *products*, as already determinate effects. The imaginary management of theatrical space, which represses the causality of the enactments, is withheld – not effaced or deconstructed, but withheld. The narrator's voice is presented: "It will not be raised or lowered ..."

The script of the television play breaks down into three parts: (1) "Pre-action"; (2) "Action"; (3) "Re-action". The sole characters are the Female Voice, Male Figure and the Small Boy. The music heard is from the largo of Beethoven's fifth piano trio ("The Ghost").

There is a pause after, "Good evening. Mine is a faint voice. Kindly tune accordingly," after which, "Good evening. Mine is a faint voice. Kindly tune accordingly." Pause. "Look." Long pause. "The familiar chamber." Pause. "At the far end, a window." The description continues.

At some point: "Now look closer"; and the image cuts to a rigidly formalistic, frontal high-angle view of a rectangle that supposedly represents "the floor" or "the wall". In these closer views ("look closer") we are given a less naturalistic view, one *not* coinciding with what we might have approximated, if based on inferences from the initial longshot of the space, which is the first shot we see – a room with a bed and a door and a window and a stool and a man sitting. Here, thus, is a second disjunction of the real or the imagined real.

As the camera moves in on the seated figure, music slowly fades in, getting louder as the camera gets closer; as the camera recedes, the music fades out; then, in silence, the camera keeps receding, until it gets back where it started, in frontal medium-long-shot. The question arises as to the 'nature' of the protagonist, the antagonist. This *agonist*, a present absence: is the camera a metaphor for a present absence? The very existence of a mobile unit to change the reproduction of a viewed scene ineluctably recalls another figure, a viewer, and is thus an anthropomorphism. And our own positioning through that becomes problematically inscribed through the making present – the foregrounding – of precisely such camera movements into a scene 'out there'. In other words, since the camera movement *does not* efface itself as the method of producing a certain kind of narrative seamlessness or narrativization for the viewer, the camera does give itself a durational hold upon the scene. This camera movement blocks that flow, *making difficult* a 'natural viewing' that would see nothing but the effect – the final play, an effect without cause, magically produced. The camera movement does not hold itself, unquestioned as to meaning, or mode of production, or ideological desire toward certain ends ... It does not efface itself toward repressing the knowledge of how a material is worked through to produce such-and-such effects. So we are left in an unavoidably problematic area, whether or not the camera becomes a protagonist or agonist or a mechanism of differentiating from the scene as given, and no more than that – merely another function in the mechanism that produces this video-play *Ghost Trio*. This problematic area must be borne in mind as an entanglement that cannot simply be left to its power as possible and obvious metaphor. That would be the too unproblematic consumption, one which the text *Ghost Trio* in the particularity of its production as a television-play denies, although metaphorical/symbolic readings/interpretations always come to hand quickest precisely because, being merely substitutive, they slip into their pregiven meanings most easily and exclude labour processes from their construction. Such meanings are, then, never given as *effects*; they are given precisely as *pregiven*. So everything stays as it is, and we have a metaphysic of absent presence, in the case of the camera described above, which would cover all blockings ... and hold them together in the imaginary unity of the natural – in whatever style the 'natural' for each specific production might be defined.

"He will now think he hears her," says V (Voice). *We* are thereby positioned in an insecure perception, fraught with the will for knowledge: who is "her"? Thus, we perceive (aurally) that we do *not* know who this she is. The disembodied voice is the voice of *a* "her", a woman, but is it the her referred to? Then, also is it the voice of a her at all – of a woman, a body, a figure, present or not – or is it simply *voice*, a different kind of character maintained from the usual one necessitating a figure? The voice that is articulated, outside of this television-play as well as, possibly, 'inside' it, is after all, not necessarily reposited inside anything *other* or *different*, anything *else*. Nor is it necessarily a part or a fragment. It may, in fact, not be disembodied; nor does it have to be embodiment of a figure, contracted into a metaphoric voice. It may be voice as articulating a specific set of words, with certain meanings – in no way a voice *of*, or *from*, or *for*. Voice may thus be 'prehistorical' and in the position of forming its history at the moment of articulation, a flow of the very material of voice, a history rememorating itself, but only from the now, the point, *now*, of inception. The material history of the voice is defined only from the moment it exists in its specific determination as voice, and not carrying in any way the baggage of a poetics, resonances of theatre-art, or life or whatever. V: "No one." "Again." Voice directs the protagonist's actions or listening for her whom he thinks he hears, whom we hear.

When the actor "raises head sharply, turns still crouched to door, fleeting face" (Beckett's instructions in the script), he is acting within the gesture (*die Geste*) in the strictly Brechtian sense. This by now overly familiar notion has hardly been sufficiently realized theatrically to warrant its being designated a cliché. The rigid freeze of an action into a pose, which, as unposed, relapses into movement (towards), then reholds itself into the gesture ("fleeting face, tense pose ... 'again' raises head sharply, turns still crouched to door, fleeting face ..."): such gesture relapses into movement and then reholds itself as gesture. That distancing is *not* evidence of a mechanistic understanding of Brechtian theory as meaning merely a distance that is only to be overcome afterward by reentry into the imaginary transparent reality of whatever fiction or pseudo-documentary is at hand. That distancing is of a truly Brechtian type often unacknowledged by Brecht in his lesser writings and in most Brecht productions. It has been affirmed, however, in the present Beckett piece as well as in the production of *Waiting for Godot* that Samuel Beckett directed at the Schiller Theater in Berlin in early 1975, with Estragon played by Horst Bollmann, Wladimir by Stefan Wigger, Lucky by Klaus Herm and Bozzo by Carl Raddatz, and which played in London in 1976, and in the same year in his production of *Footfalls* with Billie Whitelaw. Work on the relation between such Brechtian technique and the work of the Bavarian comic Karl Valentin has yet to be undertaken. Brecht started in Valentin's troupe, and worked closely with him on a codirected film *Mysterien eines Frisiersalons* (1923). He also credited Valentin with the "invention" of the distancing-technique, in his *Arbeitsjournal* and in often quoted notes on theatre. Some of the dialogues in *Godot* sound straight out of Valentin (which is no insult to either). Beckett had seen Valentin perform in 1938: "Yes, I saw K.V. in a shabby café-théâtre outside Munich. Evil days for him. I was very moved."[4]

4   Samuel Beckett, Letter to Peter Gidal, 12 September 1972.

The window of the set is not a glass pane; it is a painted-grey 'window'. But the bench can be sat on, the door can be opened, the pallet (a mattress on the floor) can be lain upon, the cassette recorder can be listened to, the mirror can be looked into.

As the camera moves in on the sitting figure, a cassette in his hand is unrecognizable at first. The camera stops, pauses, starts moving in further, with the sound faint, then louder, with the moving closer of the camera. Then the camera recedes with it. "He will now again think he hears her." The camera stays out at the original, unmoving position, and yet the sound comes on as the man (F: Figure) listens. He lifts the cassette closer to his face: he and we hear the sound – the music – at normal television level. The script states: "faint. It grows louder". In any case, the camera this time has *not* moved in, but the music nevertheless comes on, and F and we hear it. V: "Stop". Music stops. V: "Repeat". Sound comes on; image cuts to near shot; and *moving camera equals louder sound*. F raises his head sharply, as if hearing something; at that instant the sound stops. Head back into opening pose, sound returning with it. Thus the Figure controls the sound now – an effect without cause, but *given to be seen by us as without cause*. Thus we are not given an effect, some image magically produced and, therefore, an idealism, without cause. We are given the causelessness itself. Just prior to this sequence *Voice* controlled the sound with its (her) "Stop".

In viewing this durational section, and in allowing for the contradictions of the controlling element to reinforce our *lack* of knowledge *in direct conjunction with the precision of our perception*, we are placed in a position of no longer searching for a kernel of truth. No longer is a layer of meaning being unveiled to show underneath some other fabrication given as unfabricated, some whole and cohesive analogue to the real or a metaphor for such. Instead – as if we had a choice, given the material at hand – we are placed, contradictorily, in the face of such confusion, or rather, of such lapses in the internal coherences of the narrative.

We are disabled in the figuration of the plot. We are disabled in the figuring-out, the figuring-in; both are denied. Thus a fragment is given that is for once *not* a fragment of a whole that can be 'spontaneously', 'immediately', reconstituted in imagination. A fragment is given that does *not* control the meaning and stand for the meaning of the reconstituted whole. We are given a fragmentation that does not define itself through mere difference from some apprehendable, understandable whole from which it happens to be disjoined. Therefore: the fragment is not given a cohesiveness and imaginary unity of materiality and meaning through a closure of its *place* in the whole of the narrative to be identified *with* and identified *into*. Nor is the fragment given to stand in for, and represent, another, as if in the completeness of another's absence. Thus the two essential recuperations are made impossible tactics – impossible, period.

The nonidentificatory positions invoked by the mechanism of this television-play, as described so far, rely on articulating a degree of convention inside certain dominant codes. To ignore those codes totally would simply place the drama in an arena of high style, in a stylistic outside of dominant codes that would, however, thereby reallow dramatic identification through fiction, plot, character. In the case of a specific form of expression, the stylistic, outside of the dominant codes would allow identification of, and into, the scene, the space, to be withheld for a time, after which the style is merely another code for understanding and, in fact, facilitates it. Thus, *The Cabinet of Dr. Caligari* is no more 'difficult' than *Gertrud*, *The Man with a Movie Camera*, *Jaws*, *In the Realm of the Senses* or *Grease*.

On the other hand, the code of a kind of hyper-subjectivity is necessitated precisely to make possible the complex distancing as I have been trying to outline it. For example, the sound becoming audible, as the head of the protagonist moves closer to the cassette, thus allows for the usual one-to-one identification into character, with the sound as 'our sound'; the move from him to us, and us to him, is a device of convention *through which*, finally, an operation of un-positioning for the viewer/listener can be constructed/imposed. It would be an error, therefore, simply to distance the characters, the plot, the camera movements, and so on, through certain devices *prior* to such an imposition. For this reason – because of the fundamental misunderstanding that usually operates *vis-à-vis* distancing – we have had precious little Brechtian/Beckettian theatre since the 1930s, in both the English- and the German-speaking countries: no materialist theatre, no dialectical theatre.

The man opens the window. *Point-of-view* shot of rain. And the sound of rain. But the fact that the rain fills the total frame (there is no window-frame, no distant landscape, nothing to hold the perspective representation in place) places the shot of the rain into a particular position, one *not specific to the place outdoors for this particular scene*. It is, namely, the position of rain, *per se*: not this rain, not this scene, not this signifier, or whatever rain would signify given the internal drama of a man in a room opening a window to find that outdoors it is raining, and that the rain has a sound which had not been heard indoors – indoors thus being, through that shot of rain, established as a vacuum of sorts. Instead: rain, an unspecific, although materialist, term, and an unspecific, although materialist, event, that is materialist precisely through its not being constructed unproblematically within a drama. Instead another space, another event, with*out*. In that sense, the rain close-shot does not serve to naturalize the dramatization further, and to bring it forward; it serves, instead, to denaturalize the space, breaking into the continuance of dramatic flow or tension.

Similarly, an extreme close-up from above the cassette showing a "small grey rectangle on larger rectangle on seat" – abstracted so that "seat is a rectangle, flat and Lissitzky-like" – denaturalizes the supposed function, within the dramatic narrative, of the cassette-recorder. By formalizing it, within this specific context of narrative drama, it becomes an other, outside, not befitting the space given for the story. The flattening of Renaissance perspective in the view perpendicularly from above breaks the possible identification with an anthropomorphic camera as metaphor or deputy for the consuming/consumed/unconsummated viewer.

A similar device is articulated later on: the Figure's point-of-view of the bed is given, then an extreme close-up of the mirror, then a medium shot of Figure, pallet, mirror; the Figure turns to the mirror. But the mirror-close-up was pre-point-of-view, given in extreme close-up, as was the cassette-recorder *before* the Figure could (inside the dramatic narrative) have been placed to see realistically (into) the mirror. Thus the construction is foregrounded by being made difficult in viewing; the placement of a shot is not dictated, yet again, by the 'psychological' necessities of character, drama, psychology, flow, rhythm, melody, form. "Cut to close-up of mirror reflecting nothing. Small grey rectangle, same dimensions as cassette, against larger rectangle of wall." Then, later, switching back to naturalism, a shot of the Figure looking at the mirror, *from* the mirror.

Another *Geste* in *Ghost Trio*: the man walks, somewhat hunched, Nosferatu-like ('old-man' posture) to his seat. During most of what has so far been described, the narrator, or Voice, has been absent. Sound (music) has been absent. The Figure takes the cassette; he hears the sound, and we hear the sound, of the Beethoven, which stops on a cut as he jerks right; he listens, and we hear footsteps. Shot 30: "F gets up, goes to door, opens it as before, looks out, stoops forward. Crescendo creak of door opening. Near shot of stool, cassette. F holding door open, stooping forward." Shot 31: "Cut to near shot of small boy full length in corridor before open door. Dressed in black oilskin with hood glistening with rain. White face raised to invisible F (five seconds). Boy shakes head faintly. Face still raised (five seconds). Boy turns and goes. Sound of receding steps, register from same position his slow recession till he vanishes in dark at end of corridor. Five seconds on empty corridor."

Back to longshot of the whole scene. Sound comes on, after a time, camera still all the way out viewing the scene. Music louder of its 'own' accord; no closing-in of the camera to get 'nearer' to the 'actual' cassette sound, nor a parallel soundtrack with its own logic throughout as something separate from the visual. Equally, it is not a matter of F's head moving closer to the cassette to hear. The volume increases over the scene, *then* the camera starts to move in, in contradistinction to the way sound operated for the hearer – us – via the camera movement or the protagonist, earlier on. As the camera moves in, the sound stays level for some moments, thus totally separated from the movement. "Hold till end of Largo." Then sound off. But even that hold on the sound, with a hold on the camera movement, does not persist. The sound, in its final hold, gets even louder, and one cannot register whether it is the sound of the video, or the music itself, as played by whomever. This confusion between the recorded movement by Beethoven, and the audio-control of the video machine at the recording stage, disallows an easy separation of presentation and representation. The actual musical text, as given off, is positioned so that the difficulty of distinguishing difference persists – the difference 'between' perception (what one hears) and knowledge (how that hearing was, what it was, in its construction or process). Thus there is also a resistance to the identificatory use of musical drama. Identification is contradicted and contraindicated by the machined operation of volume control, a break, again, in a possible naturalization of the place *of* the (musical) drama and the place *for* the viewer of that drama – hence, a break in the unquestioned flow of meaning and feeling. The construction as construction, produced as a constant antithesis, or, better, nonthesis: the nonthetic, nonmimetic resistance.

Beckett, the producer said, made some changes from the printed text, in terms of the length of shots; but, when he did, he did that to every shot, thus not affecting the structure.

My first reading/viewing of initial moments of *Ghost Trio*, in 1977, had the protagonist moving the sound control on the cassette recorder up (louder), and yet the observer did not hear anything; sound seemed to 'come in late', based on bad synchronization. The producer said it seemed all right to Beckett. It seems more than obvious now that that is an artificiality within the scene, that that time-lapse operates solely as something preventing narrative closure and cohesion, as out-of-sync sound is used, similarly, in certain experimental films.

It must, finally, be mentioned that, although this work was specifically written for television, and constitutes, to my mind, the most radical use of television as a materialist practice (together with ... *but the clouds* ... which was shown in the same program of three plays for television by Samuel Beckett), it was, in fact, filmed in 16mm, and then video-recorded. The design and structure of *Ghost Trio*, a box for 'the box', remained unimpaired by this use of film – whose greater depth, tonality and resolution befitted the precision of Beckett's written instructions – while retransmission through video befitted the conception and structure and view (point) of the work. *TRYST* indeed.

First published in Artforum, May 1979. Reprinted by kind permission of Artforum.

AGAINST SEXUAL REPRESENTATION IN FILM
1984

> For objective dialectics the absolute is also to be found in the relative. The unity, the coincidence, identity, resultant force, of opposites, is conditional, temporary, transitory, and relative.
> Lenin, "On Dialectics", 1914

> If women come out of the cinema feeling victimised then that is harm – you can't measure the norm. Men feel their own power enhanced.
> Rachel and Sarah, Women Against Violence Against Women, LBC Radio, London, 30 September 1982

The vehement determination in patriarchy to reproduce the oppression of women in the interests of male power exists in all social practices. There is no social space which is somehow exempt from the however contradictory power-relations that capitalist patriarchy is predicated upon, and which it reproduces if it is to reproduce its interests.[1] Thus the necessary institutions of oppression 'must' be constantly reproduced; the reproduction of male power in *representation* is one instance.

Representation has been taken to mean 'the ideological' as if somehow the ideological were not itself a material practice, as if the ideological were not a state apparatus, state apparatuses. Of course, 'state apparatus' is a concept that needs modification from the Althusserian definition if it is not to become totally identified with the state structure as is. In a sense, the *state* is not the final determinant of the structures of ideology nor is it necessarily

---

[1] "... structurally men are the agents and beneficiaries of the subordination of women." Diana Leonard, preface to Christine Delphy, *Close to Home, A Materialist Analysis of Women's Oppression*, Hutchinson, 1984.

always the primary structure which gives identity to the current ideological forces, as the sphere of the so-called 'private' is imbricated in, and reproductive of, specific *ideologies*. Thus, for example, the ideology and politics of private and 'free' enterprise are in some nations bases for the ideological state apparatuses, but in others the ideology of private and 'free' individualism is *countered* by the ideological state apparatuses (i.e. in socialist states). Be that as it may, the point of all this is to state (!) that representation is ideological, is a material practice, is political.

The images and sounds which you see and hear and which position you in your unconscious and conscious relations of meaning and knowledge and 'truth' and 'nature' are, precisely, images and sounds as *material* – both in the orthodox sense of mechanistic materiality (light, grain, tone, volume, timbre, duration, etc.) and in the dialectical sense of the *social*-material in problematic relation to (its) *attempted* representation. Films that do not suppress either materiality have formed an experimental/avant-garde practice in the last two decades, mainly in Britain. Structural/Materialist (and post-Structural/Materialist) film is a concrete, theoretical, *filmic* practice. Such film is *social* as it is grain, light, form, etc. and equally and simultaneously projecting the processes of representation and its attendant problematics. *Material* is thus to be understood not as a (social) story or document, but rather: material as social inasmuch as it is the *material* of attempted representation's *process*. Such film is important in what it does *not represent*. The moment the film represents, it isn't 'about' representation. In my film practice I cannot make a film that is 'about' representation while simultaneously allowing any representation to hold (thus giving itself as *natural*); yet theoretically I can posit that such filmic represent*ing* can be dialectical and historical when it problematises processes of representation.

What the films I am not describing but alluding to have an interest in, which does not suppress their materialist practice, is a concern with how the seen is not to be believed; how the seen is 'read'; how such light readings are readings which have to be seen to not be believed; how such succession of images in duration are not, is not, an unfolding, of anything prior, anterior – not even sexuality; rather, a concretion of obsessive processing. What the camera is aimed at (the profilmic) are not overdetermining signifiers.[2]

The political question to be asked, and which has been asked in Britain since the late 1960s, is how to not reproduce dominant relations in film. The film-makers working around the London Film-Makers' Co-operative who were concerned to have their experimental film practice not simply become a 'different' style, or a private individualistic expression in another form of (phallocentric) poesis, realised that the moment-to-moment work with, on and through *process* (at *each* stage of film-making) is the film. Thus no film, no representation, however 'later' analysed and discussed in its specificity, could be separated from its imbrication in its film processes – and thus a radical experimental film practice and problematic was necessarily predicated upon the film as film *process*. The processes of representation are the contradictory difficulties that occur when at one and the same time attempting to represent and attempting not to represent, not to hold any reproduction of the 'real social space' (the profilmic space the camera is aimed at). Thus the viewer is forced constantly to attempt to arrest the images, the structures, the meanings, but can never produce a satisfaction, successful mimesis, identification or possible consumption.

Such cinematic representational practice was predicated upon the radical political position that to represent the sexual of 'men' and 'women' is to reproduce dominant sexual positions and meanings and relations. At this historical juncture, the overdetermining meanings and positions given by and through sexed

2   Peter Gidal, "The Current British Avant-Garde Film: Some Problems in Context", *Undercut*, No. 2, 1981.

figuration, in advertising, TV serials and plays on television, in photography, dominant cinema and so-called 'independent cinema', in dominant and 'alternative' theatre, in graphic illustration, etc., can only be adequately dealt with if a number of idealist notions (among others, *deconstruction*) are rejected. There are numerous ways in which films can reproduce the material ideological politics of the given capitalist-patriarchal structure; a number of styles are 'open' for use which films that oppose the definitions for a radical materialist practice constantly take up. Such films, which thereby take up a reactionary position, find 'different' *styles* which simply serve to codify existing representations (within their respective style), employing themselves as decoys and pretexts. Existing representations and social relations in representation are then *re*produced, through the perceptual iconography of the known (familiar, in both senses). To work against this effect certain dominant relations have to be *filmically* denied, and what must be recalled is that arguments against such denial (i.e. 'against repression') often forget that such a concept ('against repression') is itself *political*: whose repression? for whom? against whom? 'Against repression' as a concept must be questioned, as it disavows the existence of a political, sexual, economic *power*.[3]

The notion of deconstruction (another of the previously mentioned 'number of ways of reproducing the structure') filtered through from various academic positions which sought to leave things the way they are: the world of representation in sound and image would remain and then, after the fact, interpretation would deconstruct the meanings. Thus a whole school of bourgeois semiotics found a predetermined teleology (and many careers were founded as well). A next step in deconstructive analysis was that such interpretation be taken into the filmwork itself. Thus, instead of screening *Dressed to Kill* on a

3   Peter Gidal, "On Julia Kristeva", *Undercut*, No. 10/11, 1984.

Steenbeck and interpreting deconstructive meanings ostensibly against dominant phallocracy, one would now build these into the work itself. A ready-made school of independent film-making (and an attendant academia) sprang up, in effect finding in such films built-in deconstructions that would rationalise and make *good objects* out of whatever representation was at hand. In what Lenin would have described as classic opportunism, certain analytic insights were constructed for past films (usually from the Hollywood model, along with early Dreyer, Lang, etc.): deconstructions of the narrative sexual relations of family, of traditional roles of masculinity and femininity, of conventional narrative and narrativisation, etc. Such insights were then built into the ostensibly different or independent or 'new' filmworks, so that the selfsame bourgeois semioticians and academics previously content to describe ('textual analysis') the Hollywood good object as imbricated with contradictory and therefore 'critical' or 'challenging' constructions could now find a new rationale and good conscience in reading out from new deconstructive films precisely the *same* analyses. (Constant, and endless, denial of the return of the same, in the interest of dominant pleasure and its power.) Thus, the 'deconstructions' were no longer 'gaps' and 'contradictions'[4] in a classic film text, but rather the text itself had been 'reformed'.

This thus was the second stage defence against a radically materialist avant-garde.[5] Bourgeois representation of, for example, gender relations could now be found to be different – not simply after the fact on a Steenbeck (a perverse act of will in any case!)

---

4   It's not that every representation doesn't have contradictions, but the classic text *contains* them, makes the contradictions invisible/seamless/in the interests of dominant oppressions, i.e. *material oppressions* (and their ideological powers) / *ideological oppressions* (that material).

5   Many of those who at one point wanted to make films that were 'deconstructive in themselves' (supposedly) went on to make more or less conventional cinematic product, with one eye on commerce and the other simply on avoidance of the day-to-day difficulties of working through an avant-garde/experimental film practice.

thereby justifying the capitalist/patriarchal good object as 'actually' contradictory, problematic and deconstructive of just such bourgeois relations. No, now such analyses could come directly from the perceptually and stylistically 'different' independent cinema which mechanistically built in the deconstructions and distanciations (often of a crude sub-Brechtian type) critics would then read out. The process and materiality of cinema, the apparatus in all its forms, was thereby annihilated. But, as in literature where this attitude began, these attempts at deconstruction served to reinvigorate dominant representations, dominant meanings, dominant spectatorial positions (of oppressed, and oppressor) under the cover of a new rationale.

The overdetermining dominant meanings of 'men' and 'women', the biologism and essentialising of the definitions, the power relations that are reproduced by representing them – these are the perceptual 'knowledges' that a radical film practice must militate against. The making and unmaking of meaning and meaninglessness, the constructedness of (the attempt at) each moment of reproduction and representation *and its impossibilities at each moment,* are inseparable from the filmic apparatus and process. The conflation of the perceived with 'truth' or 'knowledge' or 'nature' is opposed by a materialist film practice, not least in its positioning of the viewer/subject against the illusion of power *over* those meanings which they consume.

The paradox is that the *illusory* power given the viewer (as male) by filmic procedures of identification and narrative reproduces actual male power positions. The viewer must be positioned in constant unknowing, the not-knower, displaced, as a resistance *against*. Through that unknowing, through the impossibilities of transparent 'communication' which would obliterate the filmic process and its materialist functioning, the viewer-as-subject becomes positioned as necessarily productive. The production of meanings (and the contradictory struggles against pre-given meaning to be consumed) forces the viewer into a dialectical relation with the cinematic, and with the cinematic apparatus.[6] "Identification: mental mechanism whereby the individual attains gratification, emotional support, relief from stress by consciously or unconsciously attributing to him/herself the characteristics of another person or a particular group" *(Webster's)*. Against sexual identity would be, then, neither *difference* ('woman-as-other' against a (male) norm, outside language and power) nor *homogeneity* ('woman-as-same', assimilating the male role in patriarchy, identifying with it, such a role denying both women's subjective and objective histories, ideologies, powers.)[7]

The lack of representation of the male and female body, let alone any narratives and narrativisations which are motored by such, means unpleasure (a different kind of pleasure) is instanciated by such cinematic practices. The representation of the male and female, and the situating of the male and female viewer *in* representation, and the depiction of male and female sexuality (whatever that is) is the ideological mode of reproducing dominant relations, no matter what the 'actual' narrative ostensibly is. Because the seen, and the scene, that we re-witness, is the reproduction of positions of secure perception as to the sexualised body, that body as always the *other* against which the sexual identity of the 'I' is reproduced, in the interests of patriarchal relations as much as the reproduction of the labour power necessary for capitalist relations. We see a man and a woman on screen and we can begin at that first stage of perception to identify what is, and then identify with/through that representation.[8]

---

6   Some of my films relate to these questions, specifically *Silent Partner* (1977) and *Room Film 1973*. See Peter Gidal, "Technology and Ideology in/through/and Avant-Garde Film: An Instance", *The Cinematic Apparatus*, Teresa de Lauretis and Stephen Heath (eds.), Macmillan, 1980.

7   Such conceptualisation is both descriptive and prescriptive through its reproduction in language of that set of meanings and politics.

8   Stephen Heath / Peter Gidal, *Cambridge Tapes* (unpublished taped discussion on narrative at Jesus College, Cambridge, March 1977).

Thus the narrative of patriarchal power relations, and dominant oppressions, is set up at the initial perception stage, because the recognition of the known, and the conflation of the known with the real, the real with the true, and the whole family romance with the place for the viewer-as-subject somewhere in that, means that thereafter whatever interpretations and differences the narrative has to offer, it is still predicated upon the acceptance of the (natural, pregiven, pregiven-as-natural) existence of the sexed role and position of, and towards, the represented men and women on-screen in-frame. What is (pre)given to that scopophilia is given as natural to it: an ideological operation.[9]

We need a concept of the materiality of ideology that understands that such representation is an immediate positioning of the viewer within a certain political relation.[10] "For it is precisely the massive reading, writing, filming, of the female body which constructs and maintains a hierarchy along the lines of a sexual difference assumed as natural. The ideological complicity of the concept of the natural dictates the impossibility of a nostalgic return to an unwritten body."[11]

The positions that are given for the retention and reproduction of male (and men's) power are given precisely through dominant pleasures, consumption instigated by the ideological material of represent*ings* every moment of/in our social existence. These meanings cannot simply be critiqued as if that were enough (interpreting the world, we certainly know, is not to change it). We have to produce different positions in our representational practices, and such a beginning of a different

---

9   The demand is for a materialist analysis, to account for the historical independence of patriarchy and capitalism: "Only then is it possible to establish the material basis for the connection between the struggle against patriarchy and the struggle against capitalism." Christine Delphy, *The Main Enemy* (1970), trans. Women's Research and Resource Centre, 1977; also in Delphy, *Close to Home,* op cit.

10 Peter Gidal, "The Anti-Narrative" (1978), *Screen,* Vol. 20, No. 2, Summer 1979.

11 Mary Ann Doane, "Women's Stake: Filming the Female Body", *October,* No. 17, Summer 1981.

position is one which does not reproduce the empirical real as real, does not give perception the status of truth, does not reproduce certain perceptions at all, precisely because of the overdetermined codified meanings that prevail.

There is no law that says everything must be represented and then interpreted differently (and if there were it would have to be broken); nor is there a law that says that not to represent certain narratives is to deny their existence. Rather, it is to produce other presentations and processes, so that no 'existence' is given at all, no 'meaning' is given at all, nothing is given outside of its being/having been constructed, so that any position taken and produced is precisely that: produced, the product of labour, of politics, of ideology, of power. The structurings of a materialist procedural practice which deny the reproduction and representation of the meaningful, narrative, sexuality, are structurings that position the viewer against the dominant power, in *resistance*. Of course, for those who deny, or love, capitalism's oppression of the mass of men and women, and patriarchy's oppression of all women, there is absolutely no need for anything but what already is, with the odd stylistic difference to reinvigorate and renew the present cinematic structures, to facilitate their consumption, avoiding at all costs the production of struggle and the production through contradictions and struggles of a different power relation.

> Another problem is that women who have relationships with men can only go so far and they then have to stop or they couldn't live with the idea. They couldn't go on sleeping with men. And they have to go on sleeping with men, for all sorts of reasons (they can't be blamed for that) because they're constructed that way. Well, let's not say that: we're constructed that way. But in any case it becomes an unbearable contradiction if you take it to its logical conclusion. Because then you start questioning everything you do and you can't go on living (...) Heterosexuality as a sort of cosmic heterosexuality is absolutely coterminus with a basic world view which not

only hasn't been put into question, but if it were put into question everything would crumble down ... nobody would know who they are. You can call into question your class and ethnic identification without eliminating your sense of self. But if people are not men and women anymore, then they don't know who they are. No identity. It's not a personal problem of not having any other identity. The problem is that no other personal identity exists (...) because it is built on the basis of gender identity (...) Attacking sexuality (...) is in the end attacking the assumption that men and women are complementary somehow, at some very basic level. And that basic level is represented by coitus (...) When one questions that, one questions everyone's identity. People cannot afford to be left without an identity, so we cannot approach a question that might lead to that.[12]

Film works that do not arrest, return, and hold the viewer (in his/her conscious and unconscious positioning) to a sexual identity[13] are predicated upon and operate through processes radically opposed to sexual representation.[14]

First published in Screen, November 1984.

---

12   Christine Delphy, interviewed by Laura Cottingham, "What is Feminism", *Off Our Backs*, Vol. 14, No. 3, March 1984.

13   One issue is how the viewer is not necessarily or always a man (or a 'man'); that phallocentric view of knowledge is the hold of the cinematic, the break of which is political.

14   See also Stephen Heath, "Afterword", *Screen*, Vol. 20, No. 2, Summer 1979; and "Repetition Time: Notes around Structural/Materialist Film" in his *Questions of Cinema*, Macmillan, 1981.

FUGITIVE THESES
RE THÉRÈSE OULTON'S PAINTINGS
1984

"My politics," said I, in a glorious burst of idiot demonhood, "and that of every other woman in this room, is waiting to see what you men are going to inflict on us next. That's my politics ..."
   Joanna Russ, *On Strike Against God*, 1980

It is obvious that for the artist obsessed with his (sic) expressive vocation, anything and everything is doomed to become occasion (...) But if the occasion appears as an unstable term of relation, the artist, who is the other term, is hardly less so (...) All that should concern us is the acute and increasing anxiety of the relation itself, as though shadowed more and more darkly by a sense of invalidity, of inadequacy, of existence at the expense of all that it excludes, all that it blinds to. The history of painting, here we go again, is the history of its attempts to escape from this sense of failure, by means of more authentic, more ample, less exclusive relations between representer and representee (...)
   Samuel Beckett, *Three Dialogues*, 1949

Painting which however stylistically 'differently' needs to represent (rather than present) is painting which relies on the opportune, on pregiven meanings, and codes within which those meanings already exist, the way you are born into an ideologically determined history before being born. What is then necessary is a break: resistance and struggle. Otherwise there is a denial of the productive possibilities and the transformations of meaning that painting as a practice can inculcate. Such a denial would make of painting illustration; Oulton's painting at its best does not. In their attempt to break with the natural, any *naturalism*, her works (to varying degrees) engage with it. For example, *The*

Passions No. 6 dialectically distances ones passions ... the histrionics of the earlier paintings, their flamboyant melodramatics, overabundance, Turner-Delacroixesqueness, overabundance of style, contrast, and sheer paint, *as if they were attempts at excess*, in *The Passions No. 6* is handled with a Wagnerian intimacy.

In other words, what could crudely have been seen as a Wagnerism[1] of excess is problematized via, and *against*, the possibility of *spectacle* (the stage-set-likeness of some of her previous works). The specific passions of *The Passions No. 6*, its 'intentionality' i.e. what it does with paint, is an operation and process at each moment and in each gesture against the coming-into-being of excess. Thus this painting cannot be consumed as spectacle; it is (a) painting which disallows any easy position of recognition (recognition by definition naturalizing the recogniz*ed*).

In identification, recognition of the other takes the place of the (material) other, assimilating the other to the self (introjection) by producing the 'satisfactions' of various consumptions. That would be a reestablishment of the viewer's 'sensitivity' and narcissism, via the artist's commodity (the aesthetic object) and the artist (the human object). Such recognition is thus of a phantasmatic self. In *The Passions No. 6* the constructed impossibility

---

1 Lunacharsky (Lenin's cultural commissar) on Wagner: "However, Wagner's music is not simply organized sound. It is not even emotions translated into sound. Nietzsche reproached Wagner for being in all actuality not a musician but a mime, a man of the theatre (the use of histrionics). Yet we must delve deeper. An understanding of Wagner from a socialist point of view is a very intricate affair ... the positive and negative are closely intertwined ..." Always again the necessary death of art, the nihilism of the late 20th century dis-illusion, and the passion and texture of productive intensity ... those are the contradictory modes of which none alone will produce the necessary struggles for change. Yet without hopelessness as its base nothing but illusion upon illusion.

"Wagner's abstraction that encompasses the concrete ...", that would enable "revolutionary passions ..."

Anatoly Lunacharsky, "Richard Wagner" (1933), *On Literature and Art*, Progress Publishers, 1973.

of apprehending the painting's 'contents' as spectacle disallows the viewer that conscious *and* unconscious position.

If identity is disallowed through such painting's process, the material *work* becomes the interrogation of the *viewer* by the attempted representation as much as the interrogation of the painting's meanings *through* the viewer's conscious and unconscious processes. This is not to anthropomorphize the painting, but rather to see as material practices both paint/canvas and the viewer's historically constituted objective *and subjective* positions, *politics*.

Naming *The Passions No. 6*'s intimacy 'Wagnerian' refers to physical and verbal exchange, for example in dialogue-scenes in *Die Walküre*. In the Zubin Mehta / Filippo Sanjust (Vienna, 1981) production, translucent screens were utilized to distance and isolate monologue and gesture. Additionally, the long dialogues were foregrounded, with the 'music' as separate interference rather than complement. It came close to a kind of distanciated objectification of theatrical convention that Warhol's *The Chelsea Girls* (1967) produces, with the 'framing' process dynamically iterated as construct, unnaturalistic, arbitrary, as is all human exchange (which nevertheless desperately attempts to deny this). Politics is the necessary positioning against the arbitrary. Oulton's *The Passions No. 6* is intimate in that sense, though (and this is important) *through and via the paint process* the expansive 'theatrical' space is *un*framed, uncentred, out of 'focus', fugitive. Unapprehendable. *Through* such a process the painting problematizes both its specific representation *and* the current styles of various contemporary anti-modernists' hysterical grandiose-gestural brushwork and content.

For painting to possibly be radically materialist, it must be a denial of the academicism and bourgeoisification of capitalist modernism (and post and anti-modernism), and must produce politico-aesthetic positions (& critiques) determinately against any retrogression to decadence, excess, the body, individualism, and the commodity fetish.

The historically dominant avant-garde painting codes are problematized by Oulton in *The Passions No. 6, Copper Glance, Mortal Coil*, in each's very moment of assertion. Thus there is no retreat in these works from the (art) historically/politically necessary engagements for (and in) large and medium scale painting in the 1980s. That struggle. No retreat from oil, scale or subject. (By 'subject' I mean to include her construction of the unapprehendable through the layers of endlessly processed precise brushwork.) This can go either way. Like mid-period Jasper Johns or late Guston, representation/metaphor/(even straightforward) symbolism, could go either way: a stylistic *for* (and subsumed by) the represented 'objects' (or spaces, depths, sites, mysteries) *or* a 'problematizing *of* the signifier', shunning stylistic masquerade, a *process against naturalism* (however defined).

If the former is the case, metaphorical elements (steps, bow, water, foliage) disinterred from the painterly struggle function to psychologically 'flatten out' complexities which could dialecticize the material. This straight metaphorizing, dispensed with by 1984, is retained in Oulton's works of 1981-1983, although the other 'flattening out' (the simplified modernism of overall flatness) had always been avoided.

I do not like the early works (1981-1983), monumental three-dimensional spaces, mythical (mystical) 'archaeological' sites, symbolic scenic fixations.

What does it mean to say, "I do not like the early works"? It means the others, *The Passions No. 6, Copper Glance*, and *Rue* (all 1984) have the impetus, passion, style, paintwork to wrench away from solidified 'focus' any perspective depth of illusionist space, *and* simultaneously cause unfocussing re any desire for an apprehendable plane. (There is less three-dimensionality in Cranach, less flatness in Pollock.) What was also to be done was to make subtle and complex, and not finally static and clichéd, nor humanistic, the painterly *gesture*. Thus paint *work* rather than expression(ism). So, Oulton is neither a (New) Romantic nor a ('New') Expressionist, though the *traces* of Sturm und Drang are the traces of a romantic *impetus*. Oulton's reinsertion of this problematic refuses to deny the necessity of certain (mythological!) poetic (Rilkean?) dichotomies as basic to the practice of oil painting in the 20th century as much as in the 16th (we disagree). In the most extreme and sophisticated works, what is 'romantic', what is 'myth' is fugitive, not assimilable to a norm which would allow it any rightness of place. In that, the work is not a *representation* but, at its best, a search for the elements of a possible exhumation of sustainable imagery as an endless impossibility.

There is no synchronicity between 'the artist's search' and a painting's material 'findings', *its* processes and productions.

Hopefully Oulton's paintings become more and more difficult to like, for those who do.

What is the complex and contradictory power of *The Passions No. 6*, *Rue*, *Copper Glance*, and *Cardinal*, other than materialities already explicated? It is a power which does not allow the viewer the reproduction of her/his sexuality-based positions (for men, those of oppressor, for women those of the oppressed).

A painting can produce its subject-matters and processes in such a manner as to *r*eproduce for example (socially-constructed) male positions. The latter we know are inseparable from the social power of having a hold over the 'object', possessing (the illusion of) knowledge of and control over the seen (and perpetual untrammelled *access* to it). Illusionary or not voyeuristic satisfaction via 'control' over the painting's process and content reproduces unquestioned stabilization of the ego as patriarchally defined all-embracing consciousness. Such a structure reproduces the oppression of that sexual category defined as object of spectacle, women. Other positions are possible; lack of spectacle is resistance. When 'perception equals knowledge' (what we see is what we know) then that ideological system reinforces the power of the sex-class which proceeds by such assumptions. Under patriarchy men benefit from that regime, as their (our) structures of knowledge are based on it (with women as object, object of specular gaze, a-and-de-historicized).

To paint against that, questioning and subverting securely-placed male identified viewing, is to question and subvert the maintaining-structures of such power.[2] The viewer must *oppose* perception to knowledge, can be positioned to oppose the reproduction of dominant ideology *vis-à-vis* the seen.

In experimental film and painting (experimental referring to an attack on what preexists) certain theorists and practitioners are defining radical materialist work in terms hinted at in this essay, rather than in the reactionary ones of simply documenting 'left-wing' or 'feminist' content. The struggle is in the production process. Another struggle is in the streets. Nothing prevents anyone from engaging in, and with, both; the structures and forms of 'recognition' of the world must be smashed, overthrown, not simply interpreted differently. These structures and forms include the world of representation, the cultural place in and against which radical practice (which, as Christine Delphy has articulated, is always theoretical and polemical[3]) must operate. Otherwise 'statements' within culture, i.e. painting, film, music, etc., become mere illustration (or stories) *of* (i.e. of something *else*, not *historical* but 'about' this history or that), outside of

---

[2] Oulton's love for Titian and her interpretation of his attempted presentation of identified male self-loathing, an anti-male polemic by a male painter, formulated largely by the handling, Titian's *paint-use*, can be theoretically disinterred and connected to some of the 'formal' questions that relate to her work. We know the impetus of much culture is a deeply negative and positive imbrication in (and possible radical break from) history, precursors. (!)

[3] "It is absurd to oppose polemic to theory for one very simple reason: no new idea appears in a void." Christine Delphy, "A Materialist Feminism is Possible" in *Feminist Review*, No. 4, 1980, and in Delphy's, *Close to Home, A Materialist Analysis of Women's Oppression*, Hutchinson, 1984.

production and transformation, struggle and contradiction. The latter the motor of *every* history. It is not stories but material (production) processes, whether of language, images, or objects, that are the social practices which can subvert, and change, the state of things. Some of these problematics some of these paintings engage.

Such work is contrary to the hysterical male anti-feminist backlash of the nouveau fascists Clemente, Chia, Salle, Fischl, etc. The anti-phallocentric, anti-sexist feminist struggles in form and content scare the main enemy's avant-garde of the Right, as well as those on the Left who maintain that one group is allowed to resist oppression but only if those in power (men, in patriarchy) lose nothing, thus a selfserving 'political logic' of the oppressor.

Is there a 'truth', 'rightness', 'quality' for a painting such as *Copper Glance*? Is the series of conventions utilized for this painting-practice within imaginable and apprehendable codes that are self-defined by that grouping of Oulton's works that you see? A definition of the acceptable, based on that, or even on that plus aspects of other contemporary painters' products? Certain paintings here refuse this, disrupt the possibilities of coherent codes of understanding and apprehending 'what is'. Thus no immediate placing (naturalization) takes place for the most worked-through paintings. Using criteria condensed from some of the above arguments one can say *The Passions No. 6* and *Copper Glance* oppose *The Passions No. 7* and *Quicksilver*. *Rue* and *Mortal Coil* oppose *Galena*, differently.

The body of work does not have an automatic relation to the body of the painter, or to the body of the painter's ideas about painting. A materialist practice would not allow for such identities. However nonexistent, an idealist critique would nevertheless demand such identities! None of this is to deny that ideological (sexual/political) constructions between painter and painting must be constituted not least by painters as an attempted defence against the retrogressions of 'inspired spontaneity'. The attempt must be made to *theorize* positions, to construct links (and however contradictory relations) between practices (the practice of the painter's thoughts, the practice of painting, the practice of various ideologies and politics, etc.). Dialectical Materialism: *The theory of reality affirming the continuous transformation of matter and dynamic interconnectedness of things and concepts* according to Webster's. The painting process's meanings don't have to rely on a metaphysic!

> The Quattrocento sought, here and there, a stimulus in moving the disappearance-point of lines sideways, without ulterior rationale; not outside of the picture but towards the edge. For the Classic consciousness such dispersals are uncomfortable.
> Heinrich Wölfflin, *Classic Art*, 1893

In Oulton's *Fountain* (1983), *Galena* (1984), and *Quicksilver* (1984), there is a disturbing search for the singular perspective point, even if not centralized. It is a point slightly askew where the spectator is 'ideally' held to be. In such a definition the spectator's position mirrors *out from* the canvas the perspective disappearance point within the representation's deep space. What is disturbing is the desire and ideology to position the viewer in that way, as such a positioning of the ideal point-of-view assumes the stable consumption of a spatial wholism. Such viewing presumes the *(political)* colonization of the viewed. Askew this position may be re the paintings referred to; yet it is still a singular, even if not central, perspective point from and through which this viewing operation takes place. The shift 'askew' still assumes the implied centrality from which shifts (may) occur whilst *the norm, and its function as norm, is maintained, and reproduced*. Reproducing this illusion insures a stable order of things. Yet *The Passions No. 6*, *Rue*, *Copper Glance*, and *Cardinal* obstinately refuse such scenarios.[4]

The danger is of perspective depth remaining unproblematic, with the painting-work (hand plus brush plus paint on canvas) a veil or curtain, rather than an irrefutable process insisting that there can be no revelation. Revelation/exhumation is neither desired nor possible; the aesthetic object is the *painting*, not (un)necessary pretences.

The quest (i.e. to paint) is, finally, one of passion and disappointment. The ques*tion* for some is whether such desire ought to produce objects infused by the illusion of fulfilment. Also: is the craft 'element' or the art 'element' art's *a priori*? Is to even momentarily 'distinguish' these 'elements' to imagine the unimaginable? The process of painting, the ineluctable act of painting, is a matter of the muchness or lessness of both, terms in which when we look at Thérèse Oulton's work painting exists *qua* painting.

> In philosophy one does not only have to in each case learn *what* is to be said about an object but also *how* one must talk about it. First one must always again learn a method with which to approach it.
> Ludwig Wittgenstein, *Remarks on Colour*, 1951

---

4   These (Oulton's) refusals, it must be stressed, take place importantly without a reversion to a reductive and simplistic capitalist modernism which I would define as unquestioned perspective centrality in relation to the 'towards flatness' paintings of Noland, Morris, Olitski, mid-period Stella, or to the (frequent) wholistics of Rothko, Newman, much Pollock, etc.: objects of endless imaginary narrativization. These are distinguishable from the Soviet-based modernism of Rozanova, Popova, Stepanova, Delaunay, Malevich, Lissitzky, Kandinsky. Though each painting must be taken as a separate, specific, material process, not covered by some overall authorial or intentional 'truth' (fallacy), I am for the sake of polemic here adumbrating certain artists' 'names' to in fact signify a multitude of paintings whose differences are falsely homogenized by bourgeois criticism. A materialist critique has to take each work as separate function, use, position, meaning. The muddled concepts of 'flatness' and 'modernism' misapprehended much work including early Stella and Warhol, not to mention Cezanne and Mondrian, in an antimaterialist, undialectical form.

What is crucial is the recognition of the differentiation between A and B.

A. The use of brush-strokes in an 'expressionist' manner towards achieving an effect of (the artist's, and by identification, the viewer's) ego-projection, the symbolic metaphorization of a frenzied psyche, narcissistic ego-spectacularization (male thuggery, in short. Oulton's apt phrase).

B. The attenuated material(ist) processes of oil paint(ing)'s *presentation*, through an endless procedure brought to arbitrary 'closure' (the specific painting, stopped, ended) without an exteriorization of some quasi-religious, transcendental, or 'truth'-seeking motive or rationale. No more the old humanist phantasy, romance of 'the natural'. *Romance without Finance is a Nuisance.* (Charlie Parker).

Yet a phantasized transcendental *natural* subject (viewer as implicit subject of the work) and object (the painting, its marks and significations) still is in some of Oulton's works an unsolved problem rather than a dynamic problematic. The light/dark dramatics of *Fountain*, *Galena*, and *Quicksilver* betray antinomies yet in each simultaneously a compositional completion which harmonizes rather than exploding them, as if *any* object, literary meanings, or the artist's personal investments/obsessions which pre-exist the painting's production could be naturalized and contained. This closure is illusionary, yet ideologically *real*, as if some representation of a subject *exterior* to the painting process were somehow then communicable, and communicated.

Against this, *Mortal Coil* places its 'bow' or 'coil' *uneasily* within, through, and *against* the paint surfaces and depths, so that a resolution, a 'proper' (or adequate) harmony is neither established nor establishable. Precisely thereby no adequacy is given either to perspective or to other pictorial conventions engaged: frame, depth, painted shapes, etc. Because of this what grey surface-luminosity (for example) there is in this painting paradoxically determines a *deep* surface, all the more *disallowing* a frame-filling overall image-surface; the very structuring of *image* is dialecticized.

There is in the new works the *refusal* to make (what could handled badly result dangerously close to) landscape or any scape at all.

Unfortunately, the prevailing ideology of reading an image means much of all this gets missed at first viewing, or altogether, in an ideological(ly understandable) operation which 'reads' all cultural work within dominant forms and formulations, attempting to deny (through conscious suppression or unconscious regression) any radical process, any determined *difficulty* or *struggle* produced by the works' dialectic processes.

This is all in all painting which persists with the *danger* of ambiguity; also with the danger of falling to one side, or the other, of the symbolic (Lacanian or not). *The Passions No. 6, Copper Glance, Rue* and *Cardinal* (all works of 1984) produce (from that problematic) works of rare and difficult beauty in their complex and contradictory power.

First published in Thérèse Oulton: Fools' Gold, Gimpel Fils, 1984.

DIALOGUE AND DIALECTIC IN GODOT
1986

... The process of a dialogue of duets leads to the voiding of desire. The running down and out of motivated feelings, the evacuation of desire, the (constant) ending of dialogue, is what such process *is*. There is a materiality to such language-*use* which is outside of anything prior or predestined. It is language as language, used towards a position, situation, in language. The 'dialogue' has its specific ways of working, ... and those specific workings are not 'about' something described, some event prior or in the future, but rather a material language process 'between' two ciphers. In the language they are situating themselves *vis à vis* one another, and the running down and out of language ... is the effecting of *dialectic* nothingness. The nothingness towards which language takes one, that running down and out, the nihilism of the process, is not 'about' nihilism. It is not 'about' the evacuation of desire in language. It is the production of language as endless attempt to ward off the end. The dialectic strategies towards this in language in *Godot* are precisely such a process.

In all this there is much denial. There is, here, a hilariousness in denial, which functions both as denial *per se* and as reflexively about denial and its processes and strategies. Humour has no little sadism. Denial as hilarious, as in the *screamed*, and screeched, repetitions of NO NO NO NO NO NO NO NO. The attempted banishment of a phobia, or an idea, or simply any content, via the NO NO NO NO NO NO NO! Analogous to this, the *content* of the statement (in the *Godot* dialogue), "You let me go", could only be taken in a straightforward manner, without any break in identification, if accepted within a strictly Calvinist tradition or a Jewish tradition of guilt. The structure of Judaeo-Calvinist guilt's lack of hilarity is precisely *there*. The masochistic desire for the law, articulated through the word STOP or NO or DON'T

GO, the ritual game's mythic, *real*, seriousness, points to nothing but the structure of immersion in self-pity, the butt of Beckett's humour.

Whilst a reflexiveness, a reflexive consciousness, is produced in the listener-viewer-audience, this is not given as such for Estragon. Thus, for the audience, his speaking does not function as some kind of 'successful' mimesis. The more 'successful' (i.e. the more dramatically precise) his shrieking mimesis, the *less* mimetic the performance and the less the words allow the identificatory process to take place for the viewer-listener-audience. This is a formalising of a structure of speech and a content of speech via its articulation as *extreme*. Unambiguous position in the content, "You let me go", pared down form, extremity of technique in the shriek. The precision of Didi's and Gogo's mimesis forces the viewer to *not* identify-with. The fourth-wall naturalism in Beckettian theatrics foregrounds the structure, and produces the kind of constantly reflexive distanciation process which *opposes* the theatrical convention of fourth-wall naturalism: "Play it *as* fourth-wall naturalism" (Beckett, directing *Endgame*) ...

The inability in the Vladimir/Estragon duets to structure the one (Vladimir or Estragon) as dominant, forces an equation. Thus any codification, here, onto type, is a neat fiction and an impossibility. These dialogues go against the construction of archetype: in the production of *Godot* by Beckett the body's archness is supported by what Beckett called "the text's ability to claw". The quote pertained to *Endgame*, and for *Godot* the clawing is of a more subtle kind: the inability of the text's clawing to let go of the characters. They are never unbound from the text, never become realistic free-agents; they are always arch. The verbal text's speaking is, in fact, a being-spoken by each, by Didi and Gogo. And it is that which does not allow for a biological-characterological type to be produced. They speak it, it speaks them, no emanation other than the holding of the characters to the text's needs. In that sense they are marionettes without the characterological characterisational parameters that critics need to invent. Thus Didi not other of Gogo, neither are they a fusion. The need to find words, find something to say, say it, let that saying produce effects of speech, i.e. the other's speech, till it runs out and down – and the whole thing may or may not start again. Speech is therefore precisely not used as a ladder which one can utilise in order to then pull it (the ladder!) away. No vehicular notions for speech here.

Object-choice can be based on sameness, not denying 'difference' but not having to be an object-choice of such difference as to make finally of the choice a representation of manifest self-dislike.

This not a matter of moral categories, narcissism as somehow 'good' or 'bad' – simply that choosing an other on the basis of self-dislike, such masochistic narcissism, may feed short-term self-lacerating needs towards a long-term bind which in its self-piteous indulgence produces what can only be a redundancy. The ideology here is of the return of the same, outside history (one's own, for example). As opposed to what? A different kind of contract: Nagg's and Nell's, Didi's and Gogo's, Speaker's with Voice (in *Company*), first person and third person (in *A Piece of Monologue*). The contract is for the Real, the choice of necessity a neurosis but not a representation, not a characterisation of a fabled *then*; *then* is nothing other than fable, duration annihilated to seamless ends. Instead: no end, constant end, just means, meanings, meaningless, means, the words in constant material and political process. "Lick thy neighbour as thyself" (Beckett, 1931).

The constant demands of Estragon and Vladimir are monological materialisations of the impossibility of knowing the other, of 'insight'. Didi/Gogo monologues function as constant materialisations of the projection-mechanism (even!) in their constant disavowals. Non-knower, non-can-er, not non-doer. Always an act: an act of language and an act of the body in the *use* of language and the *use* of the body.

The impossibility of knowing is never anything but a political battle against the illusion of such (knowing), the smug humanistic satisfactions inducing no little catharsis, whose function is the forward-projected idealisation/sentimentalisation of a mythical past in the interests of 'less is more' or 'more is less', instead of the horrendous, and revolutionary, insight that less is less.

There are various problems with the understanding of such images. A *single* close-up, or even a single longshot, of this image can operate as a fragment-of something *else*, it can be taken as part for whole. The other possibility is that the series functions as a singular totality, 'series' being merely a manner by which to form a larger unit, collapsed into a single 'meaning'. One other possibility, neither part-for-whole, nor singular-totality, could be a series of differences, deferring singularity. The constant rearresting of an image, against a previous and future one. The latter structure's function would be without teleology, no retrospective good-conscience rationalising of means to ends. Thus each 'to end' would not be co-optable but would be, each time, each sight, each moment, a cessation against each previous and future cessation. There would be no annihilating time towards some metaphysic of finality (and attendant transcendences).

The third possibility outlined is the one inculcated by the theatre-*performance* itself. The series of differences function on the viewer as the force to take position. The act works thereby as never separable from the force to re-enact/re-act, thus a non-wholistic series of gestural acts. No en-actment, done thus, covers *other* moments, other gestures, prior, subsequent, or 'in the real world'. And no enactment, thus done, functions as metaphor.

First published in Beckett: Waiting for Godot (Casebook), Ruby Cohn (ed.), Macmillan, 1987.

THE ANTI-ZOOM
(A LITTLE POLEMIC AGAINST METAPHOR)
1987

Beckett's work betrays cinematic interests not at one with that term's meanings as commonly understood. The power of the work in theatre has been to de-dramatize, in a manner inconsistent with dominant cinema's and theatre's endless identificatory spectacularizations.

Another narrative for the humanistic viewer to rock himself (sic) off on is not what the work needs. Thus the paring down, but not towards some essence, as if such could be even properly *thought*.

Paring down to the contradictory oppositional *moment* (a time and a space) at which subjectivity, its needs, its histories, comes to clash with its oppositions, the empirical fact, a body, a sound, a gesture.

Opposites therein never congeal; neither do they repeal one another, in a kind of dramatic deconstruction, taking turns. What is, rather, given is durable constant conflict *in situ*.

And the opposites that never form an identity, never hold an identity, force a viewing which itself is no longer predicated upon identification or *self-identification*. So where in all this can 'the cinematic' be found?

In the rhetorical device of the anti-zoom we can situate a material(ist) practice of (not) coming to grips with diegesis, the imaginary mental space a cinematic scene posits. The move of the zoom lens *out*, away 'from' the 'action', is the constant receding from narrative involvement.

(Involvement, as it happens, has been utilized as a term to mean its opposite anyway: "I felt involved during that ..." means that the self-reflexive awareness of viewing-position points to *not* being involved.)

Yet the receding zoom (as much as the thrusting zoom) is ordinarily understood as metaphor for the unseen presence of a figure, the filmmaker, the omniscient observer, whatever, whether receding from narrative involvement or not.

The *anti* in all this must be, therefore, the ablation of scopophilic desire ('60s terminology has a lot to answer for!) in a defensive practice *against*.

Thus rather than the humanistic quietude which still seems to be the rampant metaphor in Beckett analyses for the complete works, jots, scribbles, snatches, one must be enabled (disabled) in positing antagonisms to the functioning (and its meanings) of such a machine (and its meanings).

Zoom referred initially to Deirdre Bair's "SB's wanting to study the zoom with Eisenstein in the 1930s," about twenty-five years before the bloody thing was invented.

But anti-zoom is adumbrated in this polemic because thereby SB's theatre works against a constant *stabile*, namely the lens, against which all else would be measured, or even could. It is that metaphorical 'quality' instanced as a quasi anthropomorphism as stand-in, decoy, that, *that!* 'Zoom lens' being an indexical sign, image and referent the same.

To adduce examples here is unnecessary, Billie Whitelaw in *Rockaby*, *Not I*, *Footfalls*. The lens obliterated as imagined stasis: fetish object. And lens obliterated as *movement* in either direction.

In reference to the fifth and sixth paragraphs, not receding, simply *not*. A not *produced*, neither essential, ontological, nor anything else. Apparatus and person desexualized by ever denying a teleological function or aptitude.

What's left? Only the rests of sound and image, the viewer as view*ing*, produced through the dialectics of non-identities, as 'described'. Little else.

First published in The Review of Contemporary Fiction, Summer 1987.

IN REPRESENTATION OR OUT?
SOME CONDENSED NOTES ON AESTHETICS AND POLITICS
1988

To endlessly denounce questions of form as irrelevant at best and elitist at worst is to play straight into the hands of dominant representation, i.e. dominant forms. By 1986 this ought no longer to have to be stated. It certainly ought not to be arguable, as the alternatives are to pander to various realisms, or to pander to carefully watered-down formal changes which are already co-opted, and do not inculcate resistance to anything. Academicism thrives precisely on such co-options, which is why, in the end, literary analysis takes over, as it did in the appalling libertarian voice of reaction of Gayatri Spivak in the debate on "Sexual Identities". Spivak's thrice-repeated denials – and I quote: "I don't dislike these British films" – is a slick marginalisation of British work, the better to dispense with its force. 'Didactic' is her condescending code word for this work. Spivak's denials also betrayed a notion of pleasure which denied the political question of the ideology of pleasure. This digestible post-modernism is in power in academia, especially in the United States, France and here.

Clare Joseph's carefully precise elucidation in "Culture and Representation" leaves me with one problem, namely, the notion of 'political identification'. I fear that the concept is not the same as solidarity, because identification destroys the objects one is ostensibly identifying with. To identify the 'other' is not the same as 'identification with'. 'Identification with' structurally excludes a political solidarity because it substitutes the self and the ego for, and in the place of, any other political identification. I think that this is important to realise, so that we don't end up with another realism as a decoy for the realism we're supposedly doing battle with, although we need realism of another kind.

What worries me is the illusion that one individual's identifications could equal solidarity, and by individual I'm referring to the viewer. That is why taking a position is a political act, but it is not based on nature, ethnicity or biology. Otherwise, being black would be *the problem*, or being a woman would be *the problem*, rather than oppression being the problem. All positions are arbitrary; this doesn't mean that they are irrelevant, but simply that they have nothing to do with a natural order or essence.

First of all I try to make films, secondly I try to make films where each image, each object, is never given the hold of any recognition. To not reproduce the given as given, to see each image, each object, each imaginary space-time narrative as imaginary projection, so that nothing takes on the status of truth. The lack of recognition, and I'm not saying that it always does, can force the construction of all representational motives as constructions, as artifice, as unnatural, as ideology, so that representation is always impossible.

There is always a split between knowledge and perception, between what we know and what we see. In other words, what we think we *know* must not be thought to be the same as what we think we *see*. That split produces a process of film which simultaneously produces a spectator and a spectating that constantly problematizes representation. I see no other way to practice film – there must be other ways, but, judging from the response in "Sexual Identities" to Lis Rhodes' film *Light Reading*, perhaps understandably, some ways of film-making find less solidarity than others. The radicality of Lis Rhodes' film is not easy. This is the difficulty we have as film-makers and theoreticians. Voyeuristic pleasure is a structure of power in certain sex interests, or, as Christine Delphy would say, sex-class interests. One can hardly expect an easy relinquishing of such power, and spectators collude, to say the least. The endless reproduction of dominant forms of 'unproblematic' voyeurism is what dominant representation is all about, that is its narrative. All I can add is that irony doesn't change a damn thing and if I hear the word desire one more time I'm going to throw up.

Materialist film, a materialist avant-garde has to get rid of difference, not fetishize it, but that can only be said to an audience that accepts avant-garde and experimental film-making as a valid process. And obliterating difference must be simultaneous to understanding its historical construction and existence. The material of film, for example acetate, and the material of ideology, produce representations which are part of the contradictions within the varying historical materialities of the act of viewing. If you reject experimental film it is of no issue to argue pro or con this concept or that. But I assume that there is some sympathy with avant-garde film here.

The concept of difference assumes a dominant male norm against which the 'other' is 'other', so it must, by definition, be obliterated for a radical process to find its expression; but without such a radical process, such a polemical, political position, the illusion of the 'possible' becomes, unfortunately, broader rather than reduced.

First published in Undercut, Spring 1988. This paper (and the others mentioned) was given at the Cultural Identities Conference in London, 1988.

ENDLESS FINALITIES
(RICHTER'S ABSTRACT PAINTINGS)
1993

> *something there somewhere outside*
> *the head ...*
> *not life*
> *necessarily*
>   Samuel Beckett, 1974

Unpainting, no image glimpsable, a NON seen and reseen bereft of hope to find an already-made. So: beyond process and construction, not (even) the biblical seeing of that which is invisible.

Why the assumption that an act of criticism or theory be free of the linguistic impossible, mired in a surfeit of probables, when faced with the ostensible, real object? Even naming this problematic makes an empirical object out of an impossibility.

If I could find knowing possible ... If not dazzled, blinded, blind,[1] then blindly facing the painting.

Always again anew and simultaneously always again from a past ineradicability, as in Richter's *Abstract Paintings*.

What becomes equally ineradicable condensation with the watercolours of the same period – the fabled superimposition of one signifier upon another, colour into colour, paint into paint – here (oils on canvas) separates itself out, colour and paint discrete, makes concrete without concretising results. Endlessly finite. Each time you try again to recognise, or try to make a space, or a form, or a colour, or a depth, or a 'painting' through which something could be, you're brought up against impossibility, the end of that process, only to be moved ineluctably to

---

1   "I felt as if your *Room Film 1973* has been made by a blind man ..., that quality of trying to see." Michael Snow to the author, in Peter Gidal, "Theory and Definition of Structural/Materialist Film", *Structural Film Anthology*, British Film Institute, 1976.

attempt that grasping again. Not that any of this engagement with the painting is undetermined; it is endlessly determined by the material there ballastless.

Whatever object, however abstract, a stretch of paint on paint could be, in one's imaginary and in the history of art's imaginary, the 'object' (avoidance of saying the 'image') in such as *Abstract Painting* 724.4 (1991) or 747.1 (1991) is pushed so far in excess or/and repletion of any given known; forcing thought it becomes concept, but at a level of abstraction that can't then be boiled down or undone. From the impossible position for the viewer/viewing to a concept of impossible position. Thus not a disintegration of meaning, of language, of the word, of the paint, but disintegration of any represented.[2]

Nothing and always again nothing, never discounting what's behind and in front of, visually and temporally. The aforementioned not undetermined but 'determined but without ballast', the determinations perceptual as much as conceptual, all material.[3]

To represent truth or a truth or untruth or an untruth or to produce it, one tries with seeing then with thought. With such painting one doesn't get far with such thoughts.

Whilst there's never an evidence which allows belief or could, there's a definiteness in the painting's specificity each time, each (I hesitate to call it) fragment finite, specific, unsettling in its definition of what you see (for only so long)[4] as that (spatial and temporal) fragment seen, and always another specific material finite of another specific material 'fragment' therethrough.[5] Thus there's no unveiling, not as a concept, not as a perceptual moment, no under or over in a work so replete with under and over and through, no through as nothing to be gone through. Ends and

---

2 At first a concept of remnant or fragment, it then dissolves by being given nothing to hang onto, contextless, becomes nothing.
3 "As much as" should read "as little as".
4 Temporal exigencies in Richter's work are not exigencies.
5 "Fragment" is the seen, never conceptually "fragment-of". No part of anything.

starts: neither temporal or spatial continuum nor the kind of discontinuum predicated thereon. Thus any 'time' inferable is given no adequacy by either 724.4 or 747.1; what separates itself out concretely has no link to 'its' temporal history in each painting, in the genesis of this. With space similarly.

The 'this' can't be called image or form. *"Everything existing and endowed with a form is whatever it is through its form, and when that form is destroyed, its whole existence terminates and is obliterated ... if God did not exist, suppose this were possible, the universe would not exist, and there would be an end to the existence of the distant causes ... the existence and continuance of all forms in the last instance depend on Him, the forms are maintained by Him, in the same way as all things endowed with forms retain their existence through their forms."* (Maimonides)[6]

It (the it prior to the above quote) can't be called image or form, let alone anything else.

Atheistic, anti-metaphoric, because whatever else process has been useful for in disinterring material from concepts of origin of which the material was otherwise meant to be somehow simply illustrative, process becomes fetish and itself metaphoric of a system of representation – whilst in these pictures process – its teleologies, its ideology of causality – is not given its freedom. One mark, move, space, shape, form, colour, density, depth, definition, is not given by effect of another, spatially or temporally (however contradictorily) prior. The endless end of each mark, move, space, shape, form, colour, density, depth, definition anti-metaphoric and atheistic thereby. No ethics to speak of.

An abruption of cause, the empiricalness of one-thing-leads-to-another. *"... the definition we have given of a free cause, which is not one which can both do and not do something, but only one which does not depend on anything else."* (Spinoza)[7]

---

6   Moses Maimonides, *The Guide for the Perplexed* (A.D. 1168), Dover, 1956.
7   Spinoza, "God, Man, and his Well-being", *Collected Works*, Edwin Curley (ed.), Princeton University Press, 1985.

There's no object to be subject of or subject to. In consequence (!) no object to be made the subject of another object, endlessly, and we're left with that powerlessness, that nothingness. (Such) surcease is not 'masculine' or 'feminine'.[8]

Painting (noun) 724.4 and 747.1 is painting (verb) not only subjectless and objectless but equally not evidentiary of process or anything else, the present never as future. What this is getting at is that: what the painting becomes for the viewer in the viewing never frames itself as a presence which could then metaphorically become an ideal. There is here no process that somehow becomes the stand-in for whatever other metaphoric substitutions this or that ideology would want, thus no process even that itself 'for itself' could be an ideal presence. This politics is a different kind of realism, a politics which refuses the possibility even of painting's possible.

something there somewhere outside
the head ...
not life
necessarily

In 747.1 and 724.4 a danger is that, in a viewing context determinately literary, the spatial envelopment of each however unstable and impossible becomes an articulated place 'within which' blindness effected – wherein a romantic loss can then occur with adequacy. Whether that envelopment, attached often to notions of darkness, is, in fact, dark, grey, light-ridden, or a gloaming red, or none of those but simply substituting for what in previous ideological realms was termed 'darkness' is of no matter. Should that be the case, that 'nothing' and 'the impossible' are literalised as 'something', it could only be opposed by a concept of the

---

8   A notion not to be developed in this text, would be of Richter's paintings not positing an imaginably gendered viewer/viewing. This act of negativity is not *in vacuo* – must be seen against most of his contemporaries' works.

nothing and the impossible as something else – outside the head ... not life necessarily.[9]

Not necessarily life, necessarily not life. The act of painting 724.4 and 747.1 not defined as some romantic loss adequately concretised, materialised, the nothing and the impossible then something. Whereas nothing and the impossible are not life necessarily. In the late twentieth century, it's almost impossible not to be the last romantic, the last Catholic, the last Gnostic, the last Jew, but not the last atheist. Endless causelessness. Endless finalities. Richter's atheist paintings are not paintings of the nothing but are, finally, nothing. Endless end, not endless endlessness. What solace in unbelief.[10]

> So it is never we who affirm or deny something of the thing; it is the thing itself that affirms or denies something of itself in us.
>
> ... the Will in humans is nothing but this or that Will, so also there is nothing but this or that Desire, which is caused by this or that perception ... not really being something it cannot really cause anything.
>
> And what we say here about words, we want applied to all other external signs ... one would have had to know already the meanings (of these words) before they were spoken ...
>
> Spinoza[11]

---

9 Not unknowingness but rather the absolute unbelievability of all possible causalities. For example, faith alone grounds Spinoza's faith, so neither orthodoxy, nor you, nor I, could prove to Spinoza that he be either a believer or an atheist. Faith is beyond or outside language. It's again the case of the as if. Lies aside.

10 So that "what can be shown cannot be said" (much maligned Wittgenstein) isn't adumbrating belief in the causalities of the unbelievable, the unconscious (Freud), the unknowable, which would be maintaining given hierarchies, the self, satisfiedly smuggled-in as subject, nor is it stating that the unspeakable is transcendent, or alternatively, as some claim, establishing an empiricism.

11 Spinoza, op. cit.

In 747.1 and 724.4 neither a blurring-of, nor an unveiling, both of which would be as if both the acts and the objects the acts refuse to forego were immutable after all is said and done. Whereas these paintings grasp endlessly and hopelessly at a destructive negation inbuilt in such beauty, and could be called exhilarating death drive, the *vacuo* not of the endless return of the same, but of its endless non-return. The said repetition of such psychic painterly processes of making and viewing (no homology pretended) links to the question of how one such painting is different from another such painting, in each case, say from a series, or a period of seemingly similar works ... on the one hand each work is different, on the other the same. That isn't the question, but rather: how in Richter's works are these differences and samenesses different or the same from such samenesses and differences in others' works?

One without essentialising a work or body of work can only assiduously live in the as-if; as if a similar nexus is a same one, letting the edges of disturbance in that lie lie where they may. Otherwise we're left with "every word, every mark changes the world,"[12] *upon which* therefore *any* act or thought is impossible. What disturbs must be the politics of that, not the 'content' of this or that form, not the analysis of this or that psychoanalytic problem termed problematic.

> My method or my expectation which, so to speak, drives me to painting, is opposition ... Just that something will emerge that is unknown to me, which I could not plan, which is better, cleverer, than I am ... the whole process does not exist for its own sake.
> Gerhard Richter[13]

---

[12] *Hyper*aestheticism is not so far from *hyper*materialism not so far from *hyper*-mysticism. A materialism devoid of the mystic is self-understood.

[13] Jeanne Siegel (ed.), *Art Talk: The Early 80s*, Da Capo Press, 1988.

Richter's discontentments bear on works' leading to naught, and (them, him, us) not wanting that – yet to sidle up to a notion of 'the painting as parable' or a notion of 'worldly equivalence', metaphor its last resort, elides the problematic of painting, viz. there always being something-there there.[14] The unattainable nothing always processed by valences not only making and unmaking simultaneously but representing and unrepresenting. As avoidable as metaphor is the fetishization of process which institutes itself first against symbol, metaphor, and their substitutive mechanisms, even those of process, and secondly perversely by seeming to disavow a metaphysics of nothingness in fact predicating a concept of material essence in opposition to "... a loss of the sayable without the comfort of a metaphysics of silence."[15] Thirdly, and as corollary, more dangerously, endless source, creator in absentia everpresent-in-process, whether *ex nihil* or not. Endless end, not to be confused with the humanistic quietudes of infinite endlessness. The something there in 724.4 or 747.1 is neither a literalisation, however 'materialist' some might assume it, for life or whatever substitutive homonym, nor an act of life.

The real world is enough the real world to not allow us that luxury of unmalice – the something there in 724.4 or 747.1 is, finally, an attack on percept by concept, and on concept by percept – leaving you and me whilst thankfully not 'an actor amongst many in this or that narrative' still inseparable from this, outside the head, not life necessarily. Less and less is more more. Here, in unembarrassed repletion, making impossible (the act of) deciphering and (the attainment of) decipherment of (any) homology of percept and concept OR of percept and painting, or concept and painting. Lesson from Duchamp and Warhol, and Nietzsche:

---

14 As opposed to Gertrude Stein's "there is no there there" (referring to her hometown, Oakland, California) here (and in the latter) there's a there there.

15 Angela Moorjani, *The Aesthetics of Loss and Lessness*, Macmillan, 1992.

> But as one doesn't know where my centre is, one will with difficulty ascertain the truth, where and when I have so far been 'eccentric' ... This task has made me ill, it will also make me healthy again ... (Yet) the passion of the last writings has something frightening to it: I read them the day before yesterday with deep astonishment, as if they were something new.
>
> Nietzsche[16]

Not only not concept-percept entanglement but not concept-percept disentanglement. (Something new always something frightening to a notion of focussed self or focussed image.)[17]

Neither perceptually nor conceptually separately either is one given anything with these paintings but the inability to process – the painting comes to an end, unmotivated, neither complete nor incomplete. What next; for Richter's painting, for painting as such? And what not? Just no rehabilitation, if nothing else.

First published in Parkett, March 1993.

---

16 Nietzsche, *Sämtliche Briefe*, Deutscher Taschenbuch Verlag, 1986.
17 This essay is 'not writing about focus', the contradictions in Richter's largely black-and-white photo works wherein something entirely unfocussable is held within the paintmark *qua* paintmark, itself unthinkable materially as anything but 'focussed' – the way Shklovsky's *Zoo, or Letters not about Love* (Berlin, 1920s) was a series to a woman whom he loved who agreed to correspond in friendship if his letters not be about love. An essay on the types of unknowing, 'from' the early black-and-white unfocus paintings 'to' the current, which haven't been seen, needs writing also, as to all the changes which are anything but a style.

THE POLEMICS OF PAINT
(RICHTER IN THE NINETIES)
1995

> It is just as true that the knower is a product of matter as that matter is a mere representation of the knower ... the intellect and the material are correlatives. We then get two absolutely first things.
> Schopenhauer, *The World as Will and Representation*[1]

I
Red

Still neither sublime nor sublimated,[2] Richter's paintings in the 1990s make no radical break with those that came before. The radical problematic of his paintings, recent and otherwise, is one of producing the unrecognitions of substance (the material of ideas, the material of paint) whilst being recognizably work by 'Richter'.

Painting against recognition is the works' radical negativity. *Red (821)*, 1994, is a series of scrapes. Persistence of vision is the after-effect of attempting to grasp and being unable. Attempting

---

1 Arthur Schopenhauer, *The World as Will and Representation*, Vol. 2., translated from the German by E. F. Payne, Dover Books, 1969.

2 Sublimation: "Process postulated by Freud to account for human activities which have no apparent connection with sexuality but which are assumed to be motivated by the force of the sexual instinct. The main types of activity described by Freud as sublimated are artistic creation and intellectual inquiry. The instinct is said to be sublimated in so far as it is diverted towards a new, non-sexual aim and in so far as its objects are socially valued ones (...) The lack of a coherent theory of sublimation remains one of the lacunae in psychoanalytic thought." J. Laplanche and J. B. Pontalis, *The Language of Psycho-Analysis*, Hogarth Press, 1973. It's no surprise that psychoanalysis comes up with such paltry stuff re: art. Psychoanalysts' authority (understandably) is more comfortable with the transference and other forms of power-retention.

to see substance, thereby to know.[3] What at one moment may be seen as veils are not veils, nothing 'above', nothing 'under' or 'behind' anything else, or if, for a moment, something, then that which that something is behind or under is itself unavailable to definition, let alone sight.

A loss of will sets in right from the start, in time. Veilless, 'the red one' (as GR refers to it) persists neither as sublime nor as sublimation; not letting you identify it, let alone identify with it, the unrecognition thereby obliterates in its tenuous substance both sublimity and sublimation, relying as they do on identities.

The chemical blue (upper left), chemical green (upper right), are each present here as a singular remnant of a scrape, a remnant from the rest of the painting. The painting a sublimate (chemical transformation); disappearings, blurrings. The residue is not a nostalgia, is not metaphor, not some barely discernable muted historical past; rather, a sharp chemical substance. Ineluctable, sharper in tone and colour than anything 'else' in the painting that is 'not residue'. Ineluctable, unerasable from any immediate memory of the picture or of however much one tries to make 'a picture' of it.

The mark (veiled, scraping, palimpsestual) moving right; the stillness underneath, through it, unimpaired. You change direction 'to make a picture'. You come to a stop to make a picture. You scrape rightwards, simultaneous veiling and unveiling, palimpsest one mark upon and through another, obliterating the previous moment and memory only then to retain marks of those marks, and what shows through strongest sometimes is the least 'there' – (sometimes not). These swathes of rightward moving colour (hesitate to say 'bands of red' as the red is hardly a band, translucent, hardly a colour, so many others, so much else, prior, simultaneous, *a posteriori*) ... they are neither palimpsest, layer upon layer, nor erasure of such; singularity is denied to any

---

3   Whether substance defined as form or content.

mark, or layer, or move. No palimpsest because 'condensation of signifiers' which determines that concept here is condensation of *signifiers-which-aren't*. Condensation (*Verdichtung*, which also means poetization) in this picture never coalesces. In German it's called *Leerlauf* ('running on empty', 'treading air'). So no *Verdichtung*.

Horizontal scrapes are measures and durations – behind in front of through and beyond which nothing condenses into a signifier, not even of endlessness, or emptiness, or void. In fact, they are neither measures nor durations of unlocatable … of *the* unlocatable. Stoppages are as arbitrary as nonstoppages.

And at the stoppages verticals are created, none locatable beyond some immediately fictive image, which language will (elsewhere) appropriate as such-and-such, whilst at that very moment given as untenable: untenable language and untenable (as) image, an unfocus not *of* something, no 'prior-stasis-allowing-definition-subsequently-blurred'. Edges not seen as 'edges of' but as coagulations, trim of one streak is edge of another, *which is not another and not an edge*. Attempt to make rhythm of continuance, however slowed down, out of streaks of colour, or scrapes, or movements. Brought forward at the left side of the painting is the bareness, scraped till the scrapes' stoppages make *vertical* the swathes of bled colour-remnants. This is not a matter of colour on canvas but of the tinting ineradicable when paint scraped away.

What rhythm there was, stoppages, durations, undone as done. The ineluctable glowing green-white at bottom, 'beneath' or through, or visible via further coagulations of red; further stoppages, as arbitrary as the preceding and following nonstoppages of red – glowing, into gloaming – near the bottom left. Not the gloaming of nature, gloaming of sublimate paint. By the continued movement dissipated into other paint, other red, other red with black with what's left invisibly of 'chemical green' or colour of some sort … is made … a dissipate gloaming. Red turn to blackblue, beneath turn to level, level turn to through, through become presence.

Presence can no longer be seen as some metaphysical existence or pre-existence, as presence in this painting becomes unpresent at the inception of sight. A level 'red' disappears into a distance, chartreuse, a sublimate; whereas *to unbe* verbalizes less inadequately the state of time and space, duration and image, neither disappearing nor coalescing. Surround surrounded.

> Assume two nows, one belonging to the object and the other to the subject, and marvel at the happy accident of their coincidence (...) The *present* alone is that which always exists and stands firm and immovable. That which, empirically apprehended, is the most fleeting of all, manifests itself to the metaphysical glance that sees beyond the forms of empirical perception as that which alone endures.
> Schopenhauer[4]

You are left with a painting of nothing, without a useful concept of sublimation or *metaphor:* substitution, one thing for another, an image for a meaning, a meaning for a psychology, a psychoanalytic for an anthropomorphic consciousness, an unconsciousness for an ideology. Without that, each moment is literally, materially, for the viewer, in the viewing, gone at its visible inception. Yet that process, whether remnant or not, is a painting, a present material nonmemory. The necessary elisions to 'make' a memory are processed through the viewer into the

---

4 Schopenhauer, op. cit. Derrida's critique of presence, which (parenthetically) he obliterates in every word written (having read but few), notwithstanding: a transcendental presence is not posited here any more than in my own forlorn, endless, attempts to establish a moment to moment position, or stance, and a politics, to viewing. Otherwise the signifier's deferment of each moment's meaning would be a philosophical ruse, determining an ideal non-moment beyond time and space whilst ostensibly attempting to undermine idealist philosophy and crude materialism in one go.

uselessness of continual use, making endless finalities.

The black cross-mark lower half, mid-picture, barely there, is not an 'X'. It almost (meaning believably at moments) reads as an 'error', i.e. the obverse of an intention. An intentional mark would be a crossing-out mark. Suspending belief and suspending disbelief become equal in the viewing.

At some moment the right third of the painting, broken off from the rest, in however subtle a manner, vertically splits the continuum without breaking anywhere the series of horizontal veilings-unveilings. So it functions like a ghost image ('like' and 'ghost image' in quotes, out of linguistic discomfort). Afterimage that is persistence of vision is however subtly imbued in the very viewing moments each moment. What's left is the painting, the overwhelming impossibility of making coherence *or* fragmentation-of *(or anything else)* the, or a, category of, or for, meaning. Leaving you as bereft as the painting.

II

How aware are these paintings by Richter of the dangers via composition of identity's illusion?

… and the subject has passed out of all relation to the will, what is thus known is no longer the individual thing as such, but the *Idea* … the person who is involved in this perception is no longer an individual … is *pure* will-less, painless, timeless *subject of knowledge* … only the idea is the adequate objectivity of the will. If therefore the ideas are to become object of knowledge, this can happen only by abolishing individuality in the knowing subject … by virtue of (which) the subject, in so far as it knows an idea, is no longer individual.

Schopenhauer[5]

5   Ibid.

Object become idea. Given that the identities one subsumes the paintings under are relentlessly avoided by Richter in selfsame paintings, composition in his works becomes the viewer's, or the culture's, projection of some assumed ideal the idealism of which the works work relentlessly against. If the identities one subsumes the paintings under are relentlessly avoided by Richter, this avoidance is concrete, a concrete abstract. Avoidance must be seen *not* as denial in the social sense of the term, as such denial signifies a believable being believably alluded to followed by the ruses of 'historicization' or 'making strange' or 'deconstruction'; rather, it is avoidance as stated.[6]

The tenuous link I am establishing between 'paintings by Richter' and identityless paintings is that the above described avoidance is inseparable from the context of all other paintings one knows to be 'by Richter'. Richter's relentlessness *(Sturheit)* in these matters is Schopenhauerian, though not his attempt at making paintings abjuring *concepts* of truth, morality another matter.[7]

"With an audacity that excites astonishment and indignation [Spinoza] declares the difference between right and wrong, and in general between good and evil, to be merely conventional, and therefore in itself hollow and empty (e.g. *Ethics*, 4, prop. 37, schol. 2). [And Spinoza demonstrates that] nature carries within itself the powers by virtue of which it appears. With this, however, ethics was bound to be lost."[8] Schopenhauer is wrong, as conventionalisation of ethics, and the impossibility of pure moral determination, is not the 'no ethics' of which he accuses, of all people, Spinoza. He misunderstands Spinoza's illusionlessness.[9]

---

6   Psychoanalytic denial, unconscious repression of the matter, a different matter.
7   GR the person might not 'agree' with this – we haven't talked about such things.
8   Schopenhauer, op. cit.
9   He misunderstands Spinoza's explication of the power of that which *is*. Appearance for Spinoza does not ensure reality, one thing cannot be known from another.

Meaninglessness without *ethics* is scarier than meaninglessness with. How to locate the chimera of 'that without ethics', that without the *timeless* morality of Christian sin or relentless guilt? The a-ethical stance of *Red* has a time and a place.

The anxiety that abjures truth does not equally abjure death and time. "For what separates the beginning from the end is simply time ..."[10] The anxiety of representing time[11] acknowledges not just entropy and egress but something else – separateness, time's stillness and its anxiety *spatially* – not excluding memory, our *temporal* and its meaning, i.e. death. Moreover, temporality itself in Richter's work is the effect of the 'realist' paintings as much as of the others.

"The Will, not really being something, cannot cause anything" (Spinoza), *appearance* of the will's effectivity notwithstanding.

Schopenhauer then goes on to propose in this particularity a near-identical system: "In this way the *moral* world-order actually enters into direct connection with the force that produces the phenomenon of the world. For the *phenomenal appearance of the will* must correspond exactly to its mode of existence ... and although it continues to exist by its own power the world receives throughout a *moral* tendency" (Vol. 2). Schopenhauer had previously utilized "in uns" (in us) to mean a differentiation from 'nature in itself' ("Natur in sich selbst (tragend)"). But in abstract as well as in empirical terms, they coincide, much as for Spinoza nature is inclusive of us. Extrapolation isn't easy, for (e.g.) Spinoza in Proposition VIII states: "The knowledge of good or evil is nothing else than the *emotion* of pleasure or pain ..." whereas in the Proof to Proposition L he states: "For he who is moved neither by reason nor pity to help others is rightly called inhuman" (*Ethics*, Part IV, 1673).

At one point, in the last two pages of Volume II, the commentary to his four books in Vol. 1, Schopenhauer sees Spinoza 'no longer' separating spirit and substance (God and world). This detour can bring us back excruciatingly to Schopenhauer's "Only *that* idea which was *perceived* before it was thought," disallowing an overriding will the possibility of aesthetic communication (Vol. 2).

10 Ibid.
11 Film-maker Hollis Frampton: "When you say 'time' you're floundering ... duration ok" (in *October*, No. 32, Spring 1985). PG (23 years later): "No. It IS time." That floundering equals time's movement, its seeming nonmovement and, for all we know of advanced physics, its seeming movement.

Cause without effect, effect without cause. Here autonomy ingratiates itself through the painting's material, i.e. painting *qua* painting. *Autonomy for painting is a question of power over appearance, against metaphor.* Richter's problem, better problematic, in the 1990s for both 'kinds' of his paintings' autonomy: how can they without idealism *be?* – the quasi romanticism of that anti-romantic wish. Pure denial won't stop the malaise. If the final nothingness of such art is not to be a remnant of the past, under the power of its appearances after all, then what?

III

Occasion

... that everything that exists for knowledge and hence the whole of this world is only object in relation to the subject, perception of the perceiver ...

That which knows all things and is known by none is the *subject*. It is accordingly the supporter of the world, the universal condition of all that appears, of all objects, and it is always presupposed: *for whatever exists*, exists only for the subject.

... that the whole essence of matter consists in action, and hence in causality: consequently, space and time must also be united in this, in other words, matter must carry within itself simultaneously the properties and qualities of time and those of space, however much the two are opposed to each other. It must unite within itself what is impossible in each of those two independently, the unstable flight of time with the rigid unchangeable persistence of space; from both it has infinite divisibility. Accordingly, through it we find co-existence first brought about. This could not be either in mere time, that knows no juxtaposition, or in mere space, that knows no before, after, or now. But the *co-existence* of many states constitutes in fact the essence of reality, for through it *permanence or duration* first becomes possible. Permanence is knowable only in the change of that which exists simultaneously with what is permanent; but also only by means of what is permanent in variations does variation receive the character of *change,* i.e. of the alteration of quality and form in spite of the persistence of substance, i.e., of *matter*.

Schopenhauer[12]

Against idealism could be an art defined as intention, defined as its own adequacy, adequate intention from within each work; an art wherein intention is no longer produced by the consciousness of the artist (a truism since the 1960s). For such artmaking, disallowing given hierarchies of meaning, the painter must still work blind.

Yet an idealism even in such a schema would be to make of this attempting 'neither sublime nor sublimation' a 'positive' negative attempt, definable and maintainable as a category before, during, and after the making of a painting. Richter's polemics of painting counters that, in process, endless, powerless.

But it is not a matter of simply not making occasion, however complexly, of that which lacks occasion,[13] as that occasionlessness's occasionlessness could become a nothing of a negative something (rather than the equally to be feared occasionlessness-as-occasion). In both, a nothing as other-*of*[14]/ different-*from*, reinveigles the dominance of the known; *different from* means we know different from what, reinveigling the seen as the knowable and seeable, knowable as seeable,[15] and then to make occasion of that. That way, 'attempting', or 'identityless

---

12 Schopenhauer, op. cit.
13 Beckett's fearful prophecy. Find better term because fearful prophecy in this oedipalised patriarchy is always authoritarian. "... for the artist obsessed with expressive vocation, anything and everything is doomed to become occasion ... I know that all that is required now, in order to bring even this horrible matter to an acceptable conclusion, is to make of this ... fidelity to failure, a new occasion, ... I know that my inability to do so places myself ... in what I think is still called an unenviable situation, familiar to psychiatrists." Samuel Beckett, "Three Dialogues", *Proust & 3 Dialogues with Georges Duthuit*, John Calder, 1965.
14 "Other", e.g. despair is not the opposite of hope – and vice versa.
15 The seen being the empirical object, *seeable* is the category of belief in such.

process' or 'working blind' become metaphors for the reversion to precisely the ideology that had been denied.

The question of occasion is not simply *solved;* rather than being dissolved *in,* what is dissolved is *Abstract Painting (810-4),* 1994. Dissolution. But whether actively or passively remains in the concretest sense unclear, that is to say viewing is lost in the layers. The right and left edges of the painting evince sharply articulated colour as if it is 'the rest' that is buckled and dispersed. It is a curious *trompe-l'oeil* as are the photo-paintings which are, complex transformations notwithstanding, *trompes-l'oeil* of the real, i.e. of a photograph (of the real ...). So that here in *Abstract Painting (810-4)* a real scrape through the cataract vision betrays a 'pure' unmixed sharp unafraid red, yellow and blue *searing,* – retaining its objectness.

Any objectness in Richter (no less than in Schopenhauer) is always duration. We are thus never given objectness as emblematic or iconic, however much the culture or illustrations in a catalogue might try to make it that. Remnants from the blur, though no less unfocussed, can be hard-edged subtractions. These are remnant shapes where rubbing past half-dry paint has taken a surface off, sharply, leaving the layer beneath. Removal here leaves the sharply outlined, turning the remnant shape into a 'negative', or solarization, because darker and 'further back' from the surface, and from you.

Equally for no natural reason, a scraping, a seemingly one-dimensional thin layer, is by no means that. It is grey/blue & grey/burgundy & dried-blood/white/grey.

The nomination 'one-dimensional single scraping' is relative to previous descriptions of other areas of paint which visually, or in a rememoration-attempt, seem a conglomeration, colouristically muddy. On closer view the latter is not a conglomerate at all; it is formed from *and results in* separable colours, swathes narrowly layered horizontally, – a *d*emerging of colour and line and shape – no less or more narrow in scope than the other segment described as scraped.

Everything starts at canvas left with a sharp colour, unmixed-paint-from-the-tube. 'Unmixed' doesn't mean inviolate; some of the Prussian blue and some of the mixed impasto retain an edge of one *apparent* colour. This clarity of colour is defined as the 'start' within a teleology that maintains across the 'buckled' tautness to what unblurred colour is locatable at canvas-right, thereby delimiting the buckled sheets of paint, their unfathomable fugitive layers. Some stability for the eyes in keeping momentarily taut what endlessly dissolves or becomes brittle, cracks, or just succumbs.

IV
Lesende

There is no likeness.[16] There is no recovery. *Lesende [Woman Reading]*, 1994, for some may remind 'of Vermeer' in its superficies. Such a thought is entirely the attempt to recover via a debased form (of likeness) by reducing the architectonic complexities of Vermeer to 'light from side of painting onto face'.[17] In fact, the young woman in *Lesende*, reading *Der Spiegel* (mirror), could not exist in a less Vermeerian space than this.

---

16 "There is no likeness. So, not only the time it takes for metaphor's instanciation breaks, but the resonances, echoes, memories, without which some say life would be less, have to go when new meanings are made, new positions taken. There is no recovery.

"The unutterable horror of such loss is not at issue. No doubt the loss of belief in an afterlife is equally unutterable, or the death of Spirit, or the end of all material, the material all. Matters of ethics confound matters of aesthetics, to the point where insistence on 'content' as a correct palliative for capitalist formalism mustn't elide the by now no longer awful insight that form is content. Then gender as metaphor (and *sexual* metaphor) is redundant." Peter Gidal, *Against Metaphor*, with eight etchings by Thérèse Oulton, Fascicle Books, 1988.

17 A postcard of Vermeer's *Woman Reading a Letter*, incidentally, is tacked up near the telephone in a corner of the ante-room to Richter's studio. Richter is aware of the extraordinary spatial sophistication and breathtaking beauty, via light producing surface and colour, in Vermeer.

The photographic reproduction, its subject/object out-of-focus, produces a one-dimensional space, barely planar. The figure in any Vermeer, no less than the complex spatiality, brought to vision through suffusion and infusion of light in equal measure, is in Richter's *Lesende* the remnant of a tradition, German romantic painting, which already in Caspar David Friedrich and others is a debased one reduced to deadweight. And yet the ideal of 'kaum einen Hauch spüren' (Goethe's 'to feel hardly a breath') is the wish for *Ruh*, i.e. rest. *Rest* is Richter's definition of his state of being when painting the photopaintings ('a rest from the abstract paintings, a rest from painting'): the *idealism*, yet the blatant 'contra' to that in *Lesende*, of wishing to paint the relinquishment of idealism. Not to be seen as some impoverishment of a Vermeer reduced to 'light on subject' within a debased form, *Lesende*'s sophistication and beauty is *painting's realist finality*, in the way that that (and the painting) needs to be looked at, and through, by the viewer; it is *reproduction* (photograph) *of a representation* (the scene) *represented.*

The historical depletion, remnant become isolate, isolate temporality in vacuo, distant, image of an image, projected as a fetish. But in contrast to Duchampian fetishism of the frozen object – hard-edged etched glass, hard-edged lifeless multiple – Richter's defocussed photo-paintings dispense with the reality of a fetish as hard and sharp as much as abjuring any single form of representation *even in one picture*. It 'itself is not 'an identity' that can be readily identified either as content ('this or that real person' or 'this or that real person in this or that real photograph') or as form ('this or that real photograph' or 'this or that real photograph in this or that real painting').

Equally, this is no mechanism for a viewer's identity to be identified for voyeuristic identification into an imaginary scenario. Abstained from too is the psychoanalytical demand insisting on such a viewer as core, vortex, phallus, centre, male. And this abstention is because of, *not in spite of*, the gendering of the fetish as a woman, whereas fetish demands denial of gender through repression, facilitated by displacement and perversion. Profoundly *not* a psychoanalytic painting in its radical refusal to deny distance between you and it. Refusing obliterative coalescence, this mechanism simultaneously disallows a 'self' any defining or otherness or difference. Thus an anti-psychoanalytic *autonomy* in spite of the classic Warholian stare (viz. *Kitchen*),[18] ours at her, the woman's 'at' the mirror, disavowed then displaced via *Der Spiegel* – here extraordinarily without a narcissism of the body, or of any object standing in for the body. The radical importance of this autonomous body operates as much in Richter's 'abstract paintings' – processes of the autonomous, as opposed to illusory causalities requiring hierarchy. The multifarious, nefarious, repressions necessary for the viewer's power (imaginary, ideological, whatever:[19] all real) are in *Lesende* absent.

V
Abstract Painting (817-1)

I am writing this segment in January 1995, in Köln, surrounded by about fifty paintings, several hundred photographs, trains, mainly freight cars, going by outside the studio window 'behind' a small 15 x 15 inch painting I've leaned against it, photos of *Lesende* on the window-sill as well as some photos of houses covered in snow, also some portraits, all stuck down on thickish A4-size paper to be added to the expanding history of Richter's *Atlas* project ... I'm trying to enter the painting and have tried yesterday. I can feel my eyes move sideways, then attempt to focus into depth even against the superimposed walls of colour, some skidded across, and attempt to focus against the image underneath the brushmarks only to come up against a colour-change which prevents that image being called image, a break in the duration where a move

---

18 See my *Materialist Film*, Routledge, 1989.
19 Not to mention any *a priori* viewer as male.

stopped – and that stoppage immediately dissipated by the fading out which is not a fading out but a lightening of colour broken into by a deep yellow underneath. This complex of appearances is caused where half-dry prior paint was *lifted* due to the hard harsh lateral movement across ...

So even one duration becomes impossible to name let alone fathom. Left with nothing, not exactly bereft, not exactly more illusionless than before, but if possible no less illusionless than before. Some kind of nothingness that becomes momentarily uncoupled[20] from bereftness.

> But the name *formation* is not really suitable, for the expenditure of effort on a thing need not always be a fashioning or shaping of it.
> Schopenhauer[21]

The careful beauty, speaking of the lower half of the picture, is that it demands a reading left to right and up to down, at the same time. Here marks are transformed at the moment of apprehension, vertical templates retained where paint-covered slats began side-swipes to the right in order to 'blur' what was prior. Yet neither present nor prior is the real focus. Neither, likewise, is any material *other*, as if the eye having found its mark could then attempt the impossible decipherment of everything else. The mark for a possible grasp is virtual and frail, more white (canvas) than blue shadow and afterimage. These are denials – this painting is a denial, in the true sense, wherein denial has depths of meaning not reduced by this or that happenstance.

Richter's work abjures *concepts* of truth and the lived historical – in this vein the Baader-Meinhof pictures, *18. October 1977*, 1988, are not history painting, they are the impossibility of history painting. The temporal exigencies that make them 'historical'

---

20 *Ungekupelt*. Using the freight cars passing for something other than historical memory which comes so easily in Germany.
21 Schopenhauer, op. cit.

are just that – and like all philosophy and aesthetics, necessarily tautologous: 'it is what it is'.

VI
Green/Blue Paintings:
Notes on Powerlessness – Abstract Paintings (793-1, -2, -3, -4)

These pictures breathe breathlessly.

This blue and this green – the fragility *not* of a lung under x-rays, no x-ray negatives. Rather: possible and impossible memory. Impossible memory: effect[22] no less than cause the unknowable, memory itself designated memory by what never was nor could have been. Thus memory itself impossible breath, memory itself an impossible breathing – nothing but powerlessness. *Ohnmacht:* without power, without consciousness.[23]

Breath, not as evidence of a body, anti-biological – not even the body of the picture – and not as a poetics of breathing, or of life (as in, e.g., possible lifelessness). So: not metaphor; instead hollows, hollowings understood as hollow, not some natural hollows 'normally understood'. This wants to mean material of hollowing, the hollowed out, a depth but not in depth; not a pictorial depth, but the process of this material.

A viewing inseparable from temporality, duration. Such materiality (not materialism) is today constantly questioned (bad). Against such materiality an essence, elsewhere, is sought (worse), and (even worse!) by those who no longer seek essences metaphor gets smuggled in, through whatever fraudulent methods, in the name of postmodern popularism. Here rather: a possible metaphorless identity without authority – as authority permits fragmentation and loss of identity only when no powerlessness for the subjects of power ensues. It's another matter for

---

22   And therein retroactively adumbrated cause.

23   The concept of *Ohnmacht* (powerlessness), the word in German containing a poetics of breath in its very speaking, as both its syllables necessitate slow exhalation.

the objects thereof.

In the 'identities' of the Green/Blue paintings – as in Richter's photo-paintings – the recognizable is not lost, only always repossessed *(entzogen)* until truth however unrecognizable is questioned through representations which give nothing, *represent* nothing, which do not exist. The Green/Blue paintings are not representations. A temporal duration bereft of ideologies of life. Time of history is then time of *this* history, this process of seeing. Duration durable and unendurable.[24]

The obliteration of the recognizable is here not via speed but via endless finalities.[25] Our fear is rightly of nothing, not because it is a stand-in for death, but because it does not manage to sustain the illusion of being anything else. The *else* is what all cultural production, or culture (neither pure nor simple), is meant not to be (in the sense of pure being) but at least to cause.

A paralysis sets in for the viewer, hidden through various mechanisms (projections, introjections). The intimation is that time stops. Death is dead if time is dead;[26] *that* these pictures don't allow. Instead: the end of a duration, stoppage, as *opposed* to the sheer non-existence of time. The paralysis of breath.

The Green/Blue paintings are as little or as much photographic as *Clouds*, 1978, *Annunciation after Titian*, 1973, or the Baader-Meinhof cycle. Nothing betrays the similarity of

24 Narrativity another matter, if at all.
25 See Peter Gidal, "Endless Finalities". In the original version, as published (with errors) in *Parkett*, No. 35, March 1993: "If I could find knowing impossible" *should read* "If I could find knowing possible". "The 'this' can't be called image of form" *should read* "The 'this' can't be called image or form". "The spatial development of each however unstable ..." *should read* "The spatial envelopment of each however unstable ..." "What solace in belief" *should read* "What solace in unbelief". And finally, "Less and less is more and more" *should read* "Less and less is more more". In spite of each word's, each letter's, importance, the textual contradictions and negations in such writing mean that e.g. "What solace in belief" and "What solace in unbelief" can produce a similar polemic stance in the reader. This makes the matter of language not less material but more.
26 Certain experimental films since 1969 have not let it come to that.

all Richter's picture-groupings other than the philosophical/aesthetic.

The unknowingness when faced with these paintings as to 'what' – and whether – one sees – is akin to the what and whether as to the photos of the photo-paintings brought out through the razorsharpness of the latter's paint *surface* vying against the out-of-focus *image*, – so that nothing is relegated securely to a time past. A picture as not a temporality-denying *surround* – so the viewer is not displaced or replaced. No 'other' identification, no other 'substitutions', of metaphor or anything else. No 'other' stories. You are not invested, not placed,[27] and not *un*placed. No need left for the hysteria that more usually accompanies unknowingness and powerlessness. Instead of the viewer's anticipatory inhalation: exhale.

What remains permissible is the photographic reversal of content and form, background and object, in the simple, primary sense: nothing fills nothing. We are not satisfied, nor are we given the illusion of such. A Wittgensteinian/Man Rayan solarisation, a colour, functions as light (or lighter), another as dark (or darker), one as 'white', one as 'black', blue 'on' (or in) green, green 'on' (or in) blue (two simple colours, two filmic layers), a negativity as the first stage of endless seeing.

Photochemical differences. Results? Causes? Quasi-solarisation (blue/green/green/blue) as the ideological mechanism of impossible reproduction of the even more impossible representation of the, or a, or a possible, recognizable.

Endless seeing: therewith our powerlessness, and that of the pictures against their 'representations'. No place or time to identify with, let alone identify. No time in the picture, no space in the picture, *time and space is the picture with us*. Tracelessness, powerlessness, ours and its. Thereby, hereby, touching ground, going to ground, as what remains is the nothing, a nothing that

---

27 No cathexis.

is not a negation of 'something'.[28] At most: association to a chemical memory, memory of chemical differences, film pictures, colour reproductions ... *and in the end, a subtraction* from all the Richter paintings that we know, and from almost everything else that we know.

VII
White

By substance I mean that which exists of itself and is conceived by itself; that is something the conception of which does not imply the conception of any other thing. The same is what I understand by attribute excepting that it is so called with a respect to our understanding, which assigns such and such a definite quality to substance. For example, I call a 'plane surface' that which reflects all the rays of light unchanged. I mean the same by saying 'white', excepting that I call it white, with regard to the person that looks at the surface.

Spinoza, Letter to Simon de Vries, 1663[29]

Rather, the question is precisely: what is the impression of white, what is the meaning of this expression, what is the logic of this concept 'white'?

Wittgenstein, *Remarks on Colour*, 1951[30]

To end with questions: Is here, *Abstract Painting (800-1)*, the whiteness a suffused atmosphere as opposed to being attached to an object?

In Baader-Meinhof and *Lesende* are suffused and infused

---

28 This is neither Godard's green or blue, nor the blue of the blue flower of whatever (Novalis). Nor even a singleminded green of the Postwarholian.
29 Benedict (Baruch) Spinoza, *Nachbildung der im Jahre 1902 noch erhaltenen eigenhändigen Briefe des Benedictus Despinoza*, W. Meijer (ed.), Mouton & Co., 1903.
30 Ludwig Wittgenstein, *Bemerkungen über die Farben*, Suhrkamp, 1979.

become one?

Do the 'abstract' and 'realist' paintings at once share a problematic *re* representation, yet differ *re* substance?

First published in Gerhard Richter: Painting in the Nineties, Anthony d'Offay Gallery, 1995.

NO EYE:
THEORETICAL REFLECTIONS ON THE EYE, METAPHOR AND FILM/VIDEO
(FOR RUBY COHN)
1995

Meaninglessness scares, religiously. When the sound in *Not I* is "a flood of sound" so that what we commonly call content flares by fast so that we can't hold its moments, and in that unholding can't construct our however momentary selves, or that of the other, onstage, with any adequacy, then identity becomes something not *a priori*.

There is no I in the me that hears, because if I cannot construct an object 'you' or a content (metaphor for the 'you') to be I-of, i.e. subject-of, then I'm left as viewer/listener in a time and a place of unknowing.

The viewer/listener as not knower. This isn't new, but what is important is that this not-knowing not become a credible unknown, some definition of the ineffable, unknowable, transcendent as adequate in its invisibility as a known would be in its visibility. With hearing the same, i.e. that it not become as adequate in its unlocatability as in prior theatrics – prior a misnomer – was location. For adequacy would then reside in the usual locutions of time and place, locations of the usual narratives.

As no eye *Not I* is not that latter.

When language's speed obliterates the temporal minimum needed for identification, that obliteration could in a different play lead simply to changing gear substituting the unknown unseen unheard for the known, seen, heard, a theological step-up which changes nothing. Thus does metaphor operate. This is not that. Here there's always enough of what attaches to the real (mental and physical) for it to be a problematic inseparable. Not a metaphor for that.

Sex was surely for Freud a metaphor. One could easily argue that the endless sexualization was only via his guilt possible AS metaphor. As if one thing were another. In *Not I* one doesn't get to *hear* the guilt, *or* hear the lack of it; one must as viewer/listener intercede throughout, distinguishing the text from the text. And this *our* act always during the (onstage) speaking. Always speech-as-spoken, just as film-as-projected, not after the fact.

"Let's not muddle our genres or we might as well go home and lie down," said SB.

Said SB maintained the autonomy of image and sound, better said image to sound, sound to image, coterminal with absolute effect one upon the other. This causality, the concept I'm trying to get to here however abstrusely, has relevance because we as viewers/listeners *infer* a causality. This sound effects that action, this (my) thought has some relation to this (my) next thought, let alone yours, or this your thought followed by this my inaction or even action. And so on. Is this so far without metaphor on my part? (Unfortunately, 'like', the substitute word that metaphor needs for its operation, we find is always a seductive possibility when explaining anything. And as you know our everyday language is replete with such. Often for example, the word 'like' on its own perversely substituting for the metaphor which it itself is meant to introduce – as in: like such and such, – so metaphor returns condensed – that structure is content [in both senses]).

The care we need to take, against metaphor, is so that one thing does not in the end stand in for another, otherwise why have the one thing in the first place if the other can be its adequate stand-in, or döppelganger, or condensation (superimposition of one signifier upon another) – these three are not the same. All three though are politically (t)here to endlessly enable that which is given (note the awful religious echoes of that phrase) to be (1) perceived (2) apprehended (3) consumed – via teleology ensuing quietude. To leave you with the illusion of knowing rather than any fact of not. There is no stand in, there is no other, there is no adequate real that also perfectly represents another adequate or inadequate real or imagined.

How then to begin interpretation or even, when against interpretation, to find a position from which meaning might be extracted, instead of nothing. Our fear is, rightly, of nothing, not because it's a stand-in for death but because it doesn't manage to sustain the illusion of being anything else. The else is what all cultural production, or culture (neither pure nor simple) is meant to if not BE, in the sense of pure being, then at least CAUSE – some effectivity.

If not that then meaninglessness, no eye, no you, and (contrary to accepted cliché) no paralysis: the whole 'Beckettian universe' defies the paralysis of befitting, slotting into, a (and this is important) by definition necessarily pre-existent 'similar'. *Not I* not allowing that allows little and leaves you with less – (and less paralysis).

Not even a gender which could somehow at least for the duration of the process allow identification of it, leading to identification *with* it, leading to (myths or not of) identity. Nor identity-fragments for however short a moment (and we know since Zeno of the infinite divisibility of the moment. Ever shorter *longeurs*). Nor a viable description of something out there either. Not even that. So, what? Not even for a man or a woman in the audience the possibility let alone probability of an identification of something there, allowing a here, via some kind of morphological recognition (female, male, food, objects, rooms, whatever) leading to descriptions of sorts. Allsorts would be better than nothing, allsorts say *Finnegans Wake*, but here we are not given that as, for MOUTH, no matter how 'gendered' – and we know it is a woman's because the script tells us the actress tells us shows us we hear it and so on – we are given no arrest beyond the initial stage facts.

Thus no representations (representation an arrest) made or unmade. No befitting sound to image which could reproduce a now known gendered speaker in (endlessly necessary) re-recognition, as here speed belies focus.

Without which's re-recognition 'what is it?' and 'why is it?' and 'who is it?' remain unquestionable unquestionables, as do self and selves, however unconscious. In consequence our positioning as viewers/listeners remains ungendered, unengendered.

All this is less than enough for my eye to not need metaphor and anthropomorph. Less than necessary to fulfil that need. What we need precisely to NOT let us move to what is called the deanthropomorphized pure abstract (wrongly) is a remnant of the real through and via which the process (a real, not a representation *of* the real; engagement therein unspeakable, it not being metaphor) and the idea, can be engaged. Otherwise we have just a fully established identity of you or me *vis-à-vis* transcendent or not this so-called pure abstract, meaning, or philosophy, or theology.

So the ends of representation need, for the obliteration to nothing, to an illusionless meaninglessness, that which though not representable is still imbricated with enough recognition to be a real. That abstract.

Again we otherwise switch genres to some notions which would diffuse a process against metaphor, – allowing metaphor its hold, via the route of the known, abstract or not.

Which is not to say this concretion of *Not I* sound and image (on TV no less) is not abstract.

Where in all this is the eye of the viewer, the ear of the listener? *When* there can be no theoretical reflections on the eye, of the eye, on the ear, of the ear, on metaphor, of metaphor, on film, of film, on video, of video, and so on.

First published in Samuel Beckett Today / Aujourd'hui, 1995.

ONCE IS NEVER:[1]
WARHOL'S SATURDAY DISASTER
& BLOW JOB
2001

No two or more substances can have the same attribute.
   Spinoza[2]

Warhol's *Saturday Disaster* cannot be perceived when you stand in front of it. The immediacy of an impossibility – caused by the substance's magnitude i.e. *size* (119 x 82 inches) *not scale*, however screened from consciousness at first moments of perception – forces a mental and physical (i.e. psychosomatic) *attempt to grasp* to be simultaneous to the extraordinary shock of the carcrash/death image(s).

Two images that seem virtually the same in vertical order ineluctably position you in relation to the filmic, that is, to time.[3] Two images wherein our immediate perception is of

---

1   Walter Benjamin, Theodor Adorno, *The Complete Correspondence 1928-1940*, Polity Press, 1999.

2   Spinoza, "Proposition VIII: Proof", *Ethics*. Defining substance itself doesn't begin to answer how an *aesthetic* moment is to be articulated against any other. So one begins with perception and conception in utter unavailability of anything else.

3   Time as distinguished from duration. "When you say time you're floundering, when you say duration I understand it." In: "Hollis Frampton/Peter Gidal, An Interview (1971)", *October*, No. 32, Spring 1985. In fact it is precisely time, not duration, that must be meant because duration is now understood as moving filmically from point A to point B (and back again?) whereas time as a concept and as a concretion doesn't allow for a rational measure of beginning and end, though producing temporality; it is this conception of time which Spinoza, to confuse matters, calls duration, in terms replete with echoes of Gertrude Stein: "Duration is indefinite continuation of existing." *Ethics*. And further: "We attribute to the human mind no duration which can be defined by time, save in so far as it expressed the actual essence of the human body, which is explained by means of duration and is defined by time, that is we do not attribute duration save as long as the body lasts." What this gets at (I think) is the usage of duration ('conceiving of things') as eternal ('wanting [in absence of/PG]

the *silkscreen hand-touch* (the thinning and thickening of the blacks, greys, whites) – virtually cutting in half the central, and at first view obscure, indecipherable upside-down body halfway across the canvas, an edge resultant from the ending of one ink-application, the beginning of another – equalled by our perception of an image as *mechanical reproduction* (its newspaper-likeness, its *Weegee/Daily News* signification), mass reproduction of the means of production of death, and – again – the cutting in half of the central upside down body where one screen 'ends'. Its being neither the one nor the other.

The illusion of movement in *Saturday Disaster*, the illusion of stillness in the film *Blow Job*; the illusion of stillness in *Saturday Disaster*, the illusion of movement in *Blow Job*.

As to the painting: this illusion of movement brings to consciousness the thought of a moment after (not necessarily beyond) death. Attempting to grasp that painting's imagery, straining to look up at the top 'half', you are (due to one panel being five feet high, i.e. human scale, two panels stacked vertically anything but) *faced* with the bottom panel first, in terms of recognition of what it represents, people, cars, an event, a moment after an accident, etc., the moment after (but not beyond) death.

Having initially, momentarily, strained to look up at the top 'half', what is then faced at human scale, the lower panel, is already a repeat in static form of something preceded and lost, already each time a memory, a memory preceding the living act of perception of the as yet new, this auratic shock of living death's mimesis. "The memory of a moment is not informed by

---

beginning and end') and time ('power of determining the existence of things') as measurable instance of the present. It is in that sense that it must be seen here; Warhol's filmic durable and unendurable temporality surfaces as much in *Saturday Disaster* as in *Blow Job*.

Warhol's extreme in relation to death and time, the 100 minute film *Henry Geldzahler*, through each re-screening disables again (and again) cursory assumptions both of "death (being) dead when time is dead" (Beckett on Proust) and of presence either by definition in time or by definition eternal each time again.

everything that has happened since; the moment which it has recorded still endures, still lives, and with it the being whose form is outlined in it. And moreover, this disintegration does not only make the dead one live, it multiplies him or her. To be consoled I would have to forget not one but innumerable Albertines. When I had succeeded in bearing the grief of losing this Albertine, I must begin again with another, with a hundred others." (Marcel Proust)[4]

When you again look up ten feet to re-see the 'same', the bottom panel retroactively enacts itself as follow-on; it is in that sense 'filmic'.

The confusion for you is: is it 'simply' double; is that more, somehow? Is it a doubling, deadening reification, thereby 'less'? Or is it neither, i.e. not the top panel somehow different from the bottom panel, but the same? The same, something twice, is impossible, producing unease. What is to be disinterred is whether time's stoppage or time's persistence is death; in time's stoppage the moment of presence becomes timeless existence, but rather than transcending death thereby, Warhol makes the image precisely one of death, conferring a terrifyingly anxious, irresolute, contradiction.

The disturbance when the image of death overwhelms you is here inseparable from the inability to define it.

In the end it is time's *passage* presaging repetition – the temporal of Warhol's process – that makes such a painting so powerful. The repetition (with whatever imagistic differences caused) being the inability of escape. Lost in that, offered no definition either that would then result in a viewing coming to an end, a viewer finding substance, it or we thereby defined as finally being 'about' something, however complex. We are not given the wherewithal of its inhering ideologies to place it.

---

[4] Marcel Proust, *The Captive and the Fugitive (In Search of Lost Time*, Vol. 5). Trans. by C. K. Scott-Moncrieff and T. Kilmartin. (Translation partially revised by the author.)

Instead, we are left with time's persistence, the image sequence.

In unlikeness to contemporary culture, the wherewithal to deal with the work is not given by the work, it is in that sense alienated from its cultural context, however blatantly at first this seems with Warhol's work not to be the case.

Saturday Disaster has – as has death – no place. *You* have to pull yourself away from *it*, powerless, rather than having been enabled to place it within a realm of meaning or the senses that would befit. Here illusion of movement and illusion of stillness[5] are never without the *simultaneity* of: the atemporal presence of *substance*; the temporal[6] presence of *being* (i.e. spatially represented[7] objects and people); and *time*, endlessly irretrievable

---

5   With materialist film, film that does not suppress its (illimitable) processes – Warhol's particularly, *Blow Job* an instance – the *illusion of stillness*, the visibly projected sixteen frames per second passage of acetate, is perceived because the subject is so still and the (other) material projected – acetate – is not (scratches, flare, dust, refraction, etc. ...). Betraying, minutely, unstoppable machine-movement.

6   For the possibilities of painting that doesn't suppress its (illimitable) processes – in Thérèse Oulton's *Static* – the temporal is produced (and perceived as such) through the continuum of samenesses because each of the painted 'film-frames' is held to its painted state – states of (repeated) stasis. When the eye descends or ascends due to light *between* frames taking attention up or down, such stasis is opposed by a viewer-become-movement. The simultaneity of states produces a temporal stasis as illusionary as its momentary relinquishing. The disturbance for viewing is the disturbance of this conceptual contradiction: continuum of samenesses. Betraying, minutely, unstoppable *painting*.

More particularly, *Static*'s 'off-screen' grey-white impinging from the left into each respective filmframe partially obliterates and *makes tense* each left frame edge. It makes vertiginous a knowing of – and relation to – *Static*'s substance: is it one painting conceptually whilst a series of paintings perceptually? "No substance in so far as it is substance, can be divided into parts." (Spinoza) Your look is down the painting (frame by frame – within which endless fractal optics – as opposed to an ocular sweeping-across) whilst attempting to see 'a' painting. Escaping thus neither into form nor into a metaphysics of process, each separate and particular contingency is given – painted – as that, the ineluctable temporal.

7   How can a spatial opposite in every determination produce the so same. (The concept – the aesthetic dynamic – of the different and the same disallows philosophical interrogation its recent *sejour*.) With Gerhard Richter's *Gehöft* size not scale is the immediate radicality: 46 x 51 cm / 18 x 20 inches. Its unlocalizability of 'content' attaches thereto: each segment of & in the painting making more impossible the

from the viewer's temporally specific, historical present.

Not making of Warhol's realities of painting a repetition of something *else*, *Saturday Disaster*'s singularity is in confronting death's irreducibility, its nonrepresentability in representation. This is not negation, it is deeper and more radical than that. It is painting about what painting cannot be.

In the thirty-minute film – content self-explanatory – *Blow Job*,[8] in the end and in the beginning, movement over stillness

---

necessary spatialities – and consequent congruences – of place. This shock of small still-life size – as was against all expectations the first perceiving of Malevich's white on white – makes you look 'into' what is 'out there'. When this into is of an out-there as with *Gehöft*, the *Unheimlichkeit* (strictly: out of home, secreted) is of the physical *turned inside out*; you paint the inside of a skull by painting the outside of a skull (mental consequences elsewhere). Apart from *Gehöft's* concrete photo-image at first instance being inapprehendable as to 'right side up', the further *immediate* inapprehendability is of e.g. the top right rectangle ('background') of the picture disallowing the real its depths. Spatial irrelations – of whatever still life is here in the end perceived – are determinately not a fall into abstraction.

Unbounded by either definition abstract or nonabstract, *the scale so condenses either reality at the moment of each's perceived inception*. Either reality is repeatedly over-painted; the canvas an over-painted fourth wall, leaving literally no three dimensional projection for you to be 'in'. "Man versucht der konkret sich forcierenden Abstraktheit zu entgehen, es ist nicht möglich, man versucht MIT der Abstraktion, oder dem Abstrakten, eine Logik oder einen Glauben oder eine Sicherheit des Sehens zu 'gewinnen' und das ist genau gleich unmöglich, denn das Reale schiebt sich sozusagen davor, an die Flache des Bildes aber auch als eine flache Konstruktion als Mauer gegen Perspektive und 'Wahrheit' oder 'Schönheit' oder 'Authentizitat'." (Peter Gidal, letter to Gerhard Richter, 25 May 2000). Richter refuses – to what in his paintings, if not in the real world, are *made* the noncompliant representational 'elements' – recognition, let alone integration as elements. "That whose knowledge does not depend on knowledge of any other thing ... each attribute is conceived through itself without the aid of another." (Spinoza, ibid.) So the picture becomes a disturbance for viewing: to make a painting that presents itself as no more a solution as to how than as a solution as to how not to represent. Painted, as that – the ineluctable spatial.

8   *Blow Job*'s thirty minutes are made up of 100 foot, 2¾ minute, 16mm filmreels. Writing this has a pleasure in that it was the first Warhol film seen by me, someone at the film society at Brandeis University showed it (on February 11, 1965 according to Callie Angell) along with some long-forgotten feature; radically shocking as it seemed on one level of the temporal, still, entropic, yet befitting an ideology of the poetics of Hölderlin and Trakl, Rimbaud and Genet, for someone who had "recently come

– however slight the (camera) movement, however slight the subject's stillness – is preceded and followed by film flare-out's *material* flickering and fogging. Flare-out, lasting perhaps six or seven seconds, wherein light enters, unequally, the edges of the 16mm filmreels as they're being loaded into the camera, produces effects of partially whited out imagery whereas what the camera + lens is aimed at produces the photochemical imprint necessary for photomechanical reproduction. Flare-out: extremes of white and shade, and light and its absence, upon and through whatever image is at that moment represented; these material (quantitative) effects surpass any (Wölfflinian) form or (post-Freudian/Lacanian) *to-be-analysed* contents – thwarting analysis equally of the possible Gnostic epistemology white/dark.[9]

What remains? Presence and its filmic problematics. *Object*. Entropic stillness is how distinguished from essence or transcendence regardless of form? By *object* being film and the filmed, not an existential cool or hot of a distanced-or-not phenomenal object (e.g. the person seen). Thus one of the concrete effects – theoretical and practical – in the real world of this work was to make the category viewer/view*ing* inseparable. Film as projected rather than film as deconstructed. The processing of such ideologies. Conventional cinema has instantiated the viewer as

---

down from the Zugerberg [near Zurich], an isolated mountain in Switzerland with a school, some farmers, trees, cows, and Alpine flowers, it was a beautiful and fascinating film ..." (Peter Gidal, *Andy Warhol, Film and Paintings*, Studio Vista/Dutton, 1971, reprint with introduction, Da Capo Press, 1991). Writing this has a pleasure too in that the first Warhol painting seen by me was *Saturday Disaster*, at the Rose Art Museum at Brandeis, fifty metres from my hall of residence, viewed with a sense of strangeness over and over in 1965 ...

9   Can a representation be a representation without being a *representation-of*. This problematic attached itself in analysis of Warhol's *Hammer and Sickle* paintings wherein the questionable is of a shadow being a shadow *of*, as much as in the shadow paintings themselves. See Peter Gidal, "Some Problems 'relating to' Warhol's *Still Life 1976*", *Artforum*, May 1978. Contiguously see also, "the eradication of representation as much by light as by dark" in London Film Co-op Catalogue 1974, Notes on Peter Gidal's *Room Film 1973*.

voyeur, within which's definition the act of viewing is disavowed. Warhol is, in this work, radically anti-voyeurist.

The radicality of that, against identification in its unconscious manifestations, against fetishization (even, importantly, of filmic process) produced in *Blow Job* representation's inadequate[10] power over the machine's durable – and unendurable – time.

Words can dissolve[11] – film, Warhol's *Blow Job*, can – a viewing apprehending as endless endless time endlessly ended. That endless presence is its history – *Geschichtlichkeit* – each moment of *stare* the death of each prior and future moment. This presence of time and its simultaneous absence is the persistence, not of vision, but of nothing, a state of nothing neither 'to be reached' via the transcending of other states, nor, turned upside-down, made into a positivity ('the opposite of something'), but a machined unstoppable presence – the I at odds.

Repetition's effect of near-stasis – stilling – paradoxically belies its vacuity as pneuma for our knowledge and belief, power and control. Said differently, the film as embodied trace of use, and exchange, value is denied. The filming is in obscure relation to the body: it is precisely the *intervening* spectator's speechlessness[12] that constitutes the radical dialectical moment – identities no less in crisis than identifications, (anti-)voyeurism:

10 'Inadequacy' meant as the production of aesthetic effects of non-adequacy, not as a moral normative category of some lack or other.

11 e.g. in Gertrude Stein's *Tender Buttons: Rooms/Objects/Food* (1913): Words' meanings dissolving through mental intractability. Kafka's *Betrachtung* (1913): Words' meanings dissolving through their physical intractability aligned to their very mental tractableness. The linguistic dissolutions caused by the large 16 pt. letterpress text in and literally *on* the pages of Beckett's *The Lost Ones* has the 22 pt. letterpress of the original edition of *Betrachtung* as precedent.

12 Adorno strangely seems to posit an empirical spectator when theorizing the concept of (theatrical) intervention, opposing to this a posited interventionlessness of the speechlessness of silent film. "Kafka's novels are not screenplays for experimental theatre, since they lack in principle the very spectator who might intervene in such experiments. They represent rather the last and disappearing connecting texts of the silent film ... the ambiguity of gesture ... sinking into speechlessness ..."
Theodor Adorno, letter to Walter Benjamin, 1934, ibid.

without spectacle – of which Warhol's *Blow Job* a precursor, *accursed progenitor!*[13]

First published in Andy Warhol: Series and Singles, Fondation Beyeler, 2000.

---

13   Hamm to Nagg, in Samuel Beckett, *Endgame*.

AGAINST METAPHOR
1998 (REVISED 2005/2015)

> *... that we can do nothing by a decision of the mind unless we recollect having done so before, e.g. we cannot speak a word unless we recollect having done so.*
> Spinoza, *Ethics*

Without doubt it's plain to see one thing always stands in for another, a thing for a word, a word for an unformed notion, a vagary, however abstract or concrete one tells oneself this is. And outside the telling oneself, outside the language, the moment-to-moment placing and unplacing of oneself (not ones thoughts but ones fragile or not self, seeming-self) is the removal, outside language, in relation to things, objects in the world. Already recognition becomes the problematic within which transpire the questions as to reality in word or image, temporality simultaneous to it in that what is ahistorical in the present is immediately historicized by time's passage. What was present is already always past and for recognition and reduplication of a memory, real or otherwise, this presents a problem.

Whether or not the social space within which such questions take place is political – other than the political being all embracing therefore political q.e.d. – is a matter specifically of a political space of recognition forcing all representation to be outside any conceivable present due simply (!) to its having already *been*, and having already been past.

This would make for an eternal present, that illusion which in turn (turn and turn about ...) would be an annihilation of time, of precisely the mechanism (time) which exists as a concretion and

---

NB Due to the length of some of the notes to this text they are presented as endnotes, commencing on page 231.

an abstraction, to necessarily turn a history into history past and done and perversely thereby timeless.

Time regained, sort of, and the present with it, wherein it then is not so much recognition at a given moment as a being present at that moment. That would be in opposition to an endless moving, which one would think would put an end to the need to or the want to be moved.[1] Nothing more or less than the given, real material.

Wishing to even begin thoughts on metaphor one is ineluctably driven to a position *against* unless one wants to expand further the plethora of associations *so that* the conglomerate mystifications can exceed their present quantities *so as not* to disavow satisfactions sought as obtainable illusion requited *ad infinitum* simultaneous to simultaneous loss thereof. A spatial depth and temporal durée of (no) consequence. Therein the starting point would be the impossible, opposed to the simulacrum or stylistic of the impossible. Opposed in other words to an imagined teleology wherein the beginning and the end are forever, and at each moment, a conception of possibility against which impossibility always perceived as a tawdry misfortune, metaphor its palliative. Making of what's conceived of as the the illness what's conceived of as the cure. Or at least making of metaphor a detour, temporal, to the starting point's meaning or position. Meaning *and* position.

Another kind of realism is called for, realism of another kind.

Realist: that means consciously influenced by, and consciously influencing, reality. (Brecht) Reality is not not abstract.

> *... the whole idea of the integral use of silence in music is a relatively new concept, really. It started with the Bauhaus, I suppose, with the idea of the total involvement of space, including the windows and the doors that make space meaningful, and musically it started, in that sense, with Anton Webern. With wonderful analytical hindsight, people began to say "Ah, but Beethoven did it too!*

Op. 133, for instance – there are lots of silences in that. Very significant!" But with the best will in the world, you can't argue that he – Beethoven – weighed his silences with the same kind of arithmetic integrity ... with the same kind of appropriate longevity in relation to sound that Webern employed. So, since it's basically a new concept in music, it doesn't surprise me that it hasn't been applied to the spoken word, documentarily. Well of course, it has been in the theatre of Beckett ... but, in a way, that's almost a by-product of sullenness rather than the integral use of cessation in a texture as a component of that texture.[2]

Glenn Gould, *Glenn Gould Reader*, 1984

A by-product of sullenness, i.e. metaphor. *"Almost."* How does one manage, ever, to announce something, its existence (leaving aside here the question of its persistence) without at on(c)e and the same time announcing the existence of something else?

As we are constantly and irrevocably in meaning, only metaphor is possible, when nothing is separable from the chain of meanings. Does that posit an essence? The essence the chain.

Anti-essentialism can be used to critique metaphor, equally to critique non-metaphor (in word, object, system, perception, etc.).

Suddenly a critique of presence is hauled out in retaliation against the ostensible pure presence of the *non*-metaphoric, *as if arguing against metaphor is arguing for presence in some essentialistic, ahistorical, atemporal, eternal sense*. The last thirty years have been besotted by 'critiques of presence' by those whose own presence is exhaustively identified, and with. Subjects to whom others are their adequate willing objects, undeconstructed, pitiable. Against metaphor is not to find an irreducible pure presence attempting to deny time and death. But temporal ineluctableness is a system we can't imagine ourselves out of unless in certain manias. The anti-metaphor is neither its, nor any other's, essence, stand-in, decoy. It is a moment, at that moment a position, gone before perceivable as moment or position. The ungraspability of its moment, its finality, makes anti-metaphor distressing to theorize, metaphor's endlessness its obverse.

If silence, a temporal moment, is not to be a by-product of sullenness, can it be nothing happens, twice, or Webern-John Cage time, or Warhol-Gertrude Stein time, the by-product of repetition annihilating capitalist realism's for another kind of realism, the 'subject' of the writing and image emptied of its illusion of living force? The deathlike being then a necessary step for nonmetaphorical representation. Deathlike? In an essay against metaphor?

If a metaphor makes something new is it, the something-new, a metaphor? The something-new posited for however short a moment – at that 'moment' – is, though already past, still that something-new, its meaning new. That momentary position is nonmetaphoric or else it couldn't be sustained as such for a period long enough to allow recognition.

This is the major problem in the theorization of metaphor and anti-metaphor, because it is precisely recognition that obliterates the possibility of the new, if I see something, recognize it, seem to know it, however vaguely, then it is not the something-new. Yet the positing above is of a momentary position being nonmetaphoric, not sustained for a period long enough to allow recognition. *Yet otherwise it would dissolve without recognition having obtained to define it as the something new.* Yet requiring recognition, having the time to become something sustainable thereby recognized as what it is (or seems to be) for the viewer viewing, should paradoxically situate it as the *impossibility* of the new because the new is obliterated by recognition, re-cognition, seeing again. This seems a dead-end. Recognition is both necessary and unviable.

> *... that the mind, from the contemplation of one thing passes at once to the contemplation of another, namely, because the images of those things were so intertwined and so arranged that one followed another, which therefore cannot be conceived if the image be new ... The imagination of a new thing, therefore considered in itself, is of the same nature as other imaginations.*
>
> Spinoza, *Ethics*

For Spinoza, for the nonmetaphoric, a period must be sustained long enough to allow recognition, as the something-new. Were it immediately recognized, without a noticeable passage of time, its recognition would be that of the already known, the not new. Here thus recognition structures the defining of the something-new. In other words, without a definable moment of ones position there'd be nothing. So for this polemico/theoretical essay the term moment must do, an approximation that is analogous (not 'like' but parallel) to the black/white/foreground/background silhouette perception-experiment of attempting to hold a moment's recognition via eyes' focus against vibration before the 'opposite' equally momentarily embalms itself on the eyes, photochemically.

Defining non-metaphor in this manner as lynchpin ends up shoddy, speculative, relativistic, historically opportune/opportunistic. The extension to no more than this, the contraction to no less than that, allows for the new to be if not apprehended at least just barely enough recognized to position one's thoughts, feelings, imaginary self, in however problematic relation to it.

> *A shame too that ... had joined the increasing number of conductors inclined to accept a disastrous emendation to the score of Stravinsky's Les Noces instigated by Boulez: the removal of a silent bar in the final carillon, a silent bar which so dramatically throws out of sequence the bell strokes on every eighth beat to give a moment of vertigo. A film sequence exists of Boulez actually inducing the aged*

Stravinsky to delete the bar, though Stravinsky later repudiated this claiming he was drunk at the time. The point surely that what may indeed originally have been a mistake of counting had long since been accepted by Stravinsky as something compositionally enriching, in all the recordings he constructed and supervised.

"With the Best of Unintentions: on Cage's *Roaratorio*",
Bayan Northcott, *The Independent,* 21 July 1987

One does not ever understand, before they are completely created, what is happening and one does not at all understand what one has done until the moment when it is all done. Picasso said once that he who created a thing is forced to make it ugly.

Gertrude Stein, *Picasso*, 1938[3]

He commenced the long struggle not to express what he could see but not to express the things he did not see, that is to say the things everybody is certain of seeing but which they do not really see. As I have already said, in looking at a friend one only sees one feature of her face for another, in fact Picasso was not at all simple and he analysed his vision, he did not wish to paint the things that he himself did not see, the other painters satisfied themselves with the appearance, and always the appearance, which was not at all what they could see but what they knew was there.

Ibid.

The astonishing thing about Stein's aesthetic insight herein is that she clearly recognises ideology in forming seeing, in other painters painting and representing it, though (in the contrasted method, Picasso's) still relying on representing by painting what is there in that it is what he sees.

Unless she means "see" as *what he did not know was there but could make,* by definition that then being what he could see which in fact is not what he could have seen prior to its being made.

Such would be analogous to a penultimate argument about intention wherein some argue for intentionality visible in the artwork and some argue against it. The momentary egress from the miasma of that is to argue that everything an artwork is is by definition its, the artwork's, not some artist's, intention. Metaphor can be escaped however momentarily when a maker's consciousness is neither assumed nor extractable from the work, and when equally a seen is not represented. Thus is ineluctably necessitated a temporal system (e.g. experimental film as one such possibility) which endlessly affords momentary unrecognizables and unknowns at the moment of their integration/dissolution into the finalities of the known or the seen. Endless finalities.

Does everything have to link at some stasis to metaphor, and to a placement of the reader/listener/viewer as if to metaphor? If metaphor is 'like', at its crudest, and if it is there to inculcate a conservation of the known, whether under the rubric, and illusion, of change or not, then how can a concept of *function* be somehow outside such a syndrome? Isn't the unknown known as unknown at that very point of movement, psychical, physical, etc.? No. For to be lost is to be outside of the solidities, however arbitrary, of the illusion of knowing, of a moral position, of such a recognition.

The problem surfaces when to be really lost, to be outside, is to be vertiginous, anxious, implies fragmentation and the arbitrary not consolably adhered to as by post-Modernists in search of stability through recognition of that loss and fragmentation via deconstruction's sureties or any other manner of consolation.

One is left with not fictions, as fictions are as reassuring as fictions as nonfictions' phantasms.

So a function is a position in the subject, you, me, ucs (unconscious) or cs (conscious), without need of recourse to something other, something more or less 'like'. This could lead to a non-metaphoric category in terms of function.

Related to this, the function of sex: *In nature, libidinal strivings (are) very capable of representation, so that with repression of the normal, the perverse are strengthened and vice versa. Repression has no relation to the sexual function other than to strive for its defence* ... (Freud, *A Phylogenetic Phantasy*, in Laplanche and Pontalis, *The Language of Psychoanalysis*, J.B. Hogarth Press, 1973.) "Its." The "it" posited is a non-metaphoric *it*.[4]

So is the body you're with without being (being!!!) a metaphysical presence still not a metaphoric semiotic?[5] Can the person you are having sex with be not an 'I' in identity of self or anything else? Or the person you are talking to? Bedrock without the misbegotten identities of variegated or not I's. How do we find an object *qua* object, cipher, person, idea, thought, word, being itself that does not refer to something else, yet is not a timelessly posited being itself? This matter is always about time.

Whether 'like' or 'unlike' or 'dislike', whether moral or political position *re* all the rest of everything, can something somehow be outside of identity and self-identity, or even outside vicarious identity. Can recognition always already be unrecognition, not of one thing for another (substitution) – meanings taken over that way – but simply as non-substitutory power – one thing *not* for another – one thing for *not* an other – the one thing, this, annihilating an other? At that moment there is not metaphor, just power. Not identity, just position.

Duration ceases when created things cease to be, and begins when created things begin to exist ...
  Spinoza, *The Collected Works of Spinoza*, 1985

... from which it will be plain that these are only extrinsic denominations of things and are not attributed to things except metaphorically ...
  Ibid.

> *For then man would have had to know already the meanings of those words before they were spoken to him.*
> Ibid.

> *So if particular things have to agree with another nature, they will not be able to agree with their own, and consequently will not be able to be what they truly are.*
> Ibid.

Thus identification with the other paradoxically posits neither identity of self nor identification of an other, of an it; therefore any identification with an other is metaphoric not real. The system engaged is by definition virtual, illusory, ideological. To think otherwise is to believe in nature as the natural. For identification with self the same. As that too would necessitate a metaphor of the self to be identified with.

There is no perfect superimposition.

In the film *Yes No Maybe Maybe Not* (Malcolm Le Grice, 1967) the superimposition of the negative onto the positive coalesces only insofar as both are lost and become something else, – does not coalesce most of the time as one sequence of frames is ahead or behind. Th e two identities are ever further apart or ever closer until at moment of coalescence they are another it, no longer two, no longer subject and object, no longer I and other.

An academy is always demanding self-perpetuation as is each discourse and class. The narrativisational procreational ideology is the same that ends up reinstituting 'feminine' metaphor (metaphors of the feminine) as if that were e.g. anti-patriarchal. The political lessons are to end reproduction without fetishizing production in crude orthodox capitalist realism called socialist.

Against metaphor, against reproduction: but then the world could end! So the endless pleasures of the obverse, reproductions of various sorts and with it e.g. small adjustments, academic iterations and reiterations of everything, but no end of anything, no end to reproduction.

As in:
> the concept erasure, which has taken on the subtextual immanence of constant resurrection. A lack of originality that sees erasure as only always already being, having been, becoming a mark of absence, and the defining of that absence as therefore an *a priori* presence, betokening that human subjects seem to obligate themselves to see any denial only in Freudian terms whose every instantiating of an object or thought reaffirms what is ostensibly denied. What's confusing is that this imperialization of the material world via erasure stems from a proper antagonism to a religiousity of truth and its fetishistic codification under rubrics of erasure.

As in:
> the concept 'like', ... *I want to be like a machine* is not the same as I want to be a machine. Stating that is naming something, making that thought real, but not making a body a machine pure and simple, as a body has a name. But you don't have sex with a name. Actually you do. If the name is not being metaphor but real, and if body being machine is not being metaphor but real, those thoughts would be in opposition to the same concepts preceded by 'like'. A nonmetaphoric other so defined then unarrestable. Neither stuff the food in first, morals follow on (Brecht, *Threepenny Opera*, 1928), nor first come the morals, then stuff the food in.
>
> Non-telos without a moral. Leaving but the temporary and the political. Such relinquishing defies the conscience-and-its-negation penny-a-line-vulgarities that the aesthetico-social order insists on. Without metaphor, without the illusion of more. No metaphor. No more.

Proust's, or anyone's, memory-instigators relapse; it is time the lapsus is a cover for, lapsus thus a cover for the lapsus' own effacing of the process of memory (that time). History versus presence, temporality. *Death is dead when time is dead.* A warding off of the present, the shards, fragments, woven into a rememorated history more and more warding off anything past the now (sic), meaning anything beyond the present toward death. As if a warding off of the future – and simultaneous abnegation of the present – necessitating endless rememorations – could succeed in warding off death, the falling apart. *I never fall apart because I never felt (fell?) together.* (Warhol, no past, all present.) What need for metaphor for either of these processes?

Does the moment of presence, however attenuated, block material time's passage or does the moment itself have its own time, even the new, the not yet imagined – according to Spinoza – needing time to be perceived for what it is, resulting (though he denies cause) in an endlessness within each moment, as there is nothing before or after God.

The eternal can't suddenly have an end, God similarly, the eternal denying death.

That, a buttress against time and death, can only be metaphor when outside the mysteries of the metaphysical. But within them, it is anything but metaphor, it is real, and even true. Against such there's here the attempt at neither metaphor nor metaphysic. Presence, time, death, history of historylessness.[6]

Metaphor isn't the only problem. What is the problem is whether the lack of or absence of or eviction of metaphor leaves an essence of sorts.

Is metaphor necessary? Presumably if it solipsistically is necessary to constitute the fact, or the world view, of the perspective, i.e. necessary when necessary to create an assimilable convention.

The real corrects the metaphor, metaphor the constant approximation to something *a priori*. Useless thus as theoretical abstract, yet concrete only insofar as it is indexical, nearness to the thing referred to, in imagined similarity. Illusory function therefore is of a progress of knowledge, greater indexicality, and so on. Meanings made from meanings made. Otherwise we would be left with what we are.

If things have no origin, finally, because the origin can't be known – that's abstract pure perfect substantive thought, and properly so – then why continue solipsistic searches, self identity the goal, rationalized and humanized by generalising onto the socius? To finally relinquish those unnecessary fictions would mean being left with the nothing which dictates the seeming impulse for positions being taken. The resonances, echoes, memories without which some say life would be less have to go when new meanings are made, new positions taken. There is no likeness. There is no recovery.

The unutterable horror of such loss is (not) at issue. No doubt the loss of belief in an afterlife is equally unutterable, or the death of Spirit, or the end of all material, the material all. Matters of ethics confound matters of aesthetics, to the point where insistence on 'content' as a palliative for capitalist formalism mustn't elide the by now no longer awful insight that form is content. The *form* of the form – say 'the marketplace of ideas' as the form of a form, a metaphor for specific ideologies – overdetermining the content of the oppressions which willy-nilly fit into it is the form meant. Thereby metaphor (e.g. gender, which is a sexual metaphor) is redundant however meaningful socially.[7]

The motive for metaphor is defence against death, perversely as there is no defence.

> *Pornography has a theory to obscure the fact that it is a practice, it is a metaphor to obscure the fact that it is also a means.*
> Catharine MacKinnon, *Feminism Unmodified*, 1988

If a metaphor can obscure the fact that it is also a means (even if one questions that "also") then metaphor is a device we accept as obscurer (noun not adjective). Now either it *does* obscure something else (the fact that it is also a means) or it does not; if it *does* then as it is already embedded in that meaning, it is not obscuring it. Then it is itself metaphor-as-essence-of-itself-as-obscurer. If it doesn't obscure anything it isn't a metaphor. As it then *does not* obscure the fact that it is also a means, it is not an obscurer. Metaphor would equally obscure any radical power of aesthetic production, its viewing, its social time and space. "I did the *Hammers and Sickles* because after the Maos everyone asked if that was meant to be Communist. So I did *Hammers and Sickles* for Communism and *Skulls* for Fascism." Warhol's longtime assistant on the other hand states that the *Hammers and Sickles* were done "for no reason ... we just did them." For the "no reason" to obtain for the final work would avoidance of the term metaphor do? Obviously not, as meanings and meaninglessnesses are determinate material effects in metaphor or out. As defined a work *is* its intention,[8] investigating intention then can not somehow clarify a work's meanings or an assumed anthropomorphic consciousness embedded therein. Thus only in such solipsism ("a work is its intention") is the materiality of intention possible, positioning the aesthetico/political stance of a work.

A real that does not represent is a real against metaphor, the moment the impossible is no longer real there is nothing – perhaps the struggle is to not let that nothing be anything but that. And to not let something always be immediately something else. What spatio/temporal quantum would force metaphor's disavowal for good? Trees' leaves leaving no sound in the storms of rain and wind if no one is there to etc. etc. is still resuscitated after so many different genocides 'not participated in'. So how far from the forest does one have to be to acknowledge neither forest nor trees? Metaphor doesn't even allow you to think that you can think without it.

First published in Against Metaphor (etchings Thérèse Oulton), Fascicle Books, 1988. Revised in 2005 and 2015.

NOTES

1   For Warhol's work which looks machine made, sometimes, it is an "inefficient, slow, involving, tedious machine". Warhol's work knows of association's function in a less conscious manner than that of Freud, more akin to Rembrandt. (Gidal, *Notes on AW*, 1969 – preparatory notes for *Andy Warhol: Films and Paintings*, Studio Vista, 1971)

2   "integral use of": *integral* is material to that material, as opposed to *integrated* i.e. othernesses collapsed. You can't focus on two things at once visually. It's either or: either the donut or the hole. Either the black shape or the white. *Nicht Entzweit*. i.e. No difference (with or without an *a*). And no *differrance* as there is no *known* to defer. Unlike Derrida's "this is not a book" re his book *Glas*, this is a book. After all is said and done, all Derrida managed over three decades is to give a Joycean view of language, endless sp(l)ittings, adumbrations, a bad name. But the whole critique of presence in order to finally admit its *order* hypostasizes metaphor, a ten thousand page attempt over the years to enlarge realms of meaning, signatures, etc., until metaphor becomes not only a useful possibility but a totalized model for all and sundry processes. Without that, the discourse of his philosophical power would be vanquished. *Woman plays with truth to her own advantage, at a distance, as if it were a fetish, manipulating it, even as she refuses to believe in it.* (Derrida, *Glas*.) According to Derrida there is the impossibility of presence, or essence … except for "woman plays with …". The crudest patriarchal powerfetishism betrayed itself here. In his colossal monument to (his) self, *Glas*, Derrida tells us what is "The Jew," "The (male) Homosexual," etc. Rather pathetic hysteria, self-pitying assertions of self-identity coterminal with the embarrassingly conventionalised moan of rather humourless male paranoia: *enemies everywhere!*

3   First caesura, surcease, then lessness, meaninglessness, through language, would begin to end symbol and metaphor. Beckett saw Gertrude Stein's literature in the same light, a critique prescient of his own practice: *As we cannot eliminate language all at once, we should at least leave nothing undone that might contribute to its falling into disrepute … is there any reason why that terribly happenstance materiality of the word-surface should not be dissolved? … perhaps the logographs of Gertrude Stein are nearer to what I have in mind. At least the texture of language has become porous … (she) is doubtlessly still in love with her vehicle, albeit only in that way in which a mathematician is with figures …* ("July 9, 1937" in Samuel Beckett and Ruby Cohn, *Disjecta*, John Calder, 1983)

4   *Through bodily symptoms, repressed ideas join in the conversation, although they are distorted by mechanisms of condensation and displacement.* (Freud, op. cit.) Sex here is not posited necessarily as a metaphor for anything, or anything for it. For what "a symbolic conception" in which "through bodily symptoms repressed ideas 'join in'" might mean is that they join in for what they are, not for what they in turn

symbolically represent (for another signifier, whoever s/he may be). A nonmetaphoric possibility.

5   *... it seems no less unfair to try 'my body' as a reasonable candidate for identity, enduring-substance, and see how we get on making that the identity of the 'I': My body is meeting Peter Gidal in the park for doughnuts? ... Substituting 'my mind' doesn't seem to help much.* (Stephen Heath, "Le Père Noel", *October*, No. 23, Winter 1982)

6   A series of problems follow:
"Whilst Searle is unhappy about the details ..."
"The constructivist approach seems to threaten the distinction between the language of the poet and that of the scientist ..."
"... repudiates distinction of literal and poetic on which it is based ..."
"Black argues that some metaphors permit us to see aspects of reality that they themselves help to constitute."
"According to Rumelhard ..."
"... metaphor plays a crucial role in language acquisition. In applying old words to new objects children engage in metaphorical extension ..."
And another one: "In literary metaphors, linguistic construal – whereby the language is reinterpreted to fit the world – might be better replaced by phenomenalistic construal, wherein a reader's model of the world is changed to accommodate a literal interpretation of the metaphor." (Samuel Levin in Andrew Ortony, Introduction to *Metaphor and Thought*, Cambridge University Press, 1979) Levin's elucidation leaves no way out, he wants no longer to have language reinterpreted to fit the world, and proposes replacing it by a construal wherein a reader's model of the world (forgetting that this model is the same as language reinterpretation) is changed to accommodate a literal interpretation of the metaphor (which is predicated on that model of the world in the first place).

So many writers, agreeing with Murry that, "Metaphor is as ultimate as speech itself, and speech as ultimate as thought" rapidly draw ontological morals, while leaving the nature of metaphorical speech and thought tantalizingly obscure. Amongst the appreciators, Nowottny (*The Language Poets Use*, 1962): "Current criticism often takes metaphor *au grand serieux*, as a peephole on the nature of transcendental reality, a prime means by which the imagination can see into the life of things." She adds: "This attitude makes it difficult to see the workings of those metaphors which deliberately emphasize the frame, offering themselves as deliberate fabrications, as a prime means of seeing into the life not of things but of the creative human consciousness, framer of its own world." "Enthusiastic friends of metaphor are indeed prone to various kinds of inflation, ready to see metaphor everywhere, in the spirit of Carlyle who said: "Examine language; what if you except some primitive elements of natural sound, what is it all but metaphors, recognized as such or no longer recognized; still fluid and florid or now solid-grown and colourless? If these same primitive garments are the osseous fixtures in the Flesh Garment Language then are metaphors its muscle and living integuments." This quotation illustrates a pervasive tendency for writers to frame their basic insights in metaphorical terms. A related inflationary thrust is shown in a persistent tendency, found in Aristotle's still influential treatment, and manifest in as recent a discussion as Nelson Goodman's *Languages of Art* (1968) to regard all figurative uses of language as metaphorical, and in this way to ignore the important distinctions between metaphor and such other figures of speech as simile, metonymy and synecdoche. To make a sufficiently intricate topic still harder to handle, the deprecators tend to focus upon relatively trivial examples ('Man is a wolf') that conform to the traditional substitution view, and the special form of it that I called the comparison view whereas appreciators, in their zeal to establish that metaphor is the omnipresent principle of language (Richards, 1936) tend to dwell upon excitingly suggestive but obscure examples from Shakespeare, Donne, Hopkins or Dylan Thomas, to the neglect of simpler instances that also require attention in a comprehensive theory. It may well be a mistaken strategy to treat profound metaphors as paradigms. We are headed for the blind alley taken by those ... who have supposed metaphors to be replaceable by literal translations." (Max Black, "More about Metaphor" (1979), in Ortony, op. cit.)

If they are not replaceable by the literal then they have their own meaning that is not simply reducible. If they have their own meaning that is not simply reducible then reducible or not that meaning exists. If that meaning exists then even if it is created by the metaphor and then exists it still can not be seen to be producing something unknown. It is thus the known. The essence, the idea, are the known. The else is the power of the immediate, ineffable loss as soon as glimpsed. Less satisfying theoretically, less satisfying or reassuring in every other way. Another kind of realism. The obverse truth to God's.

7   For example: "Unter Namenslosem ein Namensloser" (last page of *Rilke* by Lou Andreas Salome). (Parenthetically: "Amongst namelessness one nameless," is not said by "Unter Namenslos*en*" (i.e. nameless ones) but by "Unter Namenslos*em*", nameless states, i.e. namelessness). "Amongst namelessness one nameless." The first part of the sentence is no metaphor, the second is. For to call Mr. Rilke nameless, "like one without a name", whether name means character, qualities, whatever, is to demand of the hearer/reader an assumption of memory and association in support for meaning from something or somewhere else. And that somewhere-else would needs encompass something prior to its specific usage here.

"I like being a vacuum; it leaves me alone to work." (Andy Warhol to Gretchen Berg, March 1967, "Andy Warhol: My True Story", *Los Angeles Free Press*) Is the "I" a metaphor? If it is then for what or whom. Labile, fragile, momentary position in the present, no sooner there than gone.

It is not a desire to be different, to be elsewhere, but to make covert that. If any word is a metaphor by definition, then, as with every signifier being a signified for another signifier, apolitical French end-of-the-20th-century theory has won, or its watered down American form. Politics, placements of power, are as if expunged from all words and images. To derealize form, metaphor is to make of nothing a *like*.

(I hope making a noun from a verb is less offensive than its opposite). Is nothing a thing? If it is then "make of nothing a like" means make metaphor of it. If nothing is not a thing, "make of nothing a like" is to make no metaphor of it.

Everyone knows words do not mean what they say. What is left are metaphorless categories of political moment. Can Father, Mother, Family, Lover be political positions outside of the associations which enable psychoanalysts to on average charge for two hours the average weekly male wage in England after tax? Warhol's notion of buying a friend comes in handy here: the concept elucidated in 1968 that one rent a person displayed in an art gallery as a friend per week at a rate far less than two sessions with an analyst. Slavery is the most appealing concept in liberal-capitalist democracies, and not coincidentally economic and sexual slavery is the sustenance without which current structures would collapse. *So is slavery a metaphor? And if so, for what?* If I now say this is not a rhetorical question it is not. Such a question says nothing about truth of any kind.

As to truth, it is reassuring that Nietzsche stated as questions: "If only I had the courage to think everything that I know ..." (Friedrich Nietzsche, *Sämtliche Werke, Kritische Studienausgabe,* Deutscher Taschenbuch Verlag/de Gruyter, 1980) Nietzsche was so aware of the instantaneous metaphoric implications of each word, of the endless supposedly 'Freudian' conscious and unconscious rememorations in the processes of meaningmaking that when referring to people which most translators even now give as "men" he writes "Menschen und Menscheninnen" and speaking of people in Berlin "Berliner und Berlinerinnen". This is – in the best sense – the politically correct paranoia in relation to metaphor's hold. In German, "Menschen" is gender free (whereas e.g. "Berliner" is not, due to masc. ending), yet even "Menschen" Nietzsche's writing realizes is already taken up socially as male; thus efforts on his part to counter this simultaneous to its usage. The radicality of this is for sexual definition and in the struggles against metaphor, producing a template in his texts – of which his letters constitute a valuable part – to divide out, more precisely rend asunder, categories. (Ibid. p. 289 and 335). This doesn't deny his hysterical misogyny elsewhere.

Aber da man nicht weiss wo mein Zentrum ist, wird man schwerlich darüber die Wahrheit treffen, wo and wann ich bisher "exzentrisch" gewesen bin. But as one doesn't know where my centre is, one will with difficulty ascertain the truth, where and when I have so far been ex-centric. (Nietzsche coined the term *Es* from whom Groddeck took it from whom Freud took it.)

Diese Aufgabe hat mich krank gemacht, sie wird mich auch wieder gesund machen. This task has made me ill, it will also make me healthy again.

Die Leidenschaft der letzten Schrift hat etwas erschreckendess: ich habe sie vorgestern mit tiefem Erstaunen und wie etwas Neues gelesen. The passion of the last writings has something frightening to it: I read them the day before yesterday with deep astonishment, as if they were something new.

8   Minus a temporal teleology.

MISCELLANY

LETTER TO ARTFORUM
1971

In a remarkably wrongheaded piece, Annette Michelson, in the June *Artforum* asserts, with reference to Michael Snow's film, *Wavelength*, "Snow has redefined filmic space as that of action". Now even the most simpleminded filmgoer such as myself knows and feels, intuitively (and rationally, if *ratio* is needed) that space has always been defined in terms of action (inner and outer). What else is a western, gangster film, situation comedy, etc.? "The object of Farber's delight, the narrative integrity of those comedies and westerns," is nothing but a reactionary, model-oriented mode of film-making indulged in by just about everyone in the commercial cinema, and certainly not indulged in by Mike Snow. The basis of Miss Michelson's hypothesis is blatantly and patently incorrect. Other, smaller assumptions seem to get carried along in the tide of shallow insight and intellectualization: "Snow, in re-introducing expectation as the core of film form", is distinguished from "the stare of Warhol". Expectation is inextricably bound to action within a defined space, whether in commercial, experimental, or any other sort of film. And nothing increases expectation more than Warhol's stare, which, in structuralist film terms, was to some extent an important basis for Snow's exploration and aesthetic. It is sad that the most important film-maker currently working (Warhol has long given up to his untalented assistants) receives much-needed and honestly-held critical attention through the dubious intelligence and aesthetically backward critical approach of Annette Michelson in *Artforum*. But the cover was beautiful. And at least she *tried*. Which is more than one can say for most ART critics.

First published in Artforum, September 1971. Reproduced by kind permission of Artforum.

LETTER TO SCREEN
1976

Just a short note apropos your last issue. Ben Brewster in his editorial wrote, "Different uses of the key terms in these discussions reveal two broad trends in film-making which opposes the narrative-representational tradition: a 'modernist' current which expels meaning in the interests of the purely filmic, and a political current which exposes the processes of signification to denaturalise ideology." He should have put quotation marks around both 'political' and 'modernist', or around neither. Also, the notion of the 'purely filmic' is a mystification.

Of the two broad trends he (and Peter Wollen) speak of, it is precisely the 'modernist' one which exposes processes of signification to denaturalise ideology. Merely superimposing some formal devices ('deconstructions' or not) over a 'political' subject matter is not the answer.

As to Peter Wollen's piece, "'Ontology' and 'Materialism' in Film": to state that "any post-Brechtian sense of materialism (must) be concerned with the significance of what is represented, itself located in the material world and in history" is to hark back to notions of given significance, found when searched for, true reality as merely exhumed. It is to see, for example, in Straub/Huillet's *History Lessons*, in the car scenes, 'reality as it is', reality as given not constructed, not as ideological (on, through, by, and for, etc.). This is far from work on the signifier. The route of significance is the route of the pregiven, which is the route of subjective interpretation of necessity felt to be correct by *each* interpret*or*. It is an ideological route that is issueless, as far as film is concerned. When the significance shines through (located 'in history' or not) we are back in the Radek/Lukács camp.

Wollen's thesis is too simplifying of the work being done ("Gidal foregrounds focussing, Le Grice foregrounds projection-procedure, etc."). Wollen's attempt to set up a single-line hierarchy (in the guise of bridges) *from* the complexities of Godard (etc.) *to* the (simple) foregrounders of this or that aspect, keeps the notions of film practice as previously acknowledged intact, with a bit of reformism at one end.

Experimental work is being done, in the most extreme form of that label, not work on 'the essence of things or being'. This of course doesn't stop one from knowing, e.g. that *duration* is non-existent as finite event in a painting; it exists in film. An ontology is not what is being expounded. Nor "an 'anti-ontology' for a medium which is 'illusionist' by nature." Whose nature?

The Brecht vogue, by the way, seems to be serving a retrograde reading of BB, supported by most productions *and* by the distance between his texts on theatre and his theatre-and-film-texts. Peter Wollen hints at a recognition of this problematic elsewhere when he writes: "A work, therefore, which recognised the primacy of the signifier in the process of signification. This would not involve the reduction of the signifier purely to the material substrate, a semiotic of pure presentation, *nor the mere interruption of a stream*, a continuum of signifieds, *by the demystificatory break, reminder or caesura of a signifier perceived as an interruption, a discontinuity within an over-riding continuity*" (p.19 – italics mine). The *nor* is to be emphasised.

I hope *Screen* will now begin to investigate in depth specific films of the avant-garde in Britain, and create a place for real theoretical discussion. (The title of my film, by the way, is *Room Film 1973*, not *Room Film*.)

First published in Screen, Summer 1976.

LETTER TO AFTERIMAGE
1976

There are some important misconceptions in Anne Cottringer's hatchet-job on my "Theory and Definition of Structural/Materialist Film".[1] I wish to clear these up briefly, as both Anne and I feel that aspects of her piece are mainly destructive and were, in her own words, "written in a fit of pique". Of course the editor ought to have been a bit careful about a piece that sets out only to find weak points and sloppy formulations (apart from setting out some weak points and sloppy formulations of its own) without attempting to bring forth or clarify some of the basic ideas in my original essay. It all sounds a bit like a take-home exam: "Find five errors in P. Gidal's article. Two hours maximum."

I am not worried about "forcing people into extreme positions" but am worried about "occasionally implicating materialism with physicality". I do in fact implicate materialism with physicality – although Cottringer thinks even the *hint* of physicality is "fatal". I do not see materialism as covered by physicality, but certainly the question of transparency and representation systems and codes has to do also with the physical transformation and reproduction of forms (the profilmic event, so to speak). This transformation has to do with codes of cinematic usage (for the most part not yet clearly delineated in the case of the avant-garde and/or Structural/Materialist film). There is no question that the dissolution of imagery through darkness and light (extreme) has to do with the flattening out of the screen surface, and brings the production of depth into play (work) against the flat screen representation-support-structure. There is no question but that the (certain) usage of grain and contrast produces itself *vis-à-vis* (into/through/with) the *image*; and the duration of that 'image',

1 Anne Cottringer, "On Peter Gidal's Theory and Definition of Structural/Materialist Film", *Afterimage*, No. 6, Summer 1976.

and 'that' image's transformation (preceded by its 'use value' to meaning and meaning production) is inseparable from the physical-material supports. This is not to say – *this is in no way to say* – that what is materialistic in film is what shows, or is, camera, lenses, graininess *per se*, flicker, slow motion, etc. But the – to my mind – idealist negation *in toto* of physicality can only lead to a blindness. Anne Cottringer is correct nevertheless in pointing out the danger of a materialism imbibed in and covered, mapped over, by pure (and only) physicality. Precisely her fear is one which ought to be elaborated *vis-à-vis* many (but not my) notions of avant-garde film practice.

As to "contradictory terminology", I do not know what that is. Perhaps I ought to be merely relaying what someone else says; surely this isn't what Anne has in mind for me? I fully see the unfortunate consequences of my own lack of clarity when, for example, I use phrases like "inner content". When one has done battle with words and phrases and with filmpractice for nearly a decade, even such sloppy phrases appear (let alone disappear) only after a great deal of effort. By "inner content" I was getting at what others have much more simply and eloquently named the profilmic event. The hangovers from an idealist culture don't disappear overnight. I think another author, Stephen Heath, has recently footnoted a long piece with that quote of mine on "inner content": I hope that's the end of it.

I wish to clarify another point: when I speak of "presence", certainly after extensively attempting to paraphrase Derrida's critique of presence, I was using "presence" as 'presence and operation of'. In other articles I used the term "presence" always placing in parenthesis that this is shorthand and must be seen in the light of Derrida's critique of the notion of presence. I think Anne Cottringer therefore picked up a moot point; I also think it best to drop the discussion about Derrida, as that would entail a truly lengthy letter.

I am grateful that Anne Cottringer attributes to me the

"instigating (of) the decisive presentation/representation and production/reproduction oppositions. These, in themselves, are not without value in the course of theoretical investigations ..." But this, in her opinion, leads nevertheless to a failure to

> adequately assess the function that representation can serve in relation to the movement and production of signification, and the transformation of raw material. Accordingly he prefers the undialectical relation, 'The content thus serves as a function upon which, time and time again, a film-maker works to bring forth the filmic event'.

A misunderstanding: when I speak of a "function upon which", I never see this as a simple laying of one thing upon another, but as a function *through* which. Thus I am admittedly bogged down in my language usage by my unfortunate experiences making films. The memory of one social practice intervenes on the formulation and attempts at theoreticisation of another (which is obviously not entirely separable). Thus a truly dialectical relation, or dialectic process, is theorised in my theory. (I must add that I'd be the first to call my "Theory and Definition etc." a theoretico/critico/polemic, and I would even acquiesce with Bellour's description of it as a "terrorist text".)

In quoting an uncharacteristically sound Benjamin text against me, Anne Cottringer is saying what I am trying to say all along:

> Epic theatre is gestural. The extent to which it can also be literary in the traditional sense is a separate issue. The gesture is its raw material and its task is the rational utilisation of this material.

Although if Anne Cottringer is truly searching for a "play of meanings" which are "revealed by editing", then we might be taking a detour back to psychologistic interpretative auteurism.

I am sure she does not intend this. It is true though that I am not interested in the "different levels upon which signification operates" – interested yes, but not for film: I see no reason to make 'Roland Barthes films' or even 'Christian Metz films' (CM either before or after his conversion from Bazin). The conservative 'Structuralist' approach to the (anthropological or other) 'object' is not my approach. Some work is being done by post-Structuralists (I am referring to what has broadly been called 'Structuralism' in France, not to Structural or Structural/ Materialism filmmaking) in constituting objects, rather than interpreting pre-constituted ones. Some work is beginning on production of meaning and constitution of the subject and the subject-relation; as well as the positioning and narrativisation and implication of the subject/viewer in such – a subject/viewer displaced, forced from position to position, and not a stasis viewing another stasis. This leads all the way to ideology as not a covering which you take off (or pull off) only to find unveiled certain meanings. Even here though, there are dangers, such as too great a notion of the constant building/construction of a subject which, misinterpreted, could lead to notions of constant renewal, consciousness force-feeding, etc. A history exists for each subject, as does re-memoration and construction/self-presentation. Investigation along these lines may be of importance to advanced filmpractice as well as to reactionary filmpractice. Here Anne Cottringer and I would probably agree (I haven't asked her yet).

Interestingly, Anne Cottringer implies a lack of interest in "the nature of the relationship between image and filmic procedures" on my part, and invokes the work of Snow by contrast. A look at my 1971 piece on *Back and Forth* and various other published notes from 1968 to the present would clarify that mistake. When she states: "the images presented are *primary* in *any* consideration of pleasure in relation to the cinema" (my italics), I would like to see some further discourse on that assertion. Although Anne Cottringer concludes correctly that "Gidal is forced to reject all narrative cinema", I have tried hard to find where she got the idea that mine is "an over-reaction to the effect of a suppression of representation". I have battled long and hard in my writings and my films to 'prove' the opposite.

I never ascribe "an unnaturalness" to narrative in relation to filmpractice (a main theoretical point I make is against naturalness, naturalisation, for clearly stated reasons); and I'm certainly not worried about narrative "because it is somehow incapable of enforcing 'presence' ..." Here we have Anne Cottringer's misunderstanding of my paper.[2] It is also not "up to the Structural/Materialist filmmaker to recover its essential nature, i.e. film as film ..." If anything, it is film's concrete existence which I am interested in; its possibilities of militating against transparency and its presentation/formation of processes of production, which have as use value precisely the meanings constructed by, through and *for*.

To end: when speaking of the 1:1 relation between viewer and viewed, I was referring to that, but in no way to what seems to have been misunderstood as long single takes. Acquaintance with my films and the films I have interest in shows this: but what I wrote shows this as well. The 1:1 relation can be set up in the most complexly edited film, when time-compression as in 'classical' narrative is not utilised as an illusionistic device. Really a simple point; in no way provocative.

Similarly non-provocative is my notion (stolen) of arbitrariness, which has nothing to do with "granting a certain fullness to an 'image-moment', where the inferences somehow come after". This Anne Cottringer just got wrong. The word moment does not mean 'full', it merely designates *moment* – not static, not essential, just moment ('a piece of time'). My rejection of

---

2   I think for reasons I can't reconstruct this wasn't Cottringer's misunderstanding of my paper but my own, as the following sentences showed. "Concrete existence" and presence are closely (thankfully) linked.

metaphysics is clear (to many) in my essay, similarly my non-rejection of psychoanalysis. What I was against (rightly quoted but wrongly understood by Anne Cottringer) is the "bourgeois ciné semiotician's *simplistic* usage of psychoanalysis [which] is a ruse". A fetishization of psychoanalytics is much further gone than the admittedly unfortunate fetishization of process. Both must be militated against. My programme notes for the NFT show of *Room Film 1973* in 1974 (Lacan on Rememoration) show in a small way how I think psychoanalytic concepts can be useful; some of the work at Edinburgh this year [1976] worked in that direction too.

To end, finally. I want to thank Anne for the work she did with/on my paper, and I do think some of the important theoretical work can be done and must be done in ways on which I am sure we agree. Certainly the fact that she bothered to take up my paper, and some of my misformulations and misconceptions, can only be of use. Still, a lengthier, more careful and more detailed piece would have been necessary.

First published in Afterimage, 1978.

EIGHT HOURS OR THREE MINUTES
1971

A film such as *Empire*'s (eight hours) emphasis is on the nature of film reality, the gradation of shades from black to white *on film*, the nature of time's (forward-) movement past a nonentity (which the Empire State Building certainly is; so 'nothing' that it attains neutrality), and the emotive connotations thereof through the description of nothingness (a traditional art-concern, by now). When one alters one's critical apparatus sufficiently, one can begin to look at film life in a totally different way, and that openness to change affects one's (viewing of) art and life. One can argue that Warhol's 'time' is relatively short: eternity is felt in three minutes in a Warhol film. Viewing the 'same' image for eight hours heightens (through use of such an extreme) the capacity of viewing for three minutes. Also, the physical and retinal reaction to eight hours is so different from the reaction to three minutes that in that difference one learns, hypnotically, about change (one's own and that of an 'other'). One can take the idea-aspects of the early Warhol films a step further; even reading about an eight-hour film alters one's capacity to respond to the three-minute one, let alone to one of eight hours' duration. Such facts have tremendous implications in terms of one's deculturalization, awakening one from bad (film-) habits, one's useless, demented, 'sane' reactions to what is different.

First published in Rules and Meanings: The Anthropology of Everyday Knowledge, Mary Douglas (ed.), Penguin, 1973.

NOTES ON MY FILM WORK
1975

Mental activation toward material analysis is the process that is relevant, whether or not actual structure is 'revealed'. (1969)

Manipulation of response and awareness thereof: through repetition and duration of image. Film situation as structured, as recorrective mechanism. (1969)

Zooming, panning, focussing to constantly 'redefine' reality and the process of seeing/filming (although the two are not the same) ... also: demystification of the subject/object relation. (1971)

Working against and with the given 'image', fragment, etc. Attempt to betray a nonhierarchical process. Attempt to force the viewer to analyse the construct. Attempt to force a dialectic. (1971) Nonhierarchical process = signifier as arbitrary. (1974)

Consciousness must not be understood as deflecting onto a mythical or mythologized subject, it must in no way imply transcendence or transcendent subjectivity; one can see it, in schematic form, as a T form, the horizontal being the work upon which functions operate (the film plane, for example), the vertical (of necessity a broken line) being the line to the complicitous (even in resistance) recipient of his/her necessary mode of inculcated dialectic operation. (1974)

Jumpcut as jumpcut, etc. (1967)

The anti-illusionist project and the materialist dialectic are no more mechanistic goals than for example Marxist political theory and practice. *Room Film 1973* is a consequent continuation and contraction of my film work, research which began with *Room* (1967). The film is not a translation of anything, it is not a representation of anything, not even of consciousness. (1973)

On *Room Film 1973*:

Each five second (90 frames, at 18fps) sequence repeated on slightly darker-green tinted stock. Operates as a five second continuity interruption *(restart)*, every 'other' five seconds. But interruptive (non-taped) splice-flashes every five seconds make vertiginous any supposed sequential consistency.

Awareness of the system (construct) through distancing through repetition.

Each (retinally) graspable (material) moment dialecticized through constant zoom focus etc. device(s) within each 'shot' (five second segment). Each shot's 'repetition' is another cipher necessitating said dialectic, is well as determining the text's shot-to-shot interruption (gap, break) and construction (i.e. not within the shot but without, between). The film is a durational text. How it is what it is, and how it is how it is what it is is determined by such devices.

A mechanistic materialism is at least as dangerous as if not more dangerous than an idealist, non (or anti) materialist operation.

Inculcated attempt to decipher the structure: dialectic mental act, with and against the 'given', it's certainly not merely an act of deconstructing potent signifiers but rather to determine the representational 'content' as less than primary and deal with (through) the operations upon that represented content. Implicit within the scope of my continuing anti-illusionist project is the notion of the arbitrariness of the signifier which is but one aspect of my film work.

(January 1973 – August 1974)

First published in Structure and Function in Time,
Rosetta Brooks (ed.), Sunderland Arts Centre, 1975.

PETER GIDAL FILMOGRAPHY

Room (Double Take), 1967, 16mm, b/w, sound, 10 minutes
Loop, 1968, 16mm, b/w, sound, 10 minutes
Still Andy, 1968, 16mm, colour, sound, 4 minutes
Key, 1968-69, 16mm, b/w, sound, 10 minutes
Hall, 1968-69, 16mm, b/w, sound, 10 minutes
Clouds, 1969, 16mm, b/w, sound, 10 minutes
Heads, 1969, 16mm, b/w, silent, 35 minutes
Focus, 1971, 16mm, b/w, sound, 7 minutes
8mm Film Notes on 16mm, 1971, 16mm, colour, silent,
    40 minutes
Movie No. 1, 1972, 16mm, colour, sound, 5 minutes
Movie No. 2, 1972, 16mm, colour, sound, 5 minutes
Upside Down Feature, 1967-72, 16mm, b/w & colour, sound,
    61 minutes
Room Film 1973, 1973, 16mm, colour, silent,
    46 minutes (at 18fps)
Film Print, 1973-74, 16mm, colour, silent, 40 minutes
C/O/N/S/T/R/U/C/T, 1974, 16mm, colour, silent, 26 minutes
Condition of Illusion, 1975, 16mm, colour, silent, 30 minutes
Silent Partner, 1977, 16mm, colour, sound, 35 minutes
Kopenhagen/1930, 1977, 16mm, b/w, silent, 40 minutes
4th Wall, 1978, 16mm, colour, silent, 45 minutes
Epilogue, 1978, 16mm, colour, silent, 9 minutes
Untitled, 1978, 16mm, colour, sound, 9 minutes
Action at a Distance, 1980, 16mm, colour, sound, 35 minutes
Close Up, 1983, 16mm, colour, sound, 70 minutes
Denials, 1986, 16mm, colour, sound, 20 minutes
Guilt, 1988, 16mm, colour, silent, 40 minutes
Flare Out, 1992, 16mm, colour, sound, 20 minutes
No Night No Day, 1997, 16mm, colour, silent, 15 minutes
Assumption, 1997, 16mm, colour, sound, 1 minute

Volcano, 2002, 16mm, b/w & colour, silent, 30 minutes
Coda I, 2013, 16mm, colour, sound, 2 minutes
Coda II, 2013, 16mm, colour, sound, 2 minutes
not far at all, 2013, 16mm, colour, sound, 15 minutes

Peter Gidal's films are distributed by LUX (London), Lightcone (Paris), and the Film-Makers' Cooperative (New York).

Please Note: Approximately a dozen films made since 1969 have been withdrawn by the film-maker.

PETER GIDAL BIBLIOGRAPHY

BOOKS BY PETER GIDAL

Andy Warhol: Films and Paintings, Studio Vista, 1971.
Bathtime Reading etc. (with Roger Hammond), self published (12 copies), 1974.
Structural Film Anthology, BFI, 1976.
Understanding Beckett: A Study of Monologue and Gesture in the Work of Samuel Beckett, Macmillan, 1986.
Against Metaphor (etchings Thérèse Oulton), Fascicle Books, 1988.
Materialist Film, Routledge, 1989.
Andy Warhol: Blow Job, Afterall Books, 2008.
Flare Out: Aesthetics 1966-2016, The Visible Press, 2016.

TEXTS BY PETER GIDAL

"... of jews, and jazz, and zwerenz' gripes", *Twen*, December 1962.
"In der Welt unserer Zeit", *Montanablatt*, No. 44, March 1963.
"Hospital", *Vagabond*, No. 7, 1966.
"Interview with Eric Burdon", *Vagabond*, No. 7, 1966.
"Who is Andy Warhol", *RCA Newsheet*, circa 1969/70.
"Peter asks Gidal", IRAT London programme note, April 1970.
"The Confrontation, a film by Miklós Jancsó", *RCA Newsheet*, May 1970.
"Steve Dwoskin", *Independent Cinema*, No. 1, May 1970.
"Underground Movies", *ARK: The Journal of the Royal College of Art*, No. 46, Spring 1970.
"Film as Materialist Consumer Product", *Cinemantics*, No. 1, 1970.
"Film as Materialist Consumer Product II", *Cinemantics*, No. 3, 1970.
"Talking Head: Problems of an Underground Filmmaker in London", *Time Out (Cinema Supplement Part 3)*, 17-31 October 1970.

"The Polluted Pseudo Political Cinema", *ARK: The Journal of the Royal College of Art*, No. 47, Winter 1970.

"Steve Dwoskin's Times For", *Time Out*, 12-26 December 1970.

Letter (response to editorial cuts), *Time Out*, 10-23 January 1971.

"Yoko Ono / Plastic Ono Band", *RCA Newsheet*, January 1971

Letter (on Charles Harrison), *Studio International*, Vol. 181, No. 929, January 1971.

Letter (on Film-Makers' Cooperative), *Studio International*, Vol. 181, No. 930, February 1971.

"Ballad of Cable Hogue", *Time Out*, 7-21 February 1971.

Letter (on Charles Harrison), *Studio International*, Vol. 181, No. 931, March 1971.

"Cinetopia", *Studio International*, Vol. 181, No. 931, March 1971.

"Warhol: Part One", *Films and Filming*, Vol. 17, No. 7, April 1971.

"Warhol: Part Two", *Films and Filming*, Vol. 17, No. 8, May 1971.

"Negative Space", *Time Out*, 14-20 May 1971.

"Lonesome Cowboys", *Time Out*, 4-10 June 1971.

"Film Culture Reader", *Time Out*, 18-24 June 1971.

"Some Notes on Underground Film", *Film*, No. 62, Summer 1971.

Letter (on Charles Harrison), *Studio International*, Vol. 182, No. 935, July/August 1971.

"Underground and Around", *Studio International*, Vol. 182, No. 935, July/August 1971.

Letter, "Foreword in Three Letters", *Artforum*, Vol. 10, No. 1, September 1971.

"Sam Beckett and Bobby Seale", *Time Out*, 5-11 November 1971.

"The London Film Makers' Co-op Cinema", *Time Out*, 17-24 September 1971.

"The London Filmmakers' Cooperative", *Time Out*, 24-30 September 1971.

"London Film Makers' Cooperative Cinema: Premiere of 8mm Films by Le Grice, Schwartz, Hammond, Gidal, Dunford", *Time Out*, 1-7 October 1971.

"The London Filmmakers Cooperative Cinema: Bruce Baillie,

Taka Iimura", *Time Out*, 8-14 October 1971.

"Kubelka, Amsterdam Co-op and Conner's Report", *Time Out*, 15 October 1971

"New Feature-Length Film at London Film Makers Cooperative Cinema: Tom Tom the Piper's Son by Ken Jacobs", *Time Out*, 29 October – 4 November 1971

"Zooms and in-fights", *Studio International*, Vol. 182, No. 938, November 1971.

"Valie Export: Viennese Action Artist", *Time Out*, 10-16 December 1971.

"Sam Fuller by Nicholas Garnham", *Time Out*, 17-23 December 1971.

"London Film-Makers Co-op: Chomont, Mekas, Dwoskin", *Time Out*, 11-17 February 1972.

"Heinrich Viel by Adolf Winkelman", *Time Out*, 3-9 March 1972.

"London Film Co-op: Ritual Anger", *Time Out*, 31 March – 6 April 1972.

Letter (co-signed with Roger Hammond), *New Statesman*, circa March 1972.

"Film Culture: An Anthology", *Art and Artists*, Vol. 6, No. 12, Issue 72, March 1972.

"Hollis Frampton's Zorn's Lemma", *Time Out*, 26 May – 1 June 1972.

"12 New International Underground Films", *Time Out*, 21-27 June 1972.

"On Hollis Frampton's Zorn's Lemma" (Pseuds Corner), *Private Eye*, No. 274, 16 June 1972.

"On Movie No. 1", *A Survey of the Avant-Garde in Britain, Vol. 3*, Gallery House, 1972.

"Parts of a Body House Book by Carolee Schneemann", *Art and Artists*, Vol. 7, No. 5, Issue 77, August 1972.

"Experimental Cinema by David Curtis", *Art and Artists*, Vol. 7, No. 6, Issue 78, September 1972.

"Film as Film", *Art and Artists*, Vol. 7, No. 9, Issue 81, December 1972. Reprinted in: *A Perspective on English Avant-Garde Film*, Arts Council of Great Britain / British Council, 1978.

"Expanded Cinema by Gene Youngblood, *Art and Artists*, Vol. 7, No. 9, Issue 81, December 1972.

"Eight Hours or Three Minutes", *Rules and Meanings: The Anthropology of Everyday Knowledge*, Mary Douglas (ed.), Penguin, 1973.

"Jackson Pollock: Energy Made Visible by B.H. Friedman", *Art and Artists*, Vol. 8, No. 2, Issue 86, May 1973.

"Beckett and Art", *Art and Artists*, Vol. 8, No. 3, Issue 87, June 1973.

"Notes on La Region Centrale by Michael Snow", *Light One*, 1973.

"Definition and Theory of the Current Avant-Garde: Materialist/Structural Film", *Studio International*, Vol. 187, No. 963), February 1974.

"Andy Warhol: New Drawings of Chairman Mao", *Studio International*, Vol. 187, No. 974, March 1974.

"Photo Collection", *Studio International*, Vol. 188, No. 968, July/August 1974.

"Beckett & Others & Art: A System", *Studio International*, Vol. 188, No. 971, November 1974.
Reprinted in: *Endlessness in the Year 2000: Samuel Beckett Today/Aujourd'hui*, No. 11, 2001.

"Angleterre, un cinéma matéraliste structurel", *Chroniques de l'art vivant*, No. 55, February 1975.

"5th Experimental Film Festival at Knokke/Heist, Belgium", *Studio International*, Vol. 189, No. 974, March/April 1975.

"Notes on my Film Work", *Structure and Function in Time*, Rosetta Brooks (ed.), Sunderland Arts Centre, 1975.

"Theory and Definition of Structural/Materialist Film", *Studio International*, Vol. 190, No. 978, November/December 1975.
Reprinted in: *Das Andere Kino*, Nos. 5/76 & 6/76, 1976.
Reprinted in: *Reading Materials of Foreign Film Theories*, Li Youzheng (ed.), Peking Film College, 1981.
Reprinted in: *Structuralism and Semiotics*, Li Youzheng (ed.), SDX Joint Publishing, 1987.
Reprinted in: *The British Avant-Garde Film 1926-1995*, Michael

O'Pray (ed.), University of Luton / Arts Council of England, 1997.
Reprinted in: *Film Theory: Critical Concepts in Media and Cultural Studies*, Philip Simpson, Andrew Utterson and K.J. Sheperdson (eds.), Routledge, 2004.

"Some Brief Notes on the Edinburgh Film Festival 1975", *Studio International*, Vol. 190, No. 978, November/December 1975.

"Straub/Huillet Talking and Short Notes on Some Contentious Issues", *ARK: The Journal of the Royal College of Art*, No. 52-01, January 1976.

"Further Footnotes", London Film-Makers' Co-operative seminar, February 1976.

Letter (on Structural Film), *Studio International*, Vol. 191, No. 981, May/June 1976.

Letter (response to "On Ontology and Materialism"), *Screen*, Vol. 17, No. 2, Summer, 1976.

"Film Print", *Arte Inglese Oggi*, British Council, 1976.

"Edinburgh Film Festival 1976", *Studio International*, Vol. 193, No. 985, January/February 1977.
Reprinted in: *Das Andere Kino*, No. 5/77, August/September 1977.

"Andy Warhol 1: Kitchen 1966", *Perspectives on British Avant-Garde Film*, Hayward Gallery, 1977.

"Identifying Non-Narrative" (discussion with Anthony Harrild and Susan Oldroyd), *Film Form*, Vol. 1, No. 2, Winter 1977.

"Victoria Ricks at RCA Diploma Show 1975", *Readings*, No. 3, 1977.

"Problems 'relating to' Warhol's Still Life 1976", *Artforum*, Vol. 16, No. 9, May 1978.
Reprinted in: *Andy Warhol: The Late Work*, Prestel, 2004.

Letter (response to "On Peter Gidal's Theory and Definition of Structural/Materialist Film"), *Afterimage*, No. 7, 1978.

"Peter Gidal at Millennium", *Millennium Film Journal*, No. 2, Spring/Summer 1978.

"Film-Maker's Statement", *A Perspective on English Avant-Garde Film*, Arts Council of Great Britain / British Council, 1978.
Reprinted in: *Una Prospettiva sul Cinema Inglese d'Avanguardia*

1967/1977, Comune di Modena, 1978.

"Zeno's Arrow by Sarah Child", *Edinburgh Film Festival*, 1978.

"Samuel Beckett's Ghost Trio", *Artforum*, Vol. 17, No. 9, May 1979.
    Reprinted in: *Transmission*, Peter d'Agostino (ed.), Tanam Press, 1985.

"The Anti-Narrative (1978)", *Screen*, Vol. 20, No. 2, Summer 1979.

Letter (response to "State of Siege"), *Time Out*, 25-31 January 1980.

"Technology and Ideology in/through/and Avant-Garde Film: An Instance", *The Cinematic Apparatus*, Teresa de Lauretis and Stephen Heath (eds.), Macmillan, 1980.

"13 MBW and Kitchen", *Undercut*, No. 1, Spring 1981.
    Reprinted in: *Andy Warhol: Film Factory*, Michael O'Pray (ed.), BFI, 1989 (as "The Thirteen Most Beautiful Women and Kitchen").

"Andy Warhol ... Factory Worker", *The Movie*, No. 65, 1981.

"The Current British Avant-Garde Film: Some Problems in Context", *Undercut*, No. 2, Summer 1981.

"On Finnegans Chin", *Undercut*, No. 5, Summer 1982.

"Politics, History, and the Avant-Garde", *Wide Angle*, Vol. 5, No. 2, March 1983.

"British Avant-Garde Film", Collective for Living Cinema programme notes, April 1983.

"(from a letter)", *Idiolects (Letters)*, No. 13, 1983.

"British Avant-Garde Film", *Millennium Film Journal*, No. 13, Fall/Winter 1983-84.

"On Julia Kristeva", *Undercut*, No. 10/11, Winter/Spring 1983-84.

"Peter Gidal Films 1967-1983", ICA, May-June 1984.

"Against Sexual Representation in Film", *Screen*, Vol. 25, No. 6, November 1984.

"Fugitive Theses re Thérèse Oulton's The Passions No. 6 and the Metals Paintings (1984)", *Thérèse Oulton: Fools' Gold*, Gimpel Fils, 1984.

"Action at a Distance" (text by Vivian Zarvis), *Feminism/Film*, No. 1, Spring 1984.

"Interview with Hollis Frampton" (1972), *October*, No. 32, Spring 1985.
  Reprinted in: *Les Cahiers du musée national d'art modern*, No. 61,
  Autumn 1997 (as "Entretien avec Hollis Frampton").
  Reprinted in: *Experimental Cinema: The Film Reader*,
  Wheeler Winston Dixon and Gwendolyn Audrey Foster (eds.),
  Routledge, 2002.
"Two Items as to the Co-op", *Light Years: A Twenty-Year Celebration*,
  London Film-Makers' Co-operative, 1986.
"Rose Lowder's Composed Recurrence" (with Lisa Cartwright),
  Millennium Film Journal, No. 16-17-18, Fall/Winter 1986-87.
"The Anti-Zoom (A Little Polemic Against Metaphor)", *Review of
  Contemporary Fiction*, Vol. 7, No. 2, Summer 1987.
"Dialogue and Dialectic in Godot", *Beckett: Waiting for Godot
  (Casebook)*, Ruby Cohn (ed.), Macmillan, 1987.
"In Representation or Out" in "Aesthetic and Politics: Working on Two
  Fronts?" (with Martina Attille, Isaac Julien and Mandy Merck),
  Undercut, No. 17, Spring 1988.
"Metastasis by The Aleinikov Brothers, Moscow: A Review", *Undercut*,
  No. 18, August 1988.
"The Riga Film Festival", *Independent Media*, No. 88, April 1989.
"Beckett and Sexuality (Terribly Short Version)", *Women in Beckett*,
  Linda Ben-Zvi (ed.), University of Illinois Press, 1991.
"Endless Finalities / Endlose Endlichkeit", *Parkett*, No. 35, March
  1993.
  Reprinted in: *Gerhard Richter, Catalogue Raisonné 1962-1993*,
  Hatje Cantz, 1993.
"NO EYE: Theoretical Reflections on the Eye, Metaphor, Film/Video",
  Samuel Beckett Today/Aujourd'hui, No. 4, 1995.
"The Polemics of Paint", *Gerhard Richter: Painting in the Nineties*,
  Anthony d'Offay Gallery, 1995.
"Peter Gidal", Centre Georges Pompidou, April 1996.
"Different and the Same", *ACT 3: Endgames: Art, Criticism, Theory*,
  Pluto Press, 1997.
Letter (response to Tom McDonaugh), *Art Journal*, Vol. 66, No. 1,

Spring 1997.

"Flashbacks: Peter Gidal", *Filmwaves*, No. 7, Spring 1999.

"Discussion with Cerith Wyn Evans", *Fig-1 38: Cerith Wyn Evans*, Fig-1, 2000.

> Reprinted in: *Fig-1: 50 Projects in 50 Weeks*, Spafax, 2001.

"Urban Rumours: Peter Gidal", *Mutations*, ACTAR, 2000.

"Once is Never: Warhol's Saturday Disaster and Blow Job", *Andy Warhol: Series and Singles*, Fondation Beyeler, 2000.

"There is no other", *Filmwaves*, No. 14, Spring 2001.

"Speaking of These Paintings" (Discussion with Thérèse Oulton), *Thérèse Oulton: Clair Obscur*, Marlborough Fine Art, 2003.

"Against Metaphor", *Drawing on Beckett*, Linda Ben-Zvi (ed.), Assaph Books, 2003.

"Time Regained (Sort of)", *Tate Magazine*, No. 6, August 2003.

"Endless Finalities, Part II", *Gerhard Richter: 4900 Colours*, Serpentine Gallery / Hatje Cantz, 2008.

"Notes from Performance of Sorts with Brecht", no-w-here / Chisenhale Gallery, 2009.

> Reprinted in: *Sequence*, No. 1, no-w-here, 2010.

> Reprinted in: *Performance of Sorts with Brecht / Volcano / Denials (DVD)*, LUX, 2011.

"Remembering (Almost Not Meeting) Beckett", *Samuel Beckett Today/ Aujourd'hui*, No. 28, 2016.

Between 1993 and 2014, Peter Gidal edited and published eight "Index Books" sales catalogues, which each contain his writings. The "Index Books Catalogue of Catalogues" was published in 2015 on the occasion of an exhibition in the 31st Biennial of Graphic Arts, Ljubljana.

WRITING ON PETER GIDAL

Andrew, Dudley, *Concepts in Film Theory*, Oxford University Press, 1984.

Armes, Roy, *A Critical History of the British Cinema*, Oxford University Press, 1978.

Auty, Chris, "State of Siege", *Time Out*, 18-24 January 1980.

Beauvais, Yann, Alain-Alcide Sudre and Rose Lowder, "An Interview with Peter Gidal", *Scratch*, No. 6, 1985.

Beckman, Karen and Jean Ma (eds.), *Still Moving: Between Cinema and Photography*, Duke University Press, 2008.

Ben-Zvi, Linda and Angela Moorjani (eds.), *Beckett at 100: Revolving it All*, Oxford University Press, 2008.

Blüher, Dominique, "Sensibilisierung für die Konstruktion der Filme", *Filmbulletin*, No. 170, April/May, 1990.

Bordwell, David, *Making Meaning: Inference and Rhetoric in the Interpretation of Cinema*, Harvard University Press, 1989.

Boynik, Sezgin, Giovanna Esposito Yussif & Kari Yli-Annala, "Practice Always Precedes Theory – Interview with Peter Gidal" *Rab-Rab: Journal for Political and Formal Inquiries in Art*, No. 2 (Vol. B), September 2015.

Branigan, Edward and Warren Buckland (eds.), *The Routledge Encyclopedia of Film Theory*, Routledge, 2013.

Christie, Ian, "Silent Partner", *Monthly Film Bulletin*, May 1978.

Clark, George, "An Overview of Shoot Shoot, Shoot", *Senses of Cinema*, No. 21, July 2002.

Comino, Jo, "Close-Up", *Time Out*, May 1984.

Cottringer, Anne, "On Peter Gidal's Theory and Definition of Structural/Materialist Film", *Afterimage*, No. 6, 1976.

Cubitt, Sean, *Videography: Video Media as Art and Culture*, Macmillan, 1993.

Curtis, David, *A History of Artists' Film and Video in Britain 1897-2004*, BFI, 2006.

Danino, Nina, and Michael Maziere (eds.), *The Undercut Reader*,

Wallflower Press, 2002.

De Bruyn, Dirk, *The Performance of Trauma in Moving Image Art*, Cambridge Scholars, 2014.

Du Cane, John, "Peter Gidal. The London Film Makers Co-op", *Time Out*, 21-27 January 1972.

———, "Upside Down Feature", *Time Out*, 1-7 December 1972.

———, "Movie No. 1", *A Survey of the Avant-Garde in Britain Vol. 3*, Gallery House, 1972.

Durgnat, Ray, "Andy Warhol: Films and Paintings. By Peter Gidal", *Art and Artists*, Vol. 6, No. 10, issue 70, January 1972.

Dusinberre, Deke, "The Ascetic Task: Peter Gidal's Room Film 1973", *Structural Film Anthology*, BFI, 1976.

———, "Consistent Oxymoron: Peter Gidal's Theoretical Strategy", *Screen*, Vol. 18, No. 2, Summer 1977.

———, *English Avant-Garde Cinema 1966-1974*, MPhil thesis, University College London, 1977.

Dwoskin, Stephen, "Peter Gidal", *Independent Film*, No. 1, 1970.

———, *Film Is*, Peter Owen, 1975.

Ellis, John, "Two New Films by Peter Gidal – *Silent Partner* and *Kopenhagen/1930*", LFMC programme note, 1971.

Errazu, Miguel, *Políticas del índice: estética y teoría de la indexicalidad en el cine y la cultura digital*, PhD thesis, Complutense University of Madrid, 2013.

Field, Simon, "Guilt", *Between Imagination and Reality: ICA Biennial of Moving Images 1990*, Tilda Swinton (ed.), ICA, 1990.

Fischer, Lucy, "The Film Image as a Mirror Image", *Soho Weekly News*, 16 January 1975.

Gow, Gordon, "Focus on 16mm", *Films & Filming*, August 1971.

Green, Darren, "All You Need is Eyes: London Filmmakers' Co-op", *Dazed and Confused*, No. 97, January 2003.

Hammond, Roger, "Bedroom – Peter Gidal", *English Independent Cinema*, NFT programme note, 1971.

———, "8mm Film Notes on 16mm", LFMC programme note, 1971.

Hammond, Roger, "8mm Notes on 16mm", *Time Out*,

19-25 November, 1971.

Hamlyn, Nicky, "From Structuralism to Imagism: Peter Gidal and his Influence in the 1980s", *Undercut*, No. 19, 1990.

———, *Film Art Phenomena*, BFI, 2003.

Heath, Stephen, "Repetition Time", *Wide Angle*, Vol. 2, No. 3, 1978.

———, "Afterword", *Screen*, Vol. 20, No. 2, Summer 1979.

———, *Questions of Cinema*, Macmillan, 1981.

Heebies-Jeebies, Artaxerxes (aka Dominique Noguez), "Peter Gidal, Du Cane, Henley, Dunford et les autres", *Chroniques de l'art vivant*, No. 55, February 1975.

Hein, Birgit, *Film im Underground*, Ullstein, 1971.

———, "Peter Gidal", *Documenta 6*, Paul Dierichs KG & Co, 1977.

Kennedy, Chris, *Peter Gidal*, Early Monthly Segments, 2010.

Kliess, Werner, "Heads", *Süddeutsche Zeitung*, February 1971.

Kuhn, Annette, "Film Print", *Perspectives on British Avant-Garde Film*, Hayward Gallery, 1977.

Laws, Catherine, *Headaches Among the Overtones: Music in Beckett/Beckett in Music*, Rodopi, 2013.

Le Grice, Malcolm, "Upside Down Feature", *Afterimage*, No. 4, 1972.

———, *Abstract Film and Beyond*, Studio Vista, 1977.

———, "Some Introductory Thoughts on Gidal's Films and Theory", *Independent Cinema Documentation File No. 1: Peter Gidal*, BFI, 1977.

Lehman, Peter, "Politics, History and the Avant-Garde: An Interview with Peter Gidal", *Wide Angle*, Vol. 5, No. 2, March 1983.

———, "The Avant-Garde: Power, Change, and the Power to Change", *Cinema Histories, Cinema Practices*, Patricia Mellencamp and Philip Rosen (eds.), University Publications of America, 1984.

Lennox-Boyd, Patricia, and Jamie Stevens (eds.), *Ciao Peter Gidal*, Benedictions, 2011.

Lennox-Boyd, Patricia, "Essay", *Peter Gidal: Condition of Illusion (DVD)*, Re:Voir, 2016.

Levi, Pavle, *Cinema by Other Means*, Oxford University Press, 2012.

Mattin, "Close-Up of What?", mattin.org, 26 April 2003.

Mekas, Jonas, "Movie Journal" (on *Room Film 1973*), *Village Voice*, 25 October 1973.

Moorjani, Angela, *The Aesthetics of Loss and Lessness*, Macmillan, 1992.

Mudie, Peter, *The Project: Structural/Materialist Film at the London Film-Makers' Co-operative (1966-83)*, PhD thesis, University of Western Australia, 2002.

Neubauer, Reinhard, "Structure/Form/Shape", *Das Andere Kino*, No. 5/76, 1976.

O'Pray, Michael, "Close Up", *Monthly Film Bulletin*, January 1984.

———, "Action at a Distance", *Monthly Film Bulletin*, March 1986.

———, "Denials", *The Elusive Sign*, Arts Council of Great Britain / British Council, 1988.

———, "Materialist Matters: Peter Gidal, Chris Welsby", *Art Monthly*, June 1988.

———, "Peter Gidal", *A Directory of British Film & Video Artists*, University of Luton / Arts Council of England, 1996.

——— (ed.), *The British Avant-Garde Film 1926-1995*, University of Luton / Arts Council of England, 1997.

———, *Avant-Garde Film: Forms, Themes and Passions*, Wallflower, 2003.

Obrist, Hans Ulrich and Cerith Wyn Evans, *The Conversation Series 24*, Walther König, 2010.

Payne, Simon, "Interview with Peter Gidal", simonrpayne.co.uk, 2001.

Penley, Constance, *The Future of an Illusion: Film, Feminism and Psychoanalysis*, University of Minnesota Press, 1989.

Peterson, James, *Dreams of Chaos, Visions of Order*, Wayne State University Press, 1994.

Philpott, Clive and Andrea Tarsia, *Live in Your Head: Concept and Experiment in Britain 1965-75*, Whitechapel Art Gallery, 2000.

Rayns, Tony, "A Directory of UK Independent Filmmakers: Peter Gidal", *Cinema Rising*, No. 1, April 1972.

Rees, A.L., "Conditions of Illusionism", *Screen*, Vol. 18, No. 3,

Autumn 1977.

———, "Silent Partner", *BFI Productions Catalogue 1977-78*, BFI, 1978.

———, *A History of Experimental Film and Video – 2nd Edition*, BFI, 2011.

Richter, Gerhard, "Interview with Hans Ulrich Obrist", *Gerhard Richter. Books*, Gregory R. Miller & Co, 2004.

Rodowick, David N., "Anti-narrative, or the Ascetic ideal", *The Crisis of Political Modernism*, Illinois University Press, 1985.

Rose, Jacqueline, *Sexuality in the Field of Vision*, Verso, 1986.

Rosenbaum, Jonathan, "Cinema at a Distance", *The Soho News*, 14 January 1981.

———, "Organizing the Avant-Garde: A Conversation with Peter Gidal", *Film: The Front Line 1983*, Arden Press, 1983.

Scheugl, Hans, and Ernst Schmidt Jr., *Eine Subgeschichte des Films*, Suhrkamp, Germany, 1974.

Simpson, Philip, Andrew Utterson and K.J. Sheperdson, *Film Theory: Critical Concepts in Media and Cultural Studies*, Routledge, 2004.

Sudre, Alain-Alcide, *L'avant-garde cinématographique britannique 1960-1980: examen des propositions des cinéastes Peter Gidal et Malcolm Le Grice, contribution à une théorie du cinéma expérimental*, PhD thesis, Université de Paris, 1981.

Swinton, Tilda (ed.), *Between Imagination and Reality: ICA Biennial of Moving Images 1990*, ICA, 1990.

Taanila, Mika, "Peter Gidal Orionissa", *Filmihullu*, No. 3, 2005.

Tofts, Darren, "Peter Gidal and Anarchic Criticism", *Journal of Beckett Studies*, Vol. 2, No. 2, Spring 1993.

Van Gelder, Lawrence, "Gidal's Two Silent Films Explore Light, Shapes", *New York Times*, 17 January 1975.

Wardill, Emily and Ian White, *We Are Behind*, Bookworks, 2010.

Webber, Mark, *Shoot Shoot Shoot (Broadsheet)*, LUX, 2002.

White, Ian, "Yet But If But If But Then But Then", luxonline.org, 2005.

Willemen, Paul (ed.), *Independent Cinema Documentation File No. 1:*

Peter Gidal, BFI, 1979.
Wollen, Peter, *Readings and Writings: Semiotic Counter-Strategies*, Verso, 1982.
Wyn Evans, Cerith, "Not Always All Ready", Tate Britain, 1998.
Youzheng, Li, *Contemporary Western Film Aesthetics*, China Social Sciences Press, 1986.